G000269667

YACHTING
MONTHLY

SOUTH WEST SPAIN & PORTUGAL

CRUISING COMPANION

A yachtsman's pilot and cruising guide
to ports and harbours from
Bayona to Gibraltar

DETLEF JENS
NAUTICAL DATA LIMITED

Cover picture: Lagos Marina

Photographs by Detlef Jens and Anke Brodmerkel

Aerial photography by Patrick Roach

Charts: Jamie Russell, Chris Stevens, Garold West

Art direction: Chris Stevens

Cruising Companion series editor: Mike Balmforth
Consultant editor: Edward Lee-Elliott

Colour reproduction: Aylesbury Studios, Bromley

Published by Nautical Data Ltd,
The Book Barn, Westbourne, Hampshire, PO10 8RS

First Edition

Copyright © Nautical Data Limited 2001

ISBN 0-333-907736

All rights reserved. No reproduction, copy or transmission of this publication may be made
without written permission. No paragraph of this publication may be reproduced, copied or transmitted
save with written permission or in accordance with the provisions of the Copyright, Designs and Patents Act 1988
(as amended). Any person who does any unauthorised act in relation to this publication may be liable to criminal
prosecution and civil claims for damages.

IMPORTANT NOTE
This Companion is intended as an aid to navigation only. The information contained within should not solely
be relied on for navigational use, rather it should be used in conjunction with official hydrographic data.
Whilst every care has been taken in compiling the information contained in this Companion, the publishers,
author, editors and their agents accept no responsibility for any errors or omissions, or for any accidents
or mishaps which may arise from its use.

Neither the publisher nor the author can accept responsibility for errors, omissions or alterations in this book.
They will be grateful for any information from readers to assist in the update and accuracy of the publication.

Readers are advised at all times to refer to official charts, publications and notices. The charts
contained in this book are sketch plans and are not to be used for navigation.
Some details are omitted for the sake of clarity and the scales have been chosen to allow best
coverage in relation to page size.

Correctional supplements are available upon request from the publishers whose address may be found on this page

Printed in Italy by Milanostampa

Typeset by Garold West

'Enterprise' enjoying perfect sailing conditions in the Straits of Gibraltar

PREFACE

Some things never change, others do so at a frightening pace. As far as the former is concerned, the magical appeal of Portugal seems timeless, although the country is undergoing significant transition in many respects. Portuguese society on the whole is becoming more modern especially in the larger cities,

but as Europe gradually grows together politically and the inner-European borders lose much of their substance, geographical and cultural regions which are not always restricted to state borders gain in importance and self awareness. In this way, regional traditions and cultural identities in Europe are enjoying something of a revival within what Euro-sceptics fear could otherwise become a more or less uniform continent.

Rapid change is particularly evident along the coast. Busy tourist areas encourage development and, in several sad cases, overdevelopment. Enthusiastic entrepreneurial activity has left its mark, particularly along the coasts of the Algarve and Andalucia, and yacht marinas seem to be climbing higher and higher on the list of desirable developments. Marinas with high-rise apartment buildings and big hotels grouped around the harbour basins seemed to be the dernier cri for property developers along these coasts at the time of research and writing – the most recent additions being Portimão in Portugal and Isla Canela in Spain. At the time of writing, there was also talk of even more marinas to come, for example in Albufeira. I cannot help but wonder about the commercial wisdom of ever more marina complexes being added to any one cruising area, or if this will enhance or spoil the coast in question. Time will no doubt tell.

On a less dramatic note, restaurants and cafés change hands in often quick succession. So something which, at the time of my visit, was a very pleasant and agreeable place with friendly service and good food could, by the time this book was printed and until you have arrived there, have turned decidedly sour. I mention this as a precautionary measure in case of a possible disappointment, but on the whole I am quite confident that really good restaurants tend to be long-lived and therefore remain unchanged for many years.

The corner of the world which is covered in this volume has a strong appeal for visitors. Portugal and southern Spain are wonderful places to sail to; they have a rich and fascinating history and culture, to be seen and experienced by anyone who wants to look beyond the fantastic beaches and pleasant restaurants. The climate is agreeable, as are most of the locals one will encounter.

If you have the time and opportunity to explore the hinterland from time to time, this will certainly make your cruise even more pleasurable and memorable. Suggestions for such diversions are made within the relevant sections of this book.

It is my sincere hope that this Cruising Companion will help to make your cruise to this superb destination a roaring success.

Fair winds and happy cruising!

Detlef Jens, November 2001

ACKNOWLEDGEMENTS

Detlef would like to thank the following for their help while researching the book: José Amaral in Aveiro (and his happy bunch of sailing friends); Wolfgang Michalsky in El Rompido; Tina and Richard Hutt in Gelves, Seville; and various tourist offices, harbour masters and fellow cruising sailors *en route*.

ABOUT THE AUTHOR

Detlef Jens is a yachting writer and travel journalist who has for many years been a regular contributor to yachting magazines in the UK and elsewhere. He has also written and translated various yachting books.

Detlef has lived in England, Germany and France as well as on his 35-foot cruising home Enterprise, aboard which he has explored mainly European waters while living permanently on board and writing along the way.

Enterprise is a Dutch designed and built (by Van Dam in Aalsmeer), one-off, medium displacement cruising boat with a round-bilge steel hull and wooden decks and coachroof which Detlef describes as "strong, simple, comfortable and reliable although not particularly fast" – in other words a near-perfect voyaging home.

Detlef Jens sailing his liveaboard home 'Enterprise'

CONTENTS

'Enterprise' at sunset off Faro

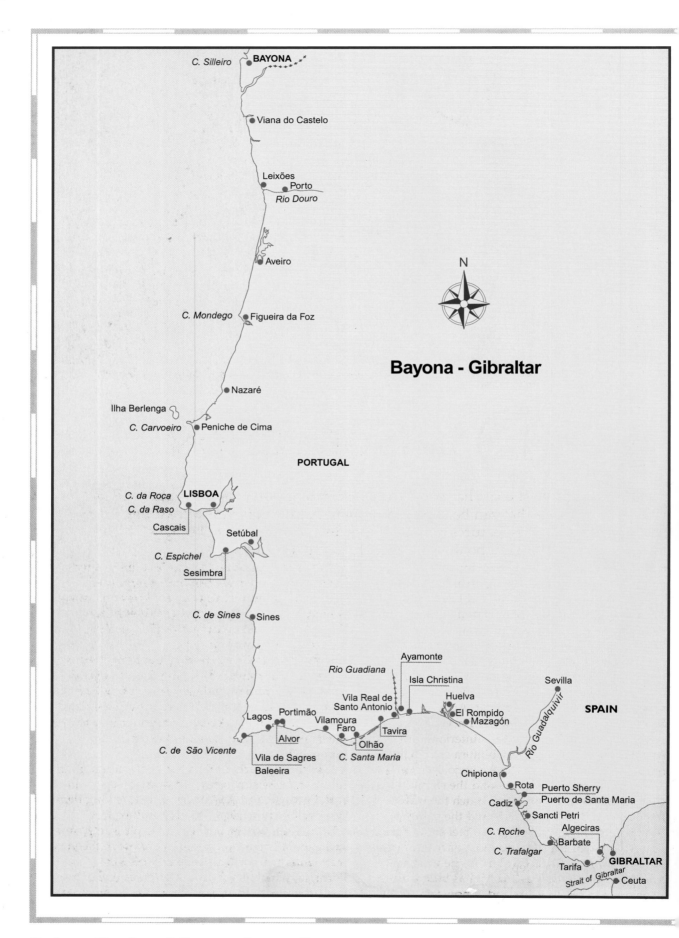

Bayona - Gibraltar

C. Silleiro ● **BAYONA**

● Viana do Castelo

Leixões
● ● Porto
Rio Douro

● Aveiro

C. Mondego ● Figueira da Foz

● Nazaré

Ilha Berlenga
C. Carvoeiro ● Peniche de Cima

PORTUGAL

C. da Roca ● **LISBOA**
C. da Raso
Cascais
Setúbal
C. Espichel
Sesimbra

C. de Sines ● Sines

Ayamonte
Rio Guadiana
Isla Christina
Huelva
Sevilla
Vila Real de
Santo Antonio
El Rompido
Mazagón
SPAIN
Lagos Portimão
Vilamoura
Faro
Tavira
Alvor
C. de São Vicente
Olhão
Vila de Sagres
C. Santa Maria
Baleeira
Chipiona
Rota Puerto Sherry
Cadiz Puerto de Santa Maria
Sancti Petri
C. Roche Algeciras
C. Trafalgar Barbate
Tarifa
Strait of Gibraltar ● Ceuta
GIBRALTAR

The Río Guadalquivir just outside Sevilla offers a friendly marina (the entrance to Puerto Gelves is to the left) and the option to anchor in the river

INTRODUCTION

The Portuguese west coast has some truly fascinating ports and towns as well as rivers and lagoons that can be explored *en route*. Admittedly, it is a coastline with few conspicuous features, few harbours and even fewer anchorages until one has rounded Cabo de São Vincente in the southwest,

but its enjoyment depends very much on what one is looking for in a cruising area.

The amazing cities of Porto and Lisboa are culturally and historically of extreme interest and still two of the most exotic towns in western Europe. Less known but just as inspiring are some smaller coastal towns, notably Viana do Castelo in the north and Sines in the south, while the lagoon of Aveiro (just S of Porto) is a wonderful area to be explored with your own boat. Apart from that, there are numerous possibilities for very rewarding excursions into the hinterland - to the ancient university town of Coimbra or into the beautiful countryside of the Alentejo, for example.

Further south, the region - and the climate - change dramatically once you reach the waters of the Algarve. Both the climate and the scenery have a decidedly Mediterranean feel about them. The coastline of the Algarve must once have been very beautiful, with steep cliffs in the west and sandy lagoons in the east, but it has been over-developed in recent years and is now fringed by

rows of grey apartment blocks and huge, ugly hotels also so often seen in the western Med. During the summer this is a very busy and noisy holiday area with associated activities ashore (Golf, Tennis) and on the water (Para-Sailing, Jet-Skiing, Windsurfing etc).

Some historically interesting and lively towns are there to be explored, notably Lagos (a good marina) and Faro (a sheltered lagoon in which to anchor). Facilities for yachts are better here than those located along Portugal's west coast, and there are the other marinas at Portimão and Vilamoura.

Marina and harbour developments designed to cater for the leisure sailor are going on apace in both Portugal and Andalucia, so before long there may well be new places to visit and explore.

During the winter, the climate is pleasantly mild and generally sunny - in stark contrast to the very wet winters in north-west Spain and west Portugal, which is why the Algarve is one of the favourite places in Europe for yachts to hibernate.

Continuing along the coast east of Faro, one encounters the Atlantic coast of south-western Spain. This land is similar to the eastern Algarve, with low-lying sand spits, marshy lagoons and deep rivers. It is still less developed ashore than the Mediterranean coast of Andalucia (which is the province of this part of Spain), but building activities are underway nearly everywhere and what appears is not very friendly to the eye - notably the same style of high and ugly apartment blocks and hotels that have already disfigured major parts of the Algarve further west and of the Mediterranean coast further east.

However, the two main navigable rivers (Río Guadiana and Río Guadalquivir) are still beautiful and flow through quite different landscapes and the most fascinating town in this part of the world is Sevilla, the capital of Andalucia (and thus also the capital of Flamenco and bull-fighting). It is the third-largest (but second-trendiest, after Barcelona) city in Spain.

Not to be missed are the ancient seafaring towns of Cádiz and, amongst other interesting places, Tarifa - with its truly fantastic beach and north African flair.

CRUISING STRATEGIES

Along the entire coastline covered in this volume, from Bayona to Gibraltar, there are no major offshore hazards and sailing is generally straightforward. The west coast is of course open to the Atlantic and often has pronounced swell. Problems can arise when cruising out of season in late autumn or winter along this coast, when there is a higher percentage of westerly and south-westerly gales. In those conditions, some harbours may be closed and others, especially Leixões and Porto, are sometimes unsafe even inside.

Sailing in summer, however, is usually very pleasant and easy-going - if coming from the north and heading south. The Portuguese Trades are northerly winds that usually blow from April or May to September or October and make for very relaxing sailing en route south. These fair winds may in fact tempt some to sail past the interesting places mentioned above, which would be a shame: it is much more difficult to turn back against the Portuguese Trades to see them later!

Coming from the UK or northern Europe, it is always best to cross Biscay at the height of the summer, say in June or July, when the weather is usually settled and the percentage of gales very small. This has the added benefit that, from Bayona southwards, the Portuguese Trades will blow you south. One should really be around Cabo de São Vincente and in the Algarve before the autumn sets in on the west coast, with its rainfalls and gales, which can be anytime from October onwards.

Every year, yachts get caught late along this coast, often having to wait for weeks on end for a window in the weather to make some more southing. The best possible strategy if too late in the season is to stay put in some harbour until there is a suitable weather window during which to cover as much ground as possible to the south. This is mainly because some harbours along the coast between Leixões and Lisboa are dangerous to enter in strong south-westerly winds - namely Aveiro, Figueira da Foz (which will be closed under those circumstances), and possibly also Nazaré and Peniche. Bearing also in mind the distance between ports, this coast is not one to be caught off in an onshore gale!

The return passage back to the UK is less straightforward, the obvious problem being the northerly winds that dominate the summer and the fact that one would wish to cross Biscay in summer. The strategies when on passage towards the north vary according to the yacht and her crew: some will sail far out into the Atlantic in search of more favourable westerly winds, others will hug the coast and harbour-hop north, often sailing or rather motor-sailing at night or early in the morning, when the north wind usually dies

The author enjoying ideal sailing conditions

Figueira da Foz fishing harbour

down to a whisper or even becomes an easterly, and spending the days in harbour.

The most attractive alternative, however, would be to continue into the Mediterranean and return via the beautiful Canal du Midi (*See W. France Cruising Companion*), thus avoiding the Portuguese Trades altogether. The passage through the Canal du Midi will take at least ten days but more often much longer, as the crew is tempted to linger along the way. In this way, one could reach Biscay via the Gironde River just south of La Rochelle at exactly the right time to cross, in early summer.

This would be a most pleasurable 12 month round-trip from the UK: Depart in May or June, head south across Biscay and along Portugal, winter in the Algarve or Southern Spain, then sail into the Mediterranean via Gibraltar, and return through the Canal du Midi in early spring, crossing Biscay again in June. Variations to this could of course include exploring the highly attractive Spanish north coast, a detour to one of the Atlantic islands (Madeira being the obvious choice) or, once inside the Mediterranean a visit to the Balearics.

It is of course possible to sail the roughly 800 miles from Falmouth to Lagos in a matter of a few days - which would be a shame. It would be equally possible to spend months *en route*, pottering along the Atlantic coasts of France, Spain and Portugal. Anything between these extremes will probably be fine for the vast majority of cruising yachts, but it will really be worth stopping at more places in Portugal than just Porto and Lisboa.

PORTS AND ANCHORAGES BETWEEN LA CORUNA AND BAYONA

Quite a few cruising yachts now choose Bayona as their first port of call after the Biscay crossing, and this is indeed a pleasant and easy place to relax in after a long passage. Boats that sail straight for Bayona will have missed the Galician Rias which are a beautiful cruising ground in their own right, but if bound further south, they have a good starting point here in which to pick up the Portuguese Trades and sail on.

However, depending on the weather and some other factors, many would prefer to make a landfall further north. La Coruña has long been a classic first port of call for any cruising yacht that has crossed Biscay. Until a few years ago, this was in fact the only harbour in north-west Spain that offered any facilities for yachts. It also had, and of course still has, the added benefit of being a large city with all travel and shopping facilities, and it has an easy approach from sea which is possible in almost any weather.

The two yacht-clubs are friendly and La Coruña is still something of a meeting-point for many long-term cruising yachts. Boats are now discouraged from using their own anchors in La Coruña, but there are moorings for visiting yachts and the berths along the floating pontoons (where boats tie up Mediterranean style, stern-to with long mooring ropes that are picked up at the pontoon and secured at the bow) are very moderately priced. If overcrowding is putting a severe strain on the marina facilities, a move to the marina at Sada might have to be considered.

Having said all that, it does make sense to

The boatyard in the fishing harbour at Lagos

choose a port already on the west coast or even past Finisterre, such as Camarinhas. Camarinhas is the bay immediately south of Cabo Villano, offers many anchorages and is becoming more and more popular with cruising boats. It is still a few miles (about 15) north of Finisterre but strategically an ideal place to make for after Biscay and before heading further south. The approach from sea is easy, with two major lights as landmarks (Cabo Villano and Cabo Toriana, with the smaller light on Punta de la Barca marking the southern tip of the entrance). There are some dangerous unmarked shoals, Las Quebrantas, off the entrance and they can be identified (during the day) by the seas breaking over them.

Once inside the Ría de Camariñhas, there is the little village of Camariñhas itself, which has a small fishing harbour with a few floating pontoons run by the local yacht club. Camariñhas also has fair shopping facilities and some services for boats. Opposite, on the south side of the Ria, is the equally small village of Mugia which has a good anchorage behind a long seawall.

About 15 miles further south is the long and impressive Cabo Finisterre. Tucked behind the peninsular that forms this Cape is the fishing village of Finisterre itself with a tiny harbour which although scenic is not ideal to relax in after a long passage or even to wait for better weather as the harbour is crowded with fishing boats. A bit easier in this respect might be the anchorages further inside the bay, the Seno de Corcubion, either off the tiny village of Sardineiro or off the slightly larger town of Corcubion.

The next good stop-over port south would really be the town of Villagarcia, although this is quite a long way up the beautiful but rock-strewn (keep to the marked channel) Ría de Arosa. Villagarcia has a marina and a yacht club with all facilities, but if bound south, it would really make more sense to continue straight to Bayona from the entrance to the Ría, as a look at the chart (BA 3633) will easily show you.

It is of course possible and would indeed make for a very memorable cruise indeed to spend weeks in these great Rias of Galicia, but that is, in part, the theme of another Cruising Companion.

LEAVING THE BOAT OR CHANGING CREW

If it should become necessary to leave the boat somewhere and return home, or to change crew, both are easily arranged in this area. Starting in the north, Viana do Castelo has a marina and good transport connection, but Porto with its international airport is perhaps the easiest place for a crew change. Unfortunately, neither the marina at Leixões nor the moorings in the Douro River at

Porto are really safe enough to leave a yacht unattended for any length of time, but this can be done at Aveiro, only a half day sail further south and half an hour's drive from the airport. In Aveiro, a yacht could be laid up for a while ashore at the local boat-yard (Ria Naval). There is also a small but sheltered marina at Torreira, in the northern part of the lagoon of Aveiro and last but not least, visiting yachts can be left on the moorings of the small but very friendly yacht club behind a lock in a small canal, if space is available here.

The next place for good travel connections is Lisboa itself. Visiting yachts have a choice of basins in which to moor, but security is, as in any major city, a concern - I would feel uneasy leaving the boat unattended for much longer than the days spent exploring this city.

There are a number of smaller harbours along the west coast such as Nazaré or Sines, where yachts have been left for quite a while. It seems safer to arrange with a local to keep an eye on the boat in a small place such as these, than in the capital itself. Along the west coast there is always the danger of winter gales making themselves felt in the harbours, and while manned boats will probably cope with that, an unattended vessel may suffer damage.

The first really secure harbour to leave the boat unattended in the water for any length of time is the marina at Lagos, which offers complete shelter in any weather. Lagos is a one hour drive from the international airport at Faro (with many cheap holiday flight connections to northern Europe) and three hours from Lisboa. Both these destinations can also be reached from Lagos by train (the train station is conveniently placed only a stone's throw from the marina) or by bus.

Vilamoura is another obvious choice to leave a boat, but for some reason, Lagos has become much more popular during the last few years - probably due to the much more attractive town, the better travel connections and the general atmosphere. At the time of publication the new marina at Portimão was not yet fully operational, so it is too early to say anything about security or shelter, although both seemed promising during our visit there.

Further along the coast, Faro has the airport but no secure moorings for unattended yachts. But there is a good marina further east on the Río Guadiana, from where Faro can easily be reached with a hire car. This is Vila Real where a boat could probably be left unattended fairly safely. Coming into Spain, there are a number of very good marinas, beginning with Ayamonte directly opposite Vila Real on the Spanish side of the Río Guadiana, which is still a fairly short drive from Faro, although, coming from Spain, a hire-car could not be left at the airport when flying out. Alternatively, the next international airport is at Sevilla, although cheap charter flights also operate out of Granada and Malaga, not too far away by car, bus or train on the Mediterranean side of Andalucia.

There is a wide choice of marinas in Andalucia - all suitable for leaving a boat (for details, see the relevant chapter in this volume). Isla Cristina is a good, safe harbour but access is a bit difficult - the large marina at Mazagon near Huelva is better. The yacht moorings in Sevilla are the marina of Puerto Gelves, situated just outside the town but comparatively cheap and quite secure, and the Club Nautico de Sevilla which has quite luxurious shoreside facilities including a swimming-pool. The Club Nautico is within walking distance of the city but much more expensive than Puerto Gelves.

There is a third mooring location, a small floating pontoon called Marina Yachting Sevilla which is located behind the lock leading to the branch of the Gualdalquivir that eventually goes through the town centre and to the Club Nautico. Marina Yachting Sevilla has some shoreside facilities such as showers, toilets, water and electricity but it is a long way from anywhere and it is almost impossible to get into the city without your own transport or using a taxi - the bus station is a long walk (1.5 kilometres).

So, Gelves is the choice of most visiting yachts. It is a pleasant quiet harbour, there is a small village close by with various bars and shops, and the bus into Sevilla runs frequently and stops right outside the marina.

There are also secure marinas in the bay of Cádiz, from where one can access the airports either at Sevilla or Malaga. Finally, for direct flights to London, Gibraltar is always a sure bet and again, a yacht can easily be left in one of the three marinas: Sheppard's Marina, Marina Bay or Queensway Quay (again, for details see under Gibraltar in the relevant chapter).

WEATHER AND TIDES

In the area covered by this volume, weather and climate varies considerably from north to south. Generally speaking, we have two main climates here - the Atlantic climate on the Portuguese west coast, and the more Mediterranean climate of the Algarve and Costa de la Luz (Spain's SW Atlantic coast).

Going into slightly more detail, we find that the weather usually changes noticeably south of the Rio Tejo, again past Cabo de São Vincente, then once more as one progresses south-east along the Algarve and Spanish coasts, and finally in the vicinity of the Strait of Gibraltar, one of the windiest places in Europe.

Tides are noticeable all along the coast but tidal streams are generally weak so that they can usually be discounted while on passage. Tidal effects do become extremely evident and important when entering and to a lesser extent when leaving nearly all harbours and rivers covered in this volume. Having up to date tide tables on board is imperative for this reason, even though for the planning of passages along the coast itself, the tides have little or no impact.

Slightly more relevant for offshore passage making (but not really so when harbour-hopping along the coast) is the Portuguese Current which flows from north to south along the coast from Finisterre to the Canaries - a section of the North Atlantic clockwise circulation of water.

The climatic system on the Portuguese coast comprises the Atlantic or Azores high, and an area of low pressure that usually forms over the Iberian peninsular in summer. The combination of the two are the ingredients for the Portuguese Trades - north winds which are wonderful if you are heading south, but less so if you are trying to go north! The Portuguese Trades usually blow from about May to October, but this is variable and in some years they do not settle in until June

The rugged coast just South of Bayona

or even July. These winds are usually amplified in summer by strong sea-breezes close to the coast, resulting in sometimes very strong or even gale force winds in the afternoons which die down to a whisper during the night. The zone of these trade winds extends about 100 miles into the Atlantic.

During the winter months, when these two systems are less pronounced, the lows that form over the North Atlantic and which normally only

Motoring up the lagoon towards Faro

land on both sides is heated up by the sun and pulls the air upwards. This phenomenon will usually be more pronounced at the downwind side of the Strait, regardless whether the wind is easterly or westerly and can increase the local wind strength by as much as two Beaufort numbers. When running downwind through the Straits, the wind will therefore increase until you shoot out at the leeward end like a cork from a champagne bottle. Whereas when you try to beat through against the wind, at least you will start off with the strongest breeze and should normally find that the wind decreases as you (hopefully) make progress towards the windward exit.

There usually is a constant flow of water into the Mediterranean through the Straits of Gibraltar, as much more water evaporates in the Mediterranean than in the Atlantic. This basic feature adds spice and interest to the tides and especially the waves encountered here, sometimes kicking up extremely nasty seas in conjunction with a wind-against-tide-against-inflow situation. The tides flow in or out, either strengthening or weakening but seldom overriding the in-going current which is also influenced by the prevailing wind of the last few days and other factors. Predicting the current through the Straits is therefore about as easy as predicting next month's weather over the British Isles or the numbers of the National Lottery. Even local experts who have been sailing here for years seldom get it right!

Tide, wind and in-flowing current must be taken into consideration when making an overall assessment of the situation. Of course even the last mentioned is not really a constant factor, as the rate of water that flows into the Med is greatly influenced by the overall weather situation, recent rainfalls and winds. As a very rough guide, the tidal flow is west-going after HW Gibraltar and east-going after LW Gibraltar. But again, the times when the tidal stream really starts to flow is influenced by many local features, see also p156.

For in-depth information about the flow of water through the Straits, I recommend the little booklet The Straits Sailing Handbook published by the charter company Straits Sailing in Gibraltar. It also gives tidal flow charts for the Straits and some examples of how best to try and determine the direction in which the surface water is moving at any given time.

The Tourist Weather (rainfalls and sunshine ashore) in Portugal and Spain is fairly simple and predictable. Northern Spain and especially Galicia have a temperate climate, cool and wet on average but with pleasant summers (much better than those in the UK!) and mild but wet and

affect more northern areas of Europe in summer, now sweep in further south, resulting in wet and windy winters, especially in Galicia and northern Portugal. South of the Rio Tejo, this generally seems less pronounced than further north, although there also can be vicious south-westerly gales here during the winter months.

In the Algarve, the northerlies are still theoretically predominant in summer, although in practice winds are far more variable than along the west coast. There are also extended periods of calm and settled weather during the winter months. Winds along the coast are often caused by land and sea breeze effects, and can be strong enough to override the gradient wind for a few hours each day.

Approaching the Straits of Gibraltar, winds generally increase in force and normally blow either straight into or straight out of the Straits. The funnelling effect accelerates all winds in this region, especially the Levante (a strong local wind blowing from the east) or an already strong westerly or south-westerly. In both cases, it will be extremely unpleasant and more often than not outright impossible for an average cruising yacht to make much progress against the wind, and any attempt at doing so must only be considered foolish, as there are good harbours on either side of the Straits in which one can wait for the right weather.

Not only is the wind increased by the funnelling effect, but also small low pressure systems which develop during the day as the

The beautiful and bizarre coast just west of Lagos

windy winters (quite similar to those in south-west England). Much the same can be said for northern Portugal as far south as Lisboa, although the summers here can get quite hot.

Summers are sunny in Portugal, statistically speaking the sun shines nearly every day in summer (true enough) and every other day in winter (this is hard to verify even after having spent many winter months in Portugal, although it could be true for the Algarve). In the south, summers are hot, often unpleasantly so in Andalucia (in Sevilla the daytime temperatures in July and August frequently touch 40 degrees Celsius) although it is always cooler along the coast. The winters are generally mild, sunny, pleasant and mainly dry along the coasts, particularly in the flat landscapes further east along the Algarve and Costa de la Luz.

Let us take a look at the statistics for Lisboa:

Minimum/maximum temperatures (Celsius)
January: 9/15; April 12/19; July 20/29; October 16/22; December 10/16.

Days of rainfall/hours of sunshine per day:
January 7/4.9; April 5/9.1; July 0/12.5; October 4/7.4; December 7/6.0.

Now looking at the Algarve and Andalucia, the average temperatures statistically vary from 10 degrees Celsius in January to 30 degrees in August. The driest months are June, July and August with the most rainfall occurring in December and January. Despite this, the winters in this part of the world are still much warmer, sunnier and drier than anywhere else in (northern) Europe and thus a favourite hibernating place for liveaboard types.

PRACTICALITIES

Fortunately, as we are in Europe there is virtually no trouble with authorities and clearance procedures or other formalities - as long as you are European citizens sailing on a European-registered yacht. The question of VAT payment on the boat can be a painful one if your vessel is not registered in the EU and cruising folk from outside the EU have had problems in this respect when staying for more than six months (easily done with first class cruising waters ranging from the Med to the Arctic Circle).

No formalities are necessary when entering Spain or Portugal for a European yacht arriving from a member state. The Portuguese Transit Log (still mentioned in some pilot books) is a thing of the past and bygone dark ages. Having said this, random customs checks (friendly unless, of course, illegal drugs or firearms are found) are sometimes made, increasing in frequency as you proceed south.

As far as documentation is concerned, some marina offices in Spain will require to see the ship's registration documents, the insurance policy number (only third-party insurance is mandatory in Spanish marinas) and the passport of the owner or captain, while the Portuguese marina officials will want to see the ship's papers and passports of every person on board, but not normally the insurance documents. In effect, as most yachts do stay in marinas nowadays, the flow of visiting yachts is thus still more or less controlled and monitored by the authorities although the hassle of doing the paperwork has thankfully been taken away from the crews and passed on to the marina staff.

Generally speaking, officials in both Spain and Portugal nowadays have a rather relaxed attitude towards yachts. It has to be said, however, that this can change dramatically if one is involved in any problems or accidents. The bottom line is that they leave you alone as long as all is well and going smoothly, but beware of legal and other hassles as soon as an incident occurs, especially if involving a local vessel. This is the moment of truth, when the laissez-faire facade will crumble away at a frightening rate...!

The waters covered in this volume are not particularly tricky ones. It is true that the west coast of Portugal basically is a dangerous Atlantic lee shore in autumn, winter and spring, with the added difficulty of frequent fog and spells of poor visibility. Also, there is a lot of inshore and offshore fishing activity and some of the fishing vessels are considered a serious threat to the safety of shipping. On the other hand, there are no major offshore dangers, no dangerous tidal overfalls or passages to be made between rocks or hidden shallows as is so often the case in many of the waters around the UK.

Typical 'Rabelo' boats in Porto – instead of these, trucks are now used to transport the Port wine down river

EQUIPMENT

Cruising the west coast of Portugal, and even more so the waters of the Algarve, does not require a specially prepared crew or boat. Therefore, any yacht and crew fit enough to cross the Bay of Biscay will definitely be well able to continue further south from Finisterre.

Alternatively, a soundly built and normally equipped coastal cruiser with a crew of some experience will be able to day sail from the UK to Gibraltar (possibly with a few overnight passages) along the west France and north Spanish coasts, avoiding a passage across Biscay altogether.

In short, any crew and yacht capable of safely coping with rough weather and the occasional short offshore passage around the UK coast will be equally capable of sailing in the area covered in this volume (Bayona to Gibraltar).

Much the same goes for equipment. No special requirements are absolutely necessary, although one or two points are worth mentioning. The first is that more and more boats get by without ever anchoring - which is fine, and their choice. Consequently, ground tackle is slipping further and further down the list of priorities on board. This has been said many times in various publications, but it is worth reiterating that good ground tackle with a heavy anchor and lots of chain and/or warp is still one of the very basic safety requirements - especially for a coastal cruiser.

An appropriately sized CQR, Delta, or Bruce with lots of chain will do the trick in most anchorages, but it is even better to carry two or even three different kinds of hooks.

When sailing south late in the season (after September) both boat and crew must be ready for some heavy and punishing weather, both on and below decks. Excellent books have been written about this subject (best of all 'Heavy Weather Sailing' by Peter Bruce and 'How to Cope with Storms' by Dietrich von Haeften) both of which are recommended as further reading, anyway. In winter, south-westerly gales are frequent and will turn the Portuguese coast into a dangerous lee shore where many harbours will then be closed or impossible to enter - so a yacht must be prepared to ride out a storm at sea.

Coming back to more pleasant aspects - in the summer, we are dealing with a rather hot cruising area (especially once past Cabo de São Vincente) and this requires some additional equipment which will greatly improve the quality of life on board. These include a good sized but easy to rig sun-awnings, wind-scoops for the hatches and, for real luxury, some kind of cooling or refrigeration system for the cold beers! It is possible to get by without refrigeration - shops for fresh supplies are plentiful and cold beers can equally easily be drunk ashore!

SUPPLIES

Which rather elegantly brings us to the general aspect of supplies and provisioning. We are in Euroland, which gives us the best of both worlds - large Hypermarkets for easy and convenient stocking up with basics, as well as delightful small local shops and markets for fun-filled exploring of local produce and specialities (which are plentiful in both Portugal and Spain - see under Eating and Drinking).

Shopping and provisioning are easy and straightforward in both Spain and Portugal as mainstream supermarkets will be found in or near to most bigger towns, and they all stock the sort of international food to which we are apparently accustomed. All the large Hypermarkets will accept credit cards as form of payment, although usually a bottom spending limit is set. There is a Tesco supermarket in the Algarve, and sailing into Gib will make home-sick Brits feel good - only UK shops and products here!

So, you do not necessarily have to embark on any culinary adventures, but it would mean missing a lot of fun and experience if you don't. As already mentioned, the small local shops - dimly lit, cool and dusty groceries, butchers and bakeries as well as the markets, especially in Portugal, are a delight. Local produce is still cheap in the markets, but in the shops and especially supermarkets, prices tend to be levelled out at a European average - although at the time of writing, provisioning in Portugal was slightly dearer than in Spain. Strangely enough, eating out was quite the reverse - generally cheaper in Portugal than in Spain.

Spares for yachts are hard to come by. Along the Atlantic coasts of Spain and Portugal, yachting has only slowly taken hold during the past few years and although new marinas have been built, there is no yachting tradition such as in the UK. Consequently, well stocked chandlers with knowledgeable staff are few and far between - most chandlers cater for the needs of the anglers and fishing boats. Ordering parts from the UK is possible, but can be a long and time-consuming exercise in Portugal or Spain, which might be character-building, but will not really be helpful for your cruising plans. Patience is a virtue easily fatigued by exercise! However, most things can be found in Gibraltar which although no longer cheaper than the rest of Europe is still more convenient than many other places in southern Europe for buying up-to-date marine hardware.

Due to the huge numbers of fishing boats, spares and repairs for diesel engines are relatively easy to organise in almost all ports. But, especially

Porto Cathedral and part of the old quarter

for advanced sail handling gear and the like, it will be worthwhile to have a good selection of spare parts on board. Remember that nearly every bit of fancy yachting hardware, other than roughly galvanised shackles of trawler dimensions, will have to be ordered from either the UK, France, or Scandinavia!

Which brings us to the always hotly discussed question of the energy-source on board for cooking. Without wanting even to touch the debate on the pros and cons of various fuels, I only have two remarks to make. Paraffin is getting more and more difficult to find, both in the UK and also in the rest of Europe. Gas is convenient if one chooses the right brand. Refilling strange bottles of gas requires a great amount of research, time and nerves in a foreign country (if it is possible at all).

Camping Gaz is available virtually all over Europe in every tiny shop and garage between the UK and Gibraltar, and although it is slightly more expensive than other forms of bottled gas, it is simply unbeatable for convenience. The same also applies for most of the Caribbean and indeed many other exotic overseas places in the French or Spanish cultural sphere.

Speaking of cultural spheres brings us to language.

Unfortunately, you cannot easily get by in English - especially in Spain. The Spaniards are almost as chauvinistic about their language as are the French, so a basic grasp of Spanish helps enormously. Other than that, the next best bet is French, which is fairly widely spoken at least in most of northern Spain.

Things are easier in Portugal - being a poorer and more humble nation, the Portuguese do not expect every visitor to master their language to perfection and some of them do speak fairly good English. One point that really helps here is that in Portugal all films, both on TV and in the cinemas, are shown in the original, sub-titled version (which is why so many Portuguese adopt a weird sort of Hollywood-movie slang). This of course, happily enables us as well to actually understand the films when we opt for an evening at the movies! However, as in any country, a basic grasp of Portuguese and an honest attempt at speaking at least a few words in their language is not only a matter of courtesy, but also helps to break the ice more quickly with the locals.

HISTORY AND CULTURE

Portugal, situated at the extreme south-west end of Europe, is a strange and multi-faceted country and is quite exotic in some ways. Historically, it

Berlenga Island – near Peniche

has always turned its attention, ambitions and hopes to the ocean on its door-step rather than looking at Europe to which, until very recently, it turned its back. So, even today, it remains a country which is decidedly different.

Throughout much of the last century Portugal had the longest fascist dictatorship in Europe. A professor of economics, Antonio de Oliveira Salazar ruled the land for forty eight years in an ultra-right, nationalistic way using classic techniques such as a secret police and informants. Despite this, the country remained neutral during the Second World War and allowed the Azores to be used by the Allied forces as a vital Atlantic base from which to operate - maybe a hint towards Portugal's traditional orientation towards the Atlantic.

Even though Salazar himself was a fascist leader, Lisboa during the war became a haven for refugees seeking to emigrate, once they had escaped from the Nazis who controlled most of the rest of Europe. In 1974, Portugal had a remarkably humane and bloodless revolution which ended the Salazar era, followed by a Marxist government for just one year during

The old town of Rota, at the northern end of the Bay of Cádiz

which the handful of rich families that had literally owned the country for centuries were divested of their wealth. Portugal and Spain have the youngest democracies in Europe.

Today, two-thirds of the population live in the areas around the two largest cities of Porto and Lisboa, but many of the old traditions can still be seen in the smaller villages along the coast and especially a little way inland. Much of Portugal's economy now depends on tourism which has its main impact along the coast, but large areas of the interior remain unchanged.

Going back in time, the early travel-writers of the 19th century found Portugal to be a strange and somewhat crude land. Lord Byron made some devastating observations, and only praised the park-like landscape around Sintra near Lisboa. Much the same goes for William Beckford, who described the Portuguese as degenerates and lashed Lisboa as being "unfit of the dignity of a capital, with its awfully steep alleys and pitifully small churches".

This was at a time when England was Portugal's strongest ally! The country, which had been conquered by Napoleon's troops and annexed by France from 1807 to 1811, was freed by the British in 1810 and 1811 and governed by them until the return of the Portuguese king from

his exile a few years later. Since that time, strong economic links have remained between Portugal and Britain, most obviously to be seen in Porto - the local port wine was exported to Great Britain in vast quantities, and many British companies had their offices here.

Earlier still, this small country on the western fringe of Europe became one of the largest colonial powers of the then known world. Historians claim that it was actually the cost of those overseas colonies that drove the motherland into poverty. Be that as it may, Portugal certainly produced some of the finest and most important

The beautifully painted bows of the 'Moliceiros' in Aveiro, the mussel boats of the Aveiro lagoon

Sines is a beautiful and largely unspoilt old town, despite the huge industrial harbour

seafarers of all times. The era of the great discoveries started when Henry (Henrique) the Seafarer (1394 to 1460) took part in Portugal's first overseas expedition, conquering Ceuta in 1415. Only a few years later, he became governor of the Algarve (from 1419 to 1457). It is here that the foundation for Portugal's expansion around the globe was laid. He initiated a nautical school in Sagres, and most of the famous voyages were started from Lagos, beginning with the discovery of Madeira, the Azores and the Cape Verdes. In 1487, Bartolomeu Dias rounded the Cape of Good Hope, but had to turn back soon after. It was not until 1498 that Vasco da Gama found the sea-route to India, while, one year later, Pedro Alvares Cabral reached Brazil, which was to become Portugal's most important colony.

The most famous voyage of all was made by a flotilla led by Fernao de Magelhaes (Magellan), whose ships were the first to circumnavigate the world (in 1519 to 1522) and thus proved once and for all that the world is round. Sadly, Magellan himself was killed during that circumnavigation.

The Portuguese themselves are a strange mix - both hot-blooded and phlegmatic, childishly optimistic and easy-going as well as melodramatic and romantic. It is not easy for

Fine buildings in the old town of Lagos

A Palazzo in Sintra

outsiders to understand their ways of thinking, although first contact is much more easily made than in Spain. The outgoing and nosy Portuguese are, however, usually quite friendly and helpful. On the other hand, conducting business is not easy, and some entrepreneurs still declare Portugal a disaster area! This is evident even in small things: we found that is was apparently impossible for an engineering company in Lagos to find a piece of aluminium tube to replace our broken spinnaker pole, although they allegedly tried for several weeks in the entire country! While the economy of neighbouring Spain has been booming for several years, nothing of that is felt in the sleepy, still often backwards, but thus also charming Portugal.

Portuguese culture as it can still be seen and felt today has two manifestations. One is the rural and still very traditionally orientated communities, where women still marry very young, have babies and are often left divorced shortly afterwards, but where families on the other hand still give vital security to the individual. The other is that of the modern cities - Porto and Lisboa.

Somewhere between these two extremes are the

Al mourol castle – Constância

smaller university towns of Coimbra, a traditional stronghold of intellectual life in Portugal, and Aveiro, where a young university attracts numerous students from other European countries, giving this interesting provincial town a strangely international atmosphere which is most obvious in the bars and discotheques at night!

In Lisboa, on the other hand, the strong influence of African culture is evident in many areas of the town. More than 800,000 people migrated to Portugal after most of the colonies were granted their independence after 1974, bringing with them black music, dancing and cooking - a welcome and spicy ingredient in the already exotic mixture that makes Portugal. Lisboa is now reputed to be the centre of black music in Europe.

Speaking of music, Fado has to be mentioned. These traditional Portuguese songs about love, heart-ache and sadness polarise the population into two camps. One says that Fado is a load of folkloristic rubbish only preserved to amuse the tourists, the other claims that it is one of the more important ingredients of Portugal's cultural heritage and in fact expresses the country's soul like nothing else.

Despite this dispute everyone loved the legendary Fado-singer Amalia Rodriguez who was given a state-burial when she died in 1999,

and another famous musician, José Afonso from Coimbra (who died in 1986). His song Grandola Vila Morena is reputed to have given the signal for the revolution of 1974, and he had already cultivated the Fado de Coimbra back in the 1950s, combining political lyrics with more traditional themes.

In the 19th century, Fado was the music of the people at the outer fringes of society – prostitutes, gangsters, adventurers – and also seamen. But, the melodramatic and fatalistic Fado really seems to have its origins with the Moors, and the music and the unique melancholy in the singing certainly reminds one of its Arabic roots. Fado can be heard in many clubs and bars, especially in Lisboa, but also in other towns around the country. Despite sometimes being degraded to cheap tourist entertainment and, at the other end of the scale, combined with elements of jazz and African music by great musicians and composers, Fado still is one way to express this strange country - just as the sparkling, proud and self-conscious Flamenco is how the neighbouring region of Andalucia expresses itself.

A look at Andalucia

Like the music, the region and the people of this southernmost province of Spain could not be more different to the Portuguese. This area, nearly as large as the whole of Portugal, has the greatest density of population in Spain, the richest culture, and the worst kind of mass-tourism along its Mediterranean coasts.

One after the other, the Phoenicians, Greeks, Romans, Vandals and Moors came and conquered the land, but the height of the Andalucian culture was under the Arab and Berber rule. During the middle ages, the Moorish culture in Andalucia was the most highly developed in the Mediterranean. Before Granada was re-conquered by the Catholic forces of Ferdinand and Isabella in 1492, the local Emirs of Cordoba, Jaen, Granada and Sevilla fought each other to the death, while at the same time rebelling against the Moors.

Interestingly, the word Flamenco not only stands for the music, but more generally for a whole attitude to life. In this sense, the Andalucians call themselves, and some individuals more than others 'Flamenco', even if these people are neither singers, musicians nor dancers. A Flamenco is therefore someone who shows his or her emotions openly and prefers having fun to having to work, who is not necessarily always strictly law-abiding, who values freedom higher than the acquisition of worldly goods, and who generally is not very much bound by convention.

Experiencing a genuine Flamenco show, this explosive firework of music, dancing and singing gives one a glimpse of the proud Andalucian soul.

Sevilla today is, after Barcelona, the second-trendiest town in Spain, and by far the most interesting place to visit in Andalucia. The historic attractions of Cádiz, dating back over 3000 years and one of the oldest cities of the western world, are a close second.

EATING AND DRINKING

Portuguese cuisine is simple and unrefined. Portugal always was a poor country and the majority of the population once lived in poverty. Food was traditionally more a matter of survival than enjoyment and people had to eat what their land produced or what they could harvest from their home waters. This is why even today, the traditional dishes are made from local produce and are usually very hearty and nourishing - no fancy nonsense here!

The main ingredients are cabbage, potatoes, carrots, tomatoes and the like. For meat, the Portuguese love chicken (of which they eat nearly everything, including the feet, which for some are nothing short of a delicacy), as well as pork (again, eating the feet and ears of the pigs) with roast suckling a true delicacy. Sometimes goat, and only more recently, beef, is also eaten.

It could be anywhere in the British Isles but this is Gibraltar's Main Street

The fish section at the market in Lagos where you are guaranteed to find the freshest fish

Despite Portugal's rich colonies, there was little exotic influence in the day-to-day cooking. Spices and dishes from overseas were exclusively for the rich, and these were a tiny minority in Portugal, although they ran the entire country for decades. It is said that until the revolution in 1974 just a handful of families *de facto* owned the entire country and controlled its economy.

Only Piri-Piri has made a breakthrough into the normal Portuguese cooking and one could not now imagine a Portuguese kitchen without these fiery, miniature peppers. Piri-Piri is added to many dishes and also served in the form of chutneys and sauces - in various degrees of hotness, from very spicy upwards!

In a traditional seafaring country whose major industry has always been fishing, fish in all guises is high on any menu. Standing out amongst all other fish is one important traditional item. Bacalhau is the one fish that can be found and eaten anywhere in Portugal. This is salted and dried cod, quite similar to the Norwegian Lutefisk. The cod was once fished by Portuguese sailing schooners as far afield as Newfoundland and Arctic waters, and it was only by salting and drying the fish that the catch could be brought back home before it had all gone bad!

There are allegedly more recipes for Bacalhau

The market at Lagos, with many exotic mussels and shellfish

Seafood on display in one of the countless seafood restaurants encoutered along the way

The cheerful crew at the Restaurant Ababuja in Alvor

than there are days in the year, but it is paramount that the Bacalhau has to be soaked and rinsed for at least 24 hours before further preparation, otherwise it will be inedible due to the strong salty taste. Once de-salted, Bacalhau can be cooked, grilled or fried and is indeed served in all ways imaginable. Some Bacalhau dishes are very tasty, others, if ill prepared, have a strong soapy and salty taste that has put many people off Bacalhau for good. It doesn't actually help these poor souls that many shops and supermarkets have the typical, strong smell of Bacalhau in its dried form.

Fortunately, a wide variety of fresh fish is also available, including Sardines, Dorade, Eel, Octopus and many more plus Mariscos and Crustaceos (mussels and shellfish). In other words - all is not lost in Portugal, even the gourmand will survive here. Freshly grilled fish with a crisp salad and a cool, soothing Vinho Verde or Branco da Mesa (ordinary table-wine but often dry and good) can still be one of the nicest meals, especially if eaten in memorable surroundings - of which there are so many in Portugal.

The people of northern Portugal love stews with beans. These are called Feijoada and often have meat, fish or chorizo (spicy sausage) as further ingredients. Also famous is the Caldeirada, a fish stew made by the fishermen from their catch and thus coming in all variations, but always thick with fish, tasty and nourishing; or the Caldo Verde, which is a potato and cabbage soup, again from northern Portugal. Not to everybody's taste and more a historic hiccough is the dish of Porto, called Tripas a moda do Porto - made famous out of pure necessity, when Henry the Navigator provisioned his fleet (with which he then proceeded to conquer Ceuta) at Porto, leaving nothing but tripes behind for the Portuense (people of Porto) to eat!

Pork is another favourite. Carne di Porco Alentejao is justly famous and actually very simple: pork stew with fried potatoes and clams. Another good one to try is Carne di Porco em vinho de alhos, which is pork in wine sauce. Leitao is roasted suckling pig always juicy and fat, but delicious.

Further south, in the Algarve, local produce comes in a richer variety and so does, consequently, the cuisine. Added to the traditional cabbages, beans and pork are figs and olives, plus even more fish than further north. Other meats frequently used in Algarve cooking are lamb, mutton, goat, and sometimes wild boar from the mountains. Also, there are more exotic spices, of which Coentros (green coriander) is

only one example.

The Spanish cuisine is altogether more bland, despite the country being traditionally more affluent and, as many people feel, livelier than their neighbours in the far west. The Spanish might love music, dramatic feelings and Fiestas, but as far as their food is concerned, the overall impression is, in comparison to other aspects of life and culture, rather disappointing. There are, of course, exceptions - notably the Basque cuisine, and some justly famous national dishes. The traditional food is still very rich in calories (lots of meat, cooked or fried in generous amounts of olive oil) but very poor in vitamins (vegetables are extremely rare items on traditional Spanish

Both Portugal and Spain have many cafes and bars, although the Café de la Prensa in Huelva is something of an exception

dishes), although, in the more metropolitan cities, things are beginning to change for the better.

Andalusian cuisine is within this cruising area. This is almost Mediterranean, with liberal use of olive oil, garlic, tomatoes and peppers. Along the coast, fish is always a good option, often coming fresh and with some variety, as well as shellfish - especially in the area around Huelva. The three Sherry towns (Jerez de la Frontera, Sanlucar de Barrameda and El Puerto de Santa Maria), Cádiz, and especially Sevilla, are famous for their Tapas - small, often delicious snacks served in bars throughout the day. They go down particularly well with a glass or two of Sherry or wine! The word "tapa" literally means lid, as these snacks traditionally came with drinks, often placed on top of the glass as a lid. Tapas can become something of an obsession - specially in Sevilla - and some chefs get quite creative about them. They consist of anything - fish, mussels, prawns, salads of all descriptions, ham, various meats and vegetables - and come in all combinations. A few Tapas taken in one or more bars can easily replace an entire meal, and often this is tastier and more entertaining than eating in a normal restaurant.

Another great speciality of the region is the famous cured ham - in almost any bar, there will usually be dozens of entire hams dangling from the ceiling. Amongst these, the Jamon Serrano is the most common and is very tasty. The next step upwards is the Jamon Iberico, from the dark Iberian pig. Best of all, but also shockingly expensive, is the Jamon Iberico de bellota, which comes from Iberian pigs which are fed only acorns. Jamon is always served in thin slices and best enjoyed as a Tapa or, maybe as a starter which can also be shared by two or more, or as a racion, which is a full dish. Hard cheeses and dry sherries (Fino from Jerez or Mazanilla from Sanlucar) make perfect companions for the Jamon.

In the poorer Andalusian mountain villages, stews were the main fare, based on thick beans or chickpeas with various types of meat (and offal) and some vegetables. This stew, called Guiso, comes in three main variations: with beef or pork, chicken, or spicy chorizo sausage). Another famous dish, although more along the Mediterranean coast, is Paella, which can be delicious. The name derives from the wide pan in which this dish is cooked, based on rice to which spices (such as saffron, which is where the yellow colour comes from) and whatever else is to hand is being added - usually seafood and rabbit or chicken. Some upmarket versions also include lobster, but that is the exception rather than the rule.

Another typical Andalusian dish and almost as

Majestic Café – Porto (above and left)

In Spain, every restaurant and bar, as indeed any enterprise dealing with tourists, has to keep a book of complaints which any customer has the right to ask for and make an entry if he feels that he has been unfairly treated. The filled in forms will, if all goes according to official proceedings, be presented to the local authority which will be a licensing body or similar.

Wine

Both Portugal and Spain produce superb wines and other world-famous specialities, such as Port wine from the Douro region or Sherry from Andalucia. Wines in both countries are generally much cheaper than in northern Europe and one will not have to spend a fortune to enjoy good quality wine.

Portugal is famous for the young Vinho Verde which comes from the northern Minho and Douro regions. The white Vinho Verde is crisp and tasty and often slightly pearly. There are also red and rosé Verdes, neither of which are aged in casks but are bottled straightaway.

The red wines from the Douro are usually very good, as are the aromatic, full-bodied and fruity reds from the Beira Alta, Beira Baixa and Beira Litoral a little way south of the Douro valley. The Alentejo produces some strong and robust reds, whilst those from the Ribatejo are generally lighter and drier.

Famous are of course the Port wines, which come as White, Red, Ruby and Tawny. All of them are strong and quite alcoholic but nevertheless delicious as either Aperitivos or, especially the sweeter and stronger Rubies and Tawnies, as dessert wines.

Spanish wines are strictly classified in terms of quality. Top of the range is the DOC (Denominacion de Origen Calificada). These have preserved high quality over a long period of time, and at present only the wines from the Rioja region in northern Spain fulfil this demanding

famous is Gazpacho, an ice cold vegetable soup consisting mainly of crushed tomatoes, cucumber, capsicums, onion, lots of garlic and oil. It often comes with breadcrumbs and a side dish of chopped raw vegetables to add. Best enjoyed on a hot and sunny day, when Gazpacho will be especially tasty and refreshing.

Now some notes on eating out in restaurants. These are generally cheaper in Portugal than they are in Spain, which is due to the difference in wages that is still quite pronounced between the two countries. Apart from the prices, also the usual meal times differ greatly. In Portugal, people usually eat their main meal in the evenings, between 18.00 and 21.00 hours. In Spain, however, the main meal of the day will often be taken during the Siesta hours of the afternoon, between 14.00 and 16.00 hours. A lighter meal will follow late in the evenings, and most restaurants will not even open before 20.00 and only foreigners and tourists will start eating before 21.00 hours - Spanish meals can even happen as late as midnight, although 22.00 is the main eating time.

Both in Portugal and Spain, the couvert of bread and butter will always automatically be served and charged extra on the bill, regardless of whether it has been ordered or not. This will usually be more opulent in Portugal, often also consisting of olives and tuna paste in addition to the bread and butter.

category. Next is the DO (Denominacion de Origen) which again says that this wine is produced to certain standards. Vino joven is young wine made for immediate drinking, such as also the vinho de mesa (table wine). Crianza has had to be stored for two years with at least six months in oak caskets (if red) or one year if white or rosé. Reserva requires longer storage, while Gran Reserva is reserved only for particularly good vintages.

Whilst the Rioja wines are surely still the best in Spain, there are a number of good regional wines from other parts of the country. Navarra, also from northern Spain, can be very good, while Aragon produces more robust reds and fruity whites.

Andalucia is famous for its sherries. These are mainly the Fino (dry whites) or Manzanilla (also dry whites from Sanlucar de Barrameda), the Oloroso (smooth and sweet), and the Amontillado (medium dry and nutty). Fino, Manzanilla and Amontillado go down well with Tapas or full meals, with the dry ones for seafood and the medium dry to accompany meat, while Oloroso is also a good dessert wine.

ABBREVIATIONS AND SYMBOLS

The following abbreviations and symbols may be encountered in this book; others may be found which are self-explanatory

	Boatyard	⊕	Hospital	⇌	Railway Station
	Boathoist/travel lift	⚓	Harbour Master	M	Sea mile(s)
Ca	Cable(s)	𝒊	Information Bureau		Showers
	Chandlery	▣	Launderette		Slip for launching, scrubbing
┼	Church	Ldg	Leading	Sp	Spring Tides
	Diesel by cans	◆	Lifeboat	SS	Traffic Signals
	Fuel Berth	Np	Neap Tides	Ⓥ 𝐕	Visitors Berth/Buoy
	Fish Harbour/Quay	✉	Post Office		
	Holding tank pumpout	✕	Restaurant		

DISTANCES

The following distances are approximate – for more detailed table see page 174

Lands End to
Bayona	510M
Viana do Castelo	537M
Leixões	565M
Lisboa	680M
Sines	726M
Lagos	797M
Gibraltar	968M

Ouessant to
Bayona	436M
Leixões	491M
Lisboa	650M
Lagos	760M
Gibraltar	934M

DISTANCES ALONG THE COAST

Bayona to
Rio Mino	20M
Viana do Castelo	31M

Viana to
Póvoa de Varzim	19M
Leixões	31M

Leixões to
Aveiro (entrance of the lagoon)	32M

Aveiro to
Figueira da Foz	34M

Figueira da Foz to
Nazaré	35M

Nazaré to
Peniche	25M

Peniche to
Cascais	45M
Lisboa (bridge)	57M

Lisboa to
Sesimbra	32M
Setubal	44M

Sesimbra to
to Sines	33M

Sines to
Rio Mino	14M
Lagos	78M

Lagos to
Portimão	8M

Portimão to
Vilamoura	20M

Vilamoura to
Faro (entrance to the lagoon)	15M

CHAPTER 1

BAYONA TO LISBOA

After a casual glance at the chart, this piece of coast may look uninspiring, stretching in a more or less even curve, slightly west of south, from the last of the great Spanish Rias, the Ria de Vigo, over a distance of roughly 230 miles to Cabo da Roca, an unspectacular headland after which one can round the corner to approach the Rio Tejo and the capital, Lisboa.

This is only a first impression. After all, cruising need not be all about deserted beaches, romantic anchorages and uninhabited islands, although admittedly all these have their merits. In this case, the attractions lie elsewhere - mainly inland, or at least ashore in some very remarkable harbour towns that can all be visited by boat, and some places further from the sea which will make enjoyable land-excursions.

The northernmost part of Portugal is aptly named the Costa Verde - the green coast. This part is indeed a lush green country, rich in vineyards that cling like narrow terraces to the steep hills along the winding banks of the Douro River. It is here that the grapes for the famous Port wines are grown, but also for the equally well-known Vinho Verde, a fresh, young wine that is especially refreshing on hot, sunny days, as well as some other very good and internationally often underrated local wines. This rich region was in fact the birthplace of the Portuguese nation, and it still has a lot of once distinguished manor-houses (Quintas) and churches scattered around the landscape. Tradition still has an important role in this part of the land, and the religious fiestas are among the more elaborate in Portugal.

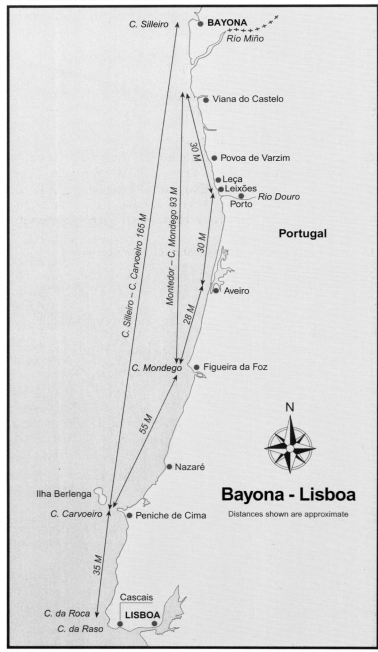

PLACES OF SPECIAL INTEREST

The first easily entered and safe Portuguese harbour, when coming from the north, is Viana do Castelo. En route, one will have passed the mouth of the Rio Mino, which is also the border between Spain and Portugal. The Rio Mino is navigable by small boats or those with little draft but has a difficult entrance. I would think that it would be a very challenging, scenically interesting and rewarding place to explore in a multihull for example, suitable for drying out once inside, but it is a no-go area for any deep-keeled monohull.

There is a small fishing harbour, Caminha, on the south bank and the entrance is marked by lights, although it frequently silts up and the depth changes from year to year. Local fishing boats might well guide a cruising yacht inside, but I would not try it unless on a calm and settled day and on a rising tide. But having said all this, there are some very nice anchorages inside the river for shoal draft vessels.

Viana do Castelo is a completely different matter, for the harbour can easily be entered under almost any conditions. Viana is a historical town of great character and charm and not to be missed on any cruise along this coast! It has the added benefits of a friendly and sheltered marina as well as a long and lively tradition in local costumes and a most delightful cuisine.

Next on the list of musts is of course Porto itself, the proud capital of this region. Visiting the town in a yacht, one has the choice of either berthing in the rather dirty marina in Leixoes, which is the commercial harbour of Porto (and, strangely enough, also an area of gastronomic treats!) and visit the city by the frequent and cheap buses, or to enter the river Douro itself and find a mooring alongside the river bank. This has, of course, the attraction of actually being in the heart of the city with the boat, but currents in the river can run swiftly, there is a significant tidal range to be taken into account when mooring, and there are no shoreside facilities in the form of showers, water or electricity such as are available in the marina at Leixoes.

A few years ago, there used to be a floating pontoon moored in the river specially for visiting yachts, which seemed like a very good idea at the time. Only when this pontoon was swept out to sea by the raging autumn ebbs (which are alleged to reach 15 knots!) while a French catamaran was still attached to it, did the authorities have second thoughts about this - the pontoon has not, so far, been replaced.

The yacht harbour with the two yacht clubs at La Coruna

Sunrise off Cabo Finisterre

Despite this horror story, the river is quite tame during the height of the summer (apart from the sometimes hair-raising entry over the shallow bar at the mouth, which should only be attempted on a rising tide in settled conditions) and is navigable fairly far inland, where it meanders (via several locks) up into the mountains and vineyards. The bridges across the Douro do not open, but if one's mast can be lowered, this is a spectacular trip that could be made by yacht.

In former times, the Barcos Rabelos - which any visitor will soon spot anchored out in the river - were used to transport grapes from the vineyards downstream to Porto, but they have only a short mast on which they set a square sail - obviously designed to more or less drift downstream on the ebb while fully laden, and to be towed back upstream by horses when empty. Also, I am sure that there were not as many bridges then as there are now.

These Barcos, by the way, are of course a great attraction for all the tourists and so they even sometimes sail what they call races on the river during the summer. Each square sail will bear the logo of one of the famous brands of Port, which somehow reminds us of the heavily sponsored scene in today's offshore racing.

So, for convenience, most cruising yachts prefer to tie up in the marina at Leixoes, while the few visitors berths in Porto itself are thus kept free for the more independent and adventurous souls among us. Porto's historical centre has recently been declared as a part of World Heritage by UNESCO, which says a lot about this charming but also exotic old quarter, with its narrow cobbled streets and stairs tumbling to the bank of the river.

Just a few miles further south is the lagoon of Aveiro which is often missed by passing cruising yachts. This may partly be the fault of the existing Pilot Books - which have discouraging things to say about the entrance to the lagoon of Aveiro. True, one English yacht came to grief here a few years ago - tragically, the boat was capsized in the entrance by the breaking waves, thrown ashore and some of the crew were drowned. It is true also that this entrance (just like the entrances to the harbours of Nazaré or Figueira da Foz) can become untenable in heavy onshore weather especially if it has been blowing for several days and if the outgoing, strong autumn tide runs against the wind. But these are conditions normally only encountered in autumn, winter and early spring - during the summer the entrance is straightforward and usually not dangerous.

Once inside, you will be on a rather special, out-of-this world lagoon of low-lying salt pans and semi-flooded marshes. Salt and seaweed is still gathered on the lagoon, but the provincial town of Aveiro is very lively, with a young university and a quite astounding night-life to go with it. It is also possible to sail a few miles to the north on the lagoon, behind the lovely sand-spit with dunes and pine-trees that separates the lagoon from the Atlantic, to a newly built, small marina at Torreira, or stop at peaceful anchorages along the way.

In the southern part, a road bridge limits access

to the busy holiday village of Costa Nova to boats with shortish masts, but the old village of Sao Jacinto, just inside the entrance, is another unusual place to visit. Beware, though - holding here is poor in places, so make sure that your anchor is well set before turning in for the night.

A land excursion to the old university town of Coimbra is certainly worth while, and this could be organised from Aveiro by train or hire car (or from Figueira da Foz, the next harbour south). The medieval town of Coimbra is one of Europe's oldest university towns and most of the city life is dominated by its students, who still wear their traditional black capes on special occasions, and where the university building with its old tower and impressive baroque library sits like a cathedral on top of the town.

A walk around the ancient streets is interesting, and there are numerous bars where the traditional Fado of Coimbra is sung. This city on the banks of the Rio Mondego (not navigable) is divided into

Figuera da Foz fishing harbour

town and gown - the lower part for commerce, the upper half the province of students and the university.

Further south, the coast has indeed little interest for the cruising yachtsman, with the exception of the Isla da Berlenga. This small red rock of an island just off the fishing town of Peniche and the Cabo Carvoeiro is a nature reserve with an abundance of bird-life and has a rather exposed anchorage on its south-east side. Berlega Grande, as this island is also called, is a paradise for divers and anglers. A spectacular walkway connects it with the Castelo de Sao Jao Baptista, dating from the 17th century when it was built as a defence against pirates and hostile warships. It now houses a hostel with a sun-terrace and a small, cheerful and unpretentious restaurant.

It is possible to anchor overnight in settled summer conditions, but if the weather is at all unsettled, it would be wiser to run for the fishing harbour of Peniche for the night. For those of us who, like me, are used to sailing in the North Sea, Berlenga Grande holds a special surprise: it looks very much like Helgoland, which could make one seriously doubt one's navigation after a couple of nights at sea!

From here, it is a longish sail of about 57 miles until one reaches the big bridge over the river Tejo, under which one of Lisboa's five yacht basins nestle.

It goes without saying that a visit to Lisboa, one of Europe's cultural capitals and the setting for EXPO 98, will be the highlight of any cruise in this area. Visitors can easily spend quite a few days - and nights - ashore and still leave without having seen it all, so adequate time should be reserved.

Dom João V library - Coimbra University

Islas Cies seen from the south, showing the main anchorage, and the small southern one

BAYONA

Bayona - 42°07.6'N / 08°50.5'W

This is a favourite haven with many cruising folk, while others think that it is somewhat over-rated. Having said that, Bayona is undoubtedly friendly enough place, and it attracts almost all cruising yachts that pass by this area so there are always plenty of yachting folk around.

The town itself is a popular holiday-resort for many Spaniards and, although small, it is interesting enough for a few days, with cosy bars and restaurants in narrow back streets but little else of real interest. Bayona has a very active and helpful Yacht Club which hosts many (some international) racing events, and it has a very nice Parador (luxury hotel) in the castle overlooking the marina - actually, the very comfortable bar of the Yacht Club is also part of the castle.

In 1493 the badly battered caravel Pinta landed here, bringing the first news of the New World and giving the town a place in history.

For those seeking the atmosphere or the facilities of a large and modern city, Vigo is just up the road by bus or taxi.

LOCATION/POSITION

Bayona is tucked away in a little bay just E of Cabo Silleiro, at the southern end of the Rias region in the entrance to the Ria de Vigo.

APPROACH AND ENTRANCE

The approach and entry to the Ria de Vigo is not difficult, either from the north through the Canal del Norte to the east of the Islas Cies, or through the Canal del Sur to the south of the islands.

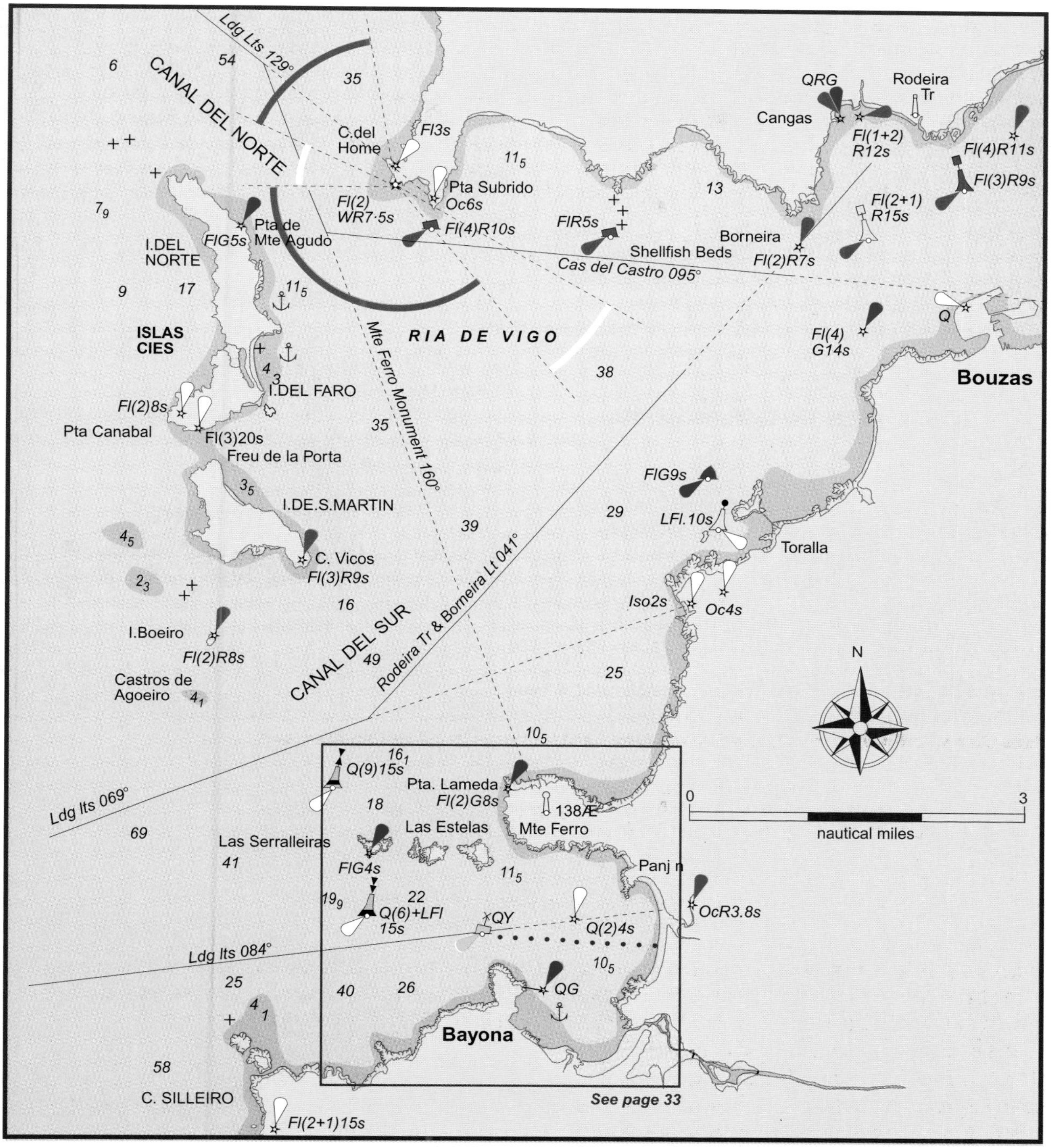
Ldg Lts 129°
CANAL DEL NORTE
C.del Home
Fl3s
Pta Subrido
Oc6s
Fl(2) WR7·5s
Fl(4)R10s
FlR5s
Shellfish Beds
Cas del Castro 095°
Borneira
Fl(2)R7s
Cangas
QRG
Rodeira Tr
Fl(1+2) R12s
Fl(4)R11s
Fl(3)R9s
Fl(2+1) R15s
Q
Fl(4) G14s
Bouzas
I.DEL NORTE
Pta de Mte Agudo
FlG5s
ISLAS CIES
I.DEL FARO
RIA DE VIGO
Mte Ferro Monument 160°
Fl(2)8s
Pta Canabal
Fl(3)20s
Freu de la Porta
I.DE.S.MARTIN
C. Vicos
Fl(3)R9s
FlG9s
LFl.10s
Toralla
Iso2s
Oc4s
I.Boeiro
Fl(2)R8s
Castros de Agoeiro
CANAL DEL SUR
Rodeira Tr & Borneira Lt 041°
N
Ldg lts 069°
Q(9)15s
Pta. Lameda
Fl(2)G8s
138Æ
Mte Ferro
0
3
nautical miles
Las Serralleiras
Las Estelas
FlG4s
Panj n
OcR3.8s
Q(6)+LFl 15s
QY
Q(2)4s
Ldg lts 084°
QG
Bayona
C. SILLEIRO
Fl(2+1)15s
See page 33

Coming from the north, local yachts pass through the Canal de la Porta between the peninsular of Monte Ferro and the innermost rock of La Estelas, although this cannot really be advised without local knowledge. In any case, it is safer and prudent to pass west of Las Selleiras, leaving all associated rocks and shoals as well as the relevant cardinal marks to port. Once inside the little bay of Bayona, sail round the headland with the castle and the mole behind it to reach the marina. The approach and the relevant buoys and pier-head are all lit, so an entry at night should not present any problems.

BERTHING

Yachts tie bow or stern to the floating pontoons with Mediterranean-style mooring ropes. Alternatively, one can pick up one of the swinging moorings which also belong to the Yacht Club. A fee is charged for the moorings, and although it is possible to anchor in the bay just off the pontoons and still be in the lee of the outer mole, cruising yachts are discouraged from doing so by the staff of the Yacht Club and often asked to move to a mooring or the pontoons instead.

If a yacht remains at anchor and thus does not pay any fees, neither the use of the Club facilities nor landing with the dinghy on the pontoons will be allowed, an attitude which seems understandable enough from the Club's point of view, as their berthing charges are actually quite moderate and they offer many amenities to their guests.

FACILITIES IN THE MARINA

The pontoons have water and electricity, fuel (yacht diesel and petrol) is also available in the marina. Ashore, the club has good showers, a launderette and a little office in the walkway beneath the castle terrace manned by helpful and friendly staff. They will also receive and hold incoming mail for visiting yachts, but only subject to prior arrangement by telephone. Upstairs on

the terrace is a first-class bar and restaurant, open to visitors from yachts staying in harbour, with fine views across the bay.

Repair facilities are limited. There is no commercial boat-yard as such, but the club has many employees who can carry out mechanical or boatbuilding repairs. Boats have been left unattended for various lengths of time without any problems, as there are always boatmen of the club around on the pontoons to see that all is well.

TRANSPORT

As far as land transportation is concerned, Bayona is a little bit out of the way and literally at the end of the road. There are buses and taxis to Vigo, where cars can be hired - there are no hire cars in Bayona - and train and bus connections exist from Vigo to other Spanish towns.

PROVISIONING

There are only a few small supermarkets in town, so for any serious provisioning, one should go to Vigo, which for this purpose would also be possible by boat. For normal, day to day shopping

Bayona, with Parador (left), the harbour (centre) and the town

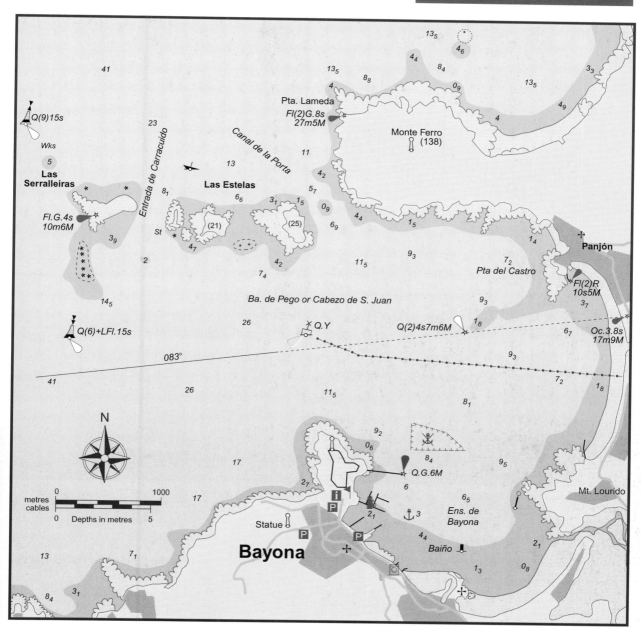

41

Q(9)15s

Wks

5
Las Serralleiras

Fl.G.4s
10m6M

3₉

2

14₅

Q(6)+LFl.15s

41

083°

26

26

23

Entrada de Carracuido

13

8₁

St

Las Estelas

Canal de la Porta

11

6₆

3₁   1₅

4₇

5₇

0₉

(21)   (25)

4₂

7₄

Ba. de Pego or Cabezo de S. Juan

11₅

Q.Y

13₅

4₆

13₅   8₈

4   0₉

Pta. Lameda
Fl(2)G.8s
27m5M

4₂

4₄

4₄   1₅

6₉

9₃

Monte Ferro
(138)

4₄

8₄

13₅

4₉

4

1₄

7₂

Pta del Castro

9₃

13₅

3₃

Q(2)4s7m6M

1₈

9₃

7₂

Panjón

Fl(2)R
10s5M

3₇

6₇   Oc.3.8s
17m9M

1₈

N

metres
cables

0   1000

0   Depths in metres   5

13

7₁

8₄   3₁

17

17

2₇

Statue

Bayona

P

P

P

i

9₂

0₆

2₁

Baiño

4₄

8₄

6

Q.G.6M

3

6₅
*Ens. de
Bayona*

1₃

9₅

2₁

0₈

Mt. Lourido

8₁

---

however, Bayona is perfectly adequate. The shops are conveniently situated in the area closest to the yacht club.

A RUN ASHORE

The Parador Conde de Gondomar is situated in the castle of Monte Real on the promontory over the marina, which dates back to 1500 and was once the residence of the governor. A stroll through the gardens is quite pleasant and will give some very nice views of the sea and the islands. Again, a walk through the town is pleasant if not wildly exciting, although there are

some picturesque and historic buildings in the old quarter. Due to its geographic position, Bayona somewhat lacks the hinterland for any interesting land excursions, except to the modern and bustling city of Vigo.

EATING OUT

Being a popular holiday resort, this is one of Bayona's strong points. In the old quarter one will find many dimly lit, romantic bars and restaurants serving Spanish food of all descriptions, from lavish menus to interesting platters of Tapas with Jamon, Fish or Chorizo.

The harbour with the yacht club and the Parador in the background. A replica of the 'Pinta' is moored on a special pontoon (mid photo) and is well worth a visit

If there is anything special to celebrate, or in case you should feel like pampering yourself with a first-class dinner, it is possible to book a table in the Parador's restaurant (Telephone 986-355000, credit cards accepted). The restaurant El Tunel in the old quarter is always a reliably good bet for high quality sea-food, as are O Moscon (Alferez Barreiro 2) and El Candil (San Juan 46).

DAYTIME ANCHORAGES NEARBY

The Islas Cies just outside Bayona are beautiful and offer some good anchorages, namely off the easterly shores of either the northern or the southern island. Holding is variable and generally better in the sand off the northern island. The large sandy bay has two beach restaurants, and as the islands are a protected area, barbecues or open fires on the beach are not allowed.

Other than that, the Ria de Vigo and Ria de Pontevedra are well sheltered areas for pottering about under sail, offering many daytime and some overnight anchorages, the latter for example in Cangas or in the Ria de Aldan.

Vigo has a marina with all facilities and a Yacht Club where visitors are welcome. As mentioned above, if serious provisioning is intended or major repairs have to be undertaken, Vigo will almost certainly be the better choice than Bayona.

USEFUL INFORMATION

Bayona Tides (Std Port Lisboa, Time Zone −0100)

	MHWS	MHWN	MLWN	MLWS
Height (metres)	3·5	2·7	1·3	0·5

Radio Telephone
Monte Real Club de Yates VHF Ch 06, 16.
Real Club Nautico de Bayona: 986-355234
Real Club Nautico de Vigo: 986-433588
Emergency and police: 091
Taxis: 986-355389

VIANA DO CASTELO

Viana do Costelo - 41°41'N / 08°50'W

The Ria de Lima looking upstream, with the marina just below the bridge

As already mentioned, this is a place full of history, character and charm - a beautiful city on the mouth of the river Lima with many fine Renaissance and Baroque buildings. There are also a number of long, sandy beaches close by. The town was founded in 1258, then called Viana da Foz do Lima, and soon prospered.

In fact, it grew so rich that it was often harassed by pirates until a fortress was built in the 16th century.

Viana today is a pleasant stop-over and a fitting introduction to the Portuguese culture.

LOCATION/POSITION

Viana is about equidistant from both Bayona and Leixoes (about 30 miles away from each).

APPROACH AND ENTRANCE

The approach and entry to the Ria de Lima is straightforward and easy by day and night and under all circumstances. The river mouth and outer harbour are protected by a mole which is lit, and once inside the harbour yachts proceed upstream to the marina which is just below the road bridge on the port side.

BERTHING

Yachts moor alongside floating pontoons with fingers. There are 140 berths, with a maximum overall length of 20 metres and a least depth of 3 metres. The harbour office can be contacted on VHF Ch 12.

FACILITIES IN THE MARINA

The pontoons have water and electricity. Fuel (diesel and petrol) is also available in the marina. Showers are situated ashore and there is a small slipway, but no facilities for hauling out of larger

Close up aerial of the marina

Viana do Castelo

yachts. Mechanical repairs can be arranged, but there are no dedicated, professional services for yachts as such.

TRANSPORT

Cars can be hired for land excursions, and the nearest international airport is Porto, a 40 minute taxi ride away.

PROVISIONING

The town centre is within easy walking distance from the marina and has all the usual shops and small supermarkets for day to day shopping. As in almost all regional towns these days, large Hypermarkets are situated in the outskirts of town and, for serious provisioning are best reached, or more essentially returned from, by taxi.

Santa Luzia sanctuary

A RUN ASHORE

Of particular interest is the Praca da Republica, one of the most picturesque, medieval squares of Portugal, if not of the entire Iberian peninsular. It is best enjoyed on a warm summer evening when the locals relax outside and the lights are on, bathing the scene in a warm glow.

A central feature is the elegant, three-storey Renaissance fountain dating back to 1553. The sinister facade of the Paco do Costelho (town hall) is inspiring enough to think a moment about the passing of history.

South-east of the square and adjacent to the ancient church Igreja Matriz (15th century) is a large house from the same era which now holds a small museum of the town's history. A walk through the streets of the historic centre, such as the Rua do Tourinho, Rua Gago Coutinho or Rua da Bandeira will reveal more historic buildings and small Baroque town palaces.

During the summer, Viana hosts numerous festivals and folk culture events, where colourful local costumes are worn. A highlight is the festival of Nossa Senhora da Agonia in August, when the entire town is in festive mood.

EATING OUT

Viana has a good reputation for its restaurants, and rightly so. Quite a few will feature Fado singing or local dancing, without becoming tacky or too touristy in the process. Typical dishes of northern Portugal feature high on the menus, with Caldo Verdhe (cabbage and potato soup), trout and any variation of Bacalhau.

Roast suckling pig is a particularly succulent delight, served as a speciality in the restaurant O Manuel (Rua do Hospital Velho, 80, telephone 82 28 85) under the name of leitao assado. Very good, although decidedly upmarket and thus not cheap restaurants are the Casa d'Armas (Largo 5 de Outubro, 30, telephone 82 49 99, closed November, no credit cards), or the Cozinha das Malheiras (Rua Gago Coutinho 19, telephone 82 36 80, major credit cards accepted). Slightly cheaper and altogether more rustic is the Os 3 Potes (Beco dos Fornos 7, telephone 82 99 28, credit cards accepted).

DAYTIME ANCHORAGES NEARBY

There are no alternative anchorages in the near vicinity, with the possible exception of the Rio Mino further north (see above).

USEFUL INFORMATION			
Viana Do Castelo Tides			
(Std Port Lisboa Time Zone 0)			
	MHWS	MHWN	MLWN MLWS
Height (metres)	3·5	2·7	1·4 0·5
Radio Telephone			
Call Porto de Viana VHF Ch 16; 11 (0900-1200; 1400-1700LT), Yacht Club VHF Ch 62.			
Local dialling code for Viana do Castelo: 258			
Harbour office: 82 90 96			
Marina: 82 00 74			

LEIXÕES

Leixões - 41°10.5'N / 08°43.3'W

The industrial harbour of Leixões, seen from the south-west

Leixões is the commercial harbour for the town of Porto. With 40,000 inhabitants, Porto is one of the two major centres in Portugal and secretly sees itself as the capital. Indeed, Porto is not only of great commercial importance, but also has a thriving cultural life which competes fiercely with that of Lisboa.

Adjacent are the towns of Leca de Palmeira and Matonishos which are both quite typically Portuguese in their liveliness and would command more attention if they weren't in the shadow of fascinating Porto itself. Leca, especially, has a reputation for some of the best restaurants in the area, and even the Portoese sometimes go there for a special meal. Frequent buses run from the marina straight into the city centre of Porto, which takes about 20 minutes.

The marina at Leixões is friendly.enough - but far from perfect. The water is always extremely dirty - something which normally does not bother us too much, but in this case it is profound, with often a film of crude oil and carcasses of cats, dogs and birds floating around! Also, it is open to the south and although tucked away in one corner of the main harbour, it is very unsheltered in any strong winds from that quarter, which are experienced frequently during autumn and winter. Boats and pontoons have often been damaged under those conditions.

However, in bad weather, when the entrance to the river Douro becomes untenable, there really is no alternative close by, and, having said all this, in normal weather conditions during the summer, the place is perfectly safe. There is also a nice beach just north of the marina with a little beach café frequented by surfers and by now the pollution may well have been washed away.

LOCATION/POSITION

Leixões harbour is 2.5 miles north of the entrance to the Douro. It can easily be located from sea by the large number of tall industrial chimneys immediately to the north.

APPROACH AND ENTRANCE

As mentioned above, Leixões harbour can easily

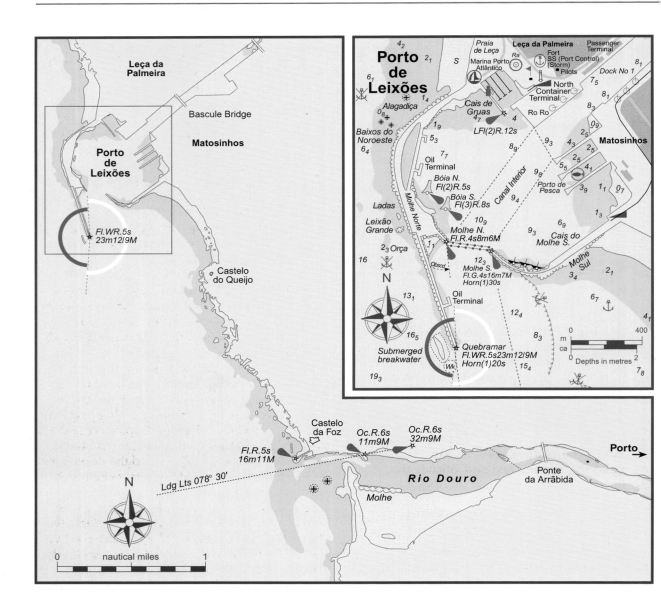

be identified from sea. There are no offlying dangers, although large commercial ships will often anchor outside and one might have to keep an eye on shipping movements.

Entry is possible under all conditions, even in very bad weather from the south-west, and at any state of the tide. The marina is tucked away behind a small mole in the north-east corner of the outer harbour.

BERTHING

Yachts moor alongside floating pontoons with fingers. There is little room to manoeuvre, and it would be not easy to do so under sail. Marina staff will usually allocate a berth and assist with berthing. When berthing, beware of a surge that often sweeps through the marina which makes the boat move back and forth quite unexpectedly.

FACILITIES IN THE MARINA

The marina has the usual facilities, such as water and electricity on the pontoons and showers and toilets ashore. Fuel is available from the first pontoon just inside the marina entrance. There are two sailing clubs and the club-house at the foot of the marina pier is quite pleasant and may be used by visiting yachtspeople. Repairs can be arranged - ask at the marina reception and they will assist as best as they can. There is a sailmaker, marine engineer and boatbuilder for repairs in town, and yachts can be hauled out by crane onto a small hard-standing space if necessary.

Leixões Marina, in the NE corner of the industrial harbour

TRANSPORT

Leixões is quite close to the international airport of Porto, so this is a good place for a crew change. Although it is easy to fly home from here, I would not recommend leaving a yacht unattended for safety reasons.

Porto has a main line railway station from which most other towns in Portugal can be reached. Cars can be hired in Leixões (inquire at the marina office), the airport is only a few minutes away by taxi (taxi rank outside the marina) or bus (inquire at marina office).

PROVISIONING

Leca de Palmeira has the usual assortment of shops associated with any small town, but the main shopping district is about 10 minutes walk from the marina. Matosinhos, on the south side of the harbour over the footbridge that leads across the docks and about 15 to 20 minutes walk away, has a very large and lively market (near the foot of the bridge) which is worth seeing. In typically Portuguese fashion, feathered livestock is kept alive until sold, whereupon the stall holder will slit their throats, let the blood run out and deliver the corpse into the buyer's hands. However fresh, this may not be everyone's ideal experience of shopping!

For serious provisioning, one should go by bus or taxi to the huge Continent Hypermarket on the main road to Porto, where literally anything in the way of food can be obtained.

A RUN ASHORE

Having already mentioned that a stroll around the quaint town of Leca de Palmeira and to the beach might be worthwhile, Porto of course beckons. The bus will drop you off in the centre of the modern part of the city, but from here it is a short and interesting walk to the old town and down to the banks of the Douro river. But before you head down there, take a look at the centre itself.

The heart of the city beats on the Praca da Liberdade, at the foot of the wide Avenida dos Aliados leading uphill to the beautiful town hall, built in the style of Flemish palaces.

The Fiesta de Sao Joao happens every year on the 24th of June, when thousands will be out on the Praca. It is their strange custom to knock each other on the heads with foam hammers, but apart from this unusual practice the Fiesta certainly is a grand spectacle.

Around the Avenida you will find the modern, fashionable shopping streets, and also some very good traditional coffee houses which are always inviting to relax in after the serious shopping has worn you out. One of the most impressive is the Majestic (Rua de Santa Catarina 112) with huge mirrors, dark wood panelling, and the general air of a Vienna coffee house straight from Sigmund Freud's times.

Close to the Praca da Liberdade is also one of the most remarkable train stations anywhere, the Estaciao Sao Bento. This building, which used to be a cloister before trains were devised, is simply beautiful. Inside, the station is more like a museum or gallery for traditional Portuguese art. The main hall is decorated with tile paintings of Portuguese life, historical scenes and images illustrating the history of transport. Even if you are not planning to leave Porto by train, go and have a look around this station!

From the station, a major road leads straight down to the bridge across the Douro, the Ponte Dom Luis I, which was built to plans of Gustave Eiffel in 1881 to 1885. It is a remarkable, two-storey affair which allegedly took 3000 tons of iron to construct.

But for us, it is far more rewarding to veer off the main road towards the right and disappear in the labyrinth of narrow, steep side streets into the old city. This is the Ribeira, the oldest quarter of Porto, which cascades down to the river bank.

The Casa do Infante is allegedly the birthplace of Henry the Seafarer, who later laid the foundations for Portugal's overseas expansion by founding the first nautical school near Sagres (see there for more information). Today, this building (Rua da Alfandega Velha) houses the Gabinete da Historia da Ciedade, the town museum. Close by is the church Igreja de Sao Francisco which is remarkable for the abundance of gold inside - all taken from Brazil in colonial times. Critics say that this is the epitome of catholic grandeur and is perhaps not to everyone's taste, but it is nevertheless impressive. Building commenced in the year 1245, but the church was not completed until 1410. It was refurbished and restyled during the 17th and 18th centuries, which is when nearly all inside surfaces were covered in gold.

Finally, down at the river banks, enjoy a pleasant stroll in the sunshine with fine views of the river, the famous bridge and the boats, which may possibly include a few adventurous cruising yachts, and the typical Barcos Rabelos which were once used to transport the grapes from the wine regions downstream to Porto. You might notice that these strange craft are steered by a huge oar from a high bridge-like structure, because when they were fully laden, the helmsman would otherwise have sailed completely blind! Once a year, these boats sail a regatta from the mouth of the Douro to the bridge (during the big Fiesta on the 23rd and 24th of June).

Along the river banks are a number of cool and dimly lit tavernas which look romantic and picturesque enough for a protracted lunch time meal, but their main appeal lies in the atmosphere rather than in the quality of the food.

Having thus fortified yourself, it is then a good idea to cross the river to the quarter of Vila Nova

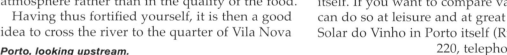
Entrance to the River Douro with the shifting sand bar

de Gaia and visit the Port wine cellars on the south bank. All famous brands of Port have their headquarters here and all of them are open for visitors (closed on Saturday afternoons and Sundays). A tour of one or two of these cellars will give an insight into the making of Port and also the chance to sample and buy the product itself. If you want to compare various brands, you can do so at leisure and at great length in the Solar do Vinho in Porto itself (Rua Entre Quintas 220, telephone 6094749) where hundreds of different types and brands of this wine can be tasted and brought.

EATING OUT

For a first class meal in memorable, grand surroundings, reserve a table at the Belle-Époque hotel Infante de Sagres (Praca Dona Filipa de Lencastre 62, telephone 3398500, credit cards accepted). You will dine exquisitely under huge wooden panels showing scenes from the life and times of Henry the Seafarer.

Porto, looking upstream.
Yachts can moor on the north side of the river just below the bridge

9952106, credit cards accepted, closed Sundays), or a simple but pleasant restaurant with good quality cooking - A Conzinha da Maria (Rua Fresca 187).

If you are stranded in Povoa de Varzim (see below), you need not despair. A two-kilometre taxi ride to the north of the harbour is the restaurant O Marinheiro (telephone (252)-682151, nautically themed and with seafood and shellfish a speciality.

ALTERNATIVE HARBOURS

Just 12 miles north of Leixões is the fishing harbour of Povoa de Varzim which offers good shelter but is also subject to some swell in strong south-westerly winds. Approach and entry are straightforward, but at night the harbour lights are nearly impossible to make out against the backdrop of the city lights. One can usually find a space in the fishing harbour and there are plans to build a marina here, so pontoons may by now be installed.

Povoa de Varzim is a small fishing town, lively but not outstanding. If for some reason you cannot make Leixões, this is a convenient harbour, but otherwise it is perhaps best to continue to Leixões.

The entrance to the Douro River is 2.5 miles south of Leixões. It has a bar and a very narrow channel over it, with seas breaking either side even in moderate conditions. However, in fine settled weather and with an ingoing flood tide beneath you the entrance should not present too many problems.

Yachts can find alongside berths on the pier beneath the old quarter of Porto, but there are no facilities whatsoever here and security might be a concern. When mooring alongside, take into account the rise and fall of the tide (differences can be as much as three metres at springs) so use very long mooring ropes led well aft and forward. Fender-boards will almost certainly be necessary.

Apart from that, there is an abundance of restaurants in Porto, but the Churrascao do Mar stands out as particularly pleasant (Rus Joao Grave 134, telephone 6096382, credit cards accepted), with seafood and shellfish a speciality, closed in August and on Sundays. Another one worth a special mention is Dom Manoel (Avenida Montevideu 384, telephone 6170179) as it is situated in an old palacio near the mouth of the Douro (this quarter is called Foz do Douro) with views over the sea and excellent food, but as is to be expected in such a palatial setting, prices are steep. For typical and cheaper meals, try one of the tavernas along the river bank, for example the popular Taverna do Bebodos.

As mentioned above, Leca de Palmeira is known for good restaurants, and if you are moored in the marina, it will be more convenient and equally enjoyable to dine out here rather than in Porto. One of the nicest small restaurants is the Flor do Castelo (Rua Santa Catarina 102, telephone 9951651, no credit cards) with very friendly service in intimate surroundings. You will not get a written menu here - just eat what the chef brings to your table, a delicious and quite lavish meal.

Another good address in Leca is the O Bem Arranjadinho (Travessa do Matinho 2, telephone

Useful Information			
Leixões Tides Std Port Lisboa Time Zone 0)			
	MHWS	MHWN MLWN	MLWS
Height (metres)	3·5	2·7 1·3	0·5

Radio Telephone Marina
Põrto Atlântico VHF Ch 62, 16.
Local dialling code for Porto: 22
Main tourism office
(Porto do Tourismo): 31 27 40 or 31 75 14
Marina office, Leixões: 9964895, VHF Ch 62
Harbour office, Povoa de Varzim:
(252)-624608 or 631464

The end of the Canal des Pyramides in the centre of Aveiro

AVEIRO

Aveiro - 40°38.5'N / 08°46'W

Aveiro is quite a remarkable and pretty provincial town. It is often called the little Venice of Portugal, as it is surrounded and criss-crossed by many small canals. Aveiro sits at one end of a bizarre lagoon with salt pans shimmering white under the sun and piles of salt on the narrow causeways between.

Seaweed is still gathered on the lagoon from large, flat-bottomed and very colourful boats which are typical of this area, but sadly they are nowadays propelled by noisy outboards rather than by oar.

The town centre is built around the main canal

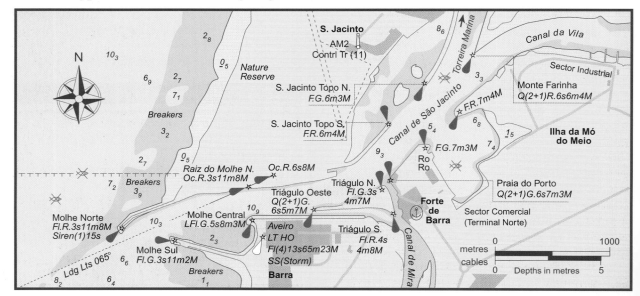

The new marina at Torreira at the northern end of the lagoon

(Canal da Cidade) which is accessible by dinghy from the Canal des Piramides. Many houses are decorated in an Art Deco style, or in the typically Portuguese fashion with colourfully painted tiles. Apart from a visit to Aveiro itself, the lagoon is nice to explore by boat and offers a few quiet anchorages.

LOCATION/POSITION

The entrance to the lagoon of Aveiro is 32 miles south of Leixoes and 34 miles north of Figueira da Foz.

APPROACH AND ENTRANCE

The entrance at the south end of a long spit with sand dunes and pine trees is sheltered by two moles and can also be identified by the conspicuous lighthouse of Barra on its south side. There are no offlying dangers, but, as the bottom shallows, the seas can become short and steep. Entry should best be made on the last half of the flood tide.

In normal conditions, this should present no problems, but things can become decidedly dangerous, and the entrance impassable, in strong on-shore winds when the seas break around and inside the entrance. When in doubt, it is possible to call the pilots at Barra on VHF Ch 16 and ask for detailed information on the conditions.

Once inside the lagoon, for Aveiro proceed past Sao Jacinto and follow the buoyed Canal da Vila.

BERTHING

There is a small floating pontoon just outside the lock to the Canal des Piramides, immediately south of the big fishing pier. Yachts can either moor here or proceed through the lock into the canal - if there is space - to the moorings of the small but very friendly Yacht Club. Boats moor between piles on both sides of the canal, and unless one is very acrobatic, the dinghy is best used to get ashore.

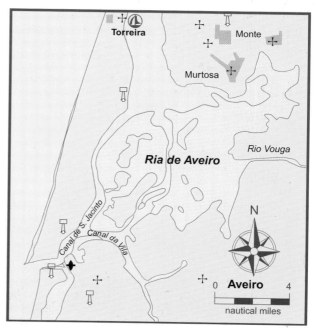

For short stays of up to a few days, no berthing fees are charged. The Yacht Club has no club house or contact address as such, but one of the members will usually greet visiting yachts sooner or later and one can take it from there.

FACILITIES

The club has installed a small pontoon with water and electricity in the canal, which might be used by visiting yachts. A boatyard also caters for yacht repairs (with a large slipway for hauling out), and is located on the south bank of the main canal leading to Aveiro.

TRANSPORT

Aveiro is only about half an hours drive from Porto international airport. It also has a train station connecting it to Coimbra, Lisboa and other towns in Portugal. There are several travel agents in town if flights need to be booked or other travel arrangements have to be made. Cars can be hired in Aveiro.

PROVISIONING

Aveiro has all the shops of a medium sized provincial town. It is however quite a long walk from the floating pontoon to the town centre, but the dinghy can be taken along the Canal des Pyramides and underneath the motorway bridge right into the Canal da Cidade and the town centre. During the winter, some streets in Aveiro are often flooded, and I remember one occasion

Canal des Piramides. Yachts can moor inside the lock, the canal continues below the low motorway bridge into the town centre

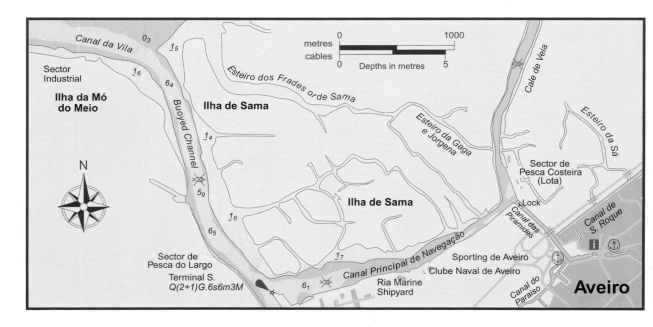

when we took the dinghy and paddled straight across the main road, tying it up literally on the doorstep of a Pizzeria, which turned out to be disappointing, by the way, despite the unusual way of getting there, so it is not otherwise mentioned!

There are small supermarkets for day to day shopping in town, but once again, for more provisions it is best to take a bus or taxi to a Hypermarket on the outskirts of town.

A RUN ASHORE

It is always pleasant to take a leisurely walk around the town, maybe starting on the central Praca da Republica, where the church and the town hall are situated. There are many small, inviting cafés to stop in, and interesting shops in which to browse. There is also a small fish market on the Praca do Peixe, north of the central canal.

The north side seems to be altogether more lively, especially at night, with many trendy and noisy bars full of students from all over Europe - apparently Aveiro university actively encourages foreign students to visit. The bars and discotheques are somewhat scattered around the place, but they are easily found by following the crowds or simply asking around.

In the southern part of the town, the Convento de Jesus now houses the town museum. Of special interest might be the exhibition about the moliceiros, the seaweed-gatherers.

Aveiro has some fine old houses close to the harbour

The beautifully painted 'Moliceiros' moored in the centre of Aveiro

found in many shops and restaurants, are the ovos molos, specially prepared, extremely sweet eggs consisting mainly of egg yolk and several tons of sugar! They are eaten with coffee in the afternoons, or as desserts - you either love them or hate them!

DAYTIME ANCHORAGES NEARBY

There are several sheltered anchorages on the lagoon, especially when following the Canal de Sao Jacinto northwards. Holding is generally not bad in sand and mud, with the exception of the anchorage in front of the little village of Sao Jacinto itself.

If you anchor off the ferry pier in the Baia de Sao Jacinto, you can reach Aveiro by foot ferry and bus, a regular service in summer.

It is also possible to visit the new, small marina at Torreira, a village set amidst dunes and pine trees, but finding one's way past the shallow bar in the Canal de Ovar north of Ilho de Monte Farinha is reported to be difficult.

The most popular and quite spectacular beaches are on the southern side of the entrance, where the little village of Costa Nova is a thriving holiday centre during the summer.

Unfortunately, access to the southern part of the lagoon is limited by a road bridge with not quite enough clearance for the average 34-foot sailing yacht.

EATING OUT

As already mentioned, Aveiro nowadays is more of a students' town with a vibrant night-life, so it is not famous for fantastic restaurants. There are many unpretentious eating-places favoured by the locals, but for a special treat, one might consider the restaurant A Cozinha do Rei in the Hotel Afonso V (Rua Dr. Manuel de Neves 65, telephone 426802). Also above average are the Salpoente (Rua Canal Sao Roque 83, telephone 382674, closed Sundays) and the O Moliceiro (Largo do Rossio 6, telephone 420858).

One speciality typical of Aveiro, which will be

Useful Information

Aveiro Tides

(Std Port Lisboa Time Zone 0)

	MHWS	MHWN	MLWN	MLWS
Height (metres)	3·3	2·6	1·4	0·6

Local dialling code for Aveiro: 234
Port Captain of Aveiro: 397230
Tourist office: 20760

FIGUEIRA DA FOZ

Figueira da Foz - 40°09′N / 08°52′W

This is a typical Portuguese harbour town and attractive seaside resort with a convenient marina and a strategic position as a stepping-stone when harbour hopping south. Also, the ancient university town of Coimbra (see above) is not many kilometres away upstream and is well worth a visit, this being simplest by hire-car.

LOCATION/POSITION

Figueira da Foz lies immediately south of Cabo Mondego, 34 miles south of Aveiro and 35 miles north of Nazaré.

APPROACH AND ENTRANCE

Cabo Mondego is easy to identify from sea. Figueira is at the mouth of the Rio Mondego, which is protected by two moles reaching out to sea. Under normal circumstances, the approach and entrance do not present any problems. However, the harbour is frequently closed in autumn and winter when the prevailing south-westerly winds become strong and can make the entrance unpassable. There is a shifting bar outside the entrance on which the seas can break heavily under those conditions. If in doubt about entering, call the harbour-office or the pilots on VHF Ch 16.

Storm signals are displayed on the fortress on the north side of the entrance: A black ball hoisted to the top (day) or three fixed lights GRG (vert) means that the port is closed. If the black ball is hoisted to the middle (day) or the lights are flashing, the entry is dangerous and prohibited for all vessels under 12 metres in length. So, when on passage south late on the year, wait for a secure window in the weather and avoid the danger of being caught out in an onshore gale along this coast at all costs.

BERTHING

The marina is on the north side of the river close to the town. Mooring is alongside on floating pontoons with fingers. There are 200 berths on the pontoons plus a 120-metre quay in case your boat is longer than 15 metres.

FACILITIES IN THE MARINA

Water and electricity on the pontoons, and there are showers ashore. Some repairs can be arranged.

PROVISIONING AND ASHORE

The marina is conveniently close to the town centre, so shops are within easy reach. One could have a wander around town and have a look at the old fortress, the Casa do Paco (a 17th century residence), and the local museum.

There is a seaside promenade, a casino and several discotheques. The beaches north of the

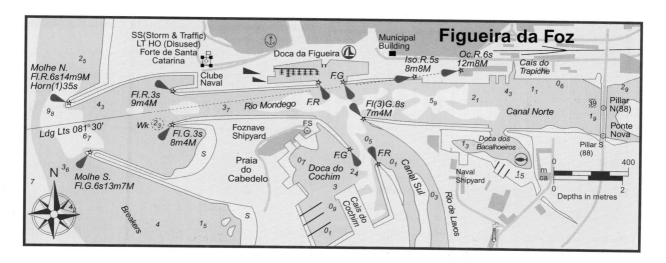

Entrance of the Rio Mondego, looking upstream with the marina to the left

entrance are also worth mentioning and they are not too far from the marina. There are a number of bars and restaurants, but none is really outstanding.

Having said that, there is one restaurant 11 kilometres south of Figueira which offers very good food at reasonable prices. This is the O Solar de Lavos (in Lavos, telephone 233-946787, closed Sunday nights, credit cards accepted). If taking a hire-car to visit Coimbra, this is a good alternative to the restaurants in Figueira itself.

Figueira da Foz lighthouse

Bridge - Figueira da Foz

USEFUL INFORMATION

Figueira da Foz Tides
(Std Port Lisboa Time Zone 0)

	MHWS	MHWN	MLWN	MLWS
Height (metres)	3·5	2·7	1·3	0·5

Radio Telephone
Port Postradfoz VHF Ch 11, 16. Marina Ch 08.

NAZARÉ

Nazaré harbour seen from the south, with the winding entrance and the yacht pontoons at the inner end

NAZARÉ

Nazaré - 39°35.5'N / 09°04.5'W

A fishing harbour with a tiny but very friendly marina and a small but quite picturesque and bustling holiday town which gets rather busy during the summer. This may also be down to the fact that the surrounding landscape is very pleasant, with long sandy beaches and pine forests.

Unfortunately, the marina is very close to the busy and noisy fishing harbour, and a long way from the town, but there is a miniature railway that connects the harbour with the town during the summer.

If you happen to be here in September, so much the better - from the 8th to 14th of September there is a big Fiesta, with fun-fairs, folk-dancing and bull-fights.

LOCATION/POSITION

Nazaré is immediately south of the headland Pontal da Nazaré, which has a lighthouse. It is 35 miles south of Figueira da Foz and 25 miles north of Peniche.

APPROACH AND ENTRANCE

The rocky headland with a fortress and lighthouse can be identified from sea. There are no offlying dangers and the harbour, for a pleasant change, does not have a bar across the entrance! First-time entry at night can still be quite interesting, as one has to come fairly close to the beach before the harbour opens up.

It is possible to enter at any state of the tide and, theoretically, in any weather. However, entering this harbour in a very strong onshore wind requires nerves, prudence and the usual bit of luck.

BERTHING

Once inside the harbour, there are a few pontoons for yachts in the south part, where one moors alongside or rafts up to other yachts. The least depth is 3.5 metres in this part of the port.

FACILITIES IN THE MARINA

The pontoons have water and electricity, and there are showers ashore. The marina staff are very friendly and helpful and will assist where they can - language is not a problem as the manager hails from the Isle of Man.

Fuel is available, and repairs could possibly be arranged. It has been reported as a suitable place to haul out and leave a yacht for a time.

PROVISIONING

Nazaré is not the perfect place to stock up with plenty of food and drink, as the marina is such a long way from the town. However, the marina staff will probably be able to organise a taxi which can take you to one of the big supermarkets a little way inland of the town itself.

A RUN ASHORE

Nazaré has some very inviting sandy beaches close to the harbour. A walk through the busy little town is quite interesting, and there are numerous bars and cafés in which to pass the time. The climb up to Monte Sitio will be rewarded with fantastic views across the bay.

Not far inland from Nazaré, at Batalha, lies the monastery of Santa Maria da Vitoria which is classified as World Heritage Site by UNESCO. This medieval monastery is world-famous, building having commenced after the battle of Aljubarrota against the Spaniards in 1385. It is a conglomeration of several very impressive buildings, amongst them a gigantic church, two chapels and various inside yards, and the overall impression is simply mind-boggling - even for those who do not normally indulge in the admiration of ancient churches.

Nazaré seen from the north; town front, and harbour in the background

EATING OUT

As Nazaré is still primarily a fishing town (at least it is in winter when the holidaymakers of summer are gone!), fish is an obvious choice for lunch or dinner. The restaurant Mar Bravo has a good quality selection of seafood and shellfish (Praca Sousa Oliveira 67-A, telephone 551180). And in case you cannot manage the walk back to the boat after over-indulgence, they also offer accommodation!

DAYTIME ANCHORAGES NEARBY

Sao Martinho do Porto

A tiny bay formed by the mouth of the Rio Salir, about 5 miles south of Nazaré. Whilst it looks like a perfect natural harbour on the chart, local sailors have warned that surf and swell run into the bay and often make entering and leaving decidedly difficult and often dangerous.

Once inside, the depths shallow rapidly from about 3 metres in the entrance to less than 2 metres. Use this anchorage only in settled summer weather and definitely not during the autumn or winter months.

Stay well off-shore until the entrance to the bay, between two rocky headlands, can be identified. There are shoals and rocks off the headlands on both sides. If possible, identify the leading pillars and enter on a course of 145°. Inside, to port, is a jetty which is used by local craft and fishermen, depth is around 2 metres at the head but shallowing rapidly. There are also underwater hazards. Ashore is a small, rather touristy, town with some shops, bars, restaurants and banks.

USEFUL INFORMATION

Nazaré Tides (Std Port Lisboa Time Zone 0)			
MHWS	MHWN	MLWN	MLWS
Height (metres) 3·3	2·5	1·4	0·6

Radio Telephone VHF Ch 11, 16 (Office Hrs).
Local dialling code for Nazaré: 262

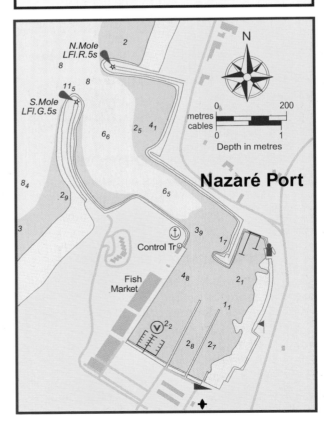

PENICHE

Peniche - 39°21'N / 09°22'W

This is another ancient fishing town that turns into a popular holiday spot during the summer. Attractively located on the rocky promontory that has Cabo Carvoeiro at its end, Peniche offers baroque churches and an ancient fort. Visitors are not only drawn here by the picturesque little town or the boats leaving for Isla da Belenga (see below), but also by the surrounding countryside, with the beaches, lagoon and historic town of Obidos not far away to the north. There is also a good marina inside the main harbour.

LOCATION/POSITION

The harbour of Peniche is tucked away in a corner immediately south-east of the promontory. It is just over 25 miles south of Nazaré and 45 miles north of Cascais (in the approaches to Lisboa).

APPROACH AND ENTRANCE

Coming from north, the channel between Isla Berlenga and Cabo Carvoeiro is wide, deep and safe. There are no dangers off the Cape and once past one can head straight for the harbour entrance. Approach and entry are usually easy, but in strong south-westerly winds it can become tricky and even dangerous.

BERTHING

Once inside the harbour the marina is on the inside of the west pier. Yachts moor to pontoons with fingers and shelter is good, although severe swell has been experienced inside the marina during winter in south-westerly gales. There are 140 berths with a least depth of 3.5 metres. The harbour-office can be called on VHF Ch 16 and 62.

FACILITIES IN THE MARINA

Water and electricity are laid on at the pontoons, with laundrette, showers and toilets ashore. Repairs can be arranged, there are some technical services, and boats can be hauled out by slipway or crane. Fuel is available in the harbour.

TRANSPORT

Buses to Obidos and other places in the region, but Obidos is certainly worth a visit (see below).

The peninsular of Peniche seen from south

PROVISIONING

Peniche is a busy little town and has a good range of shops of all descriptions.

A RUN ASHORE

A walk around the town and the promontory is time well spent. From Cabo Carvoeiro with its bizarre cliffs, some of which are allegedly shaped like a ship (although this requires some imagination to recognise), there is a grand view out to sea and to the Isla Berlenga. The fort dates back to the 16th century and can be visited. This used to be the strongest and most feared fortification facing the sea in the whole of Portugal, and building was continuous for nearly 300 years!

During the times of the dictator Salazar, political prisoners were kept (and tortured) in the very place where you can now enjoy a peaceful visit to the regional museum (open Tuesday to Sunday)!

For those interested in clerical history, the three baroque churches in town are noteworthy. These are Igreja de Nossa Senhora da Ajuda with remarkable sculptures (17th and 18th century), Igreja da Misericordia with two paintings by Josefa de Obidos from the 17th century, and Igreja de Sao Pedro which has a painted wooden ceiling.

The Isla Berlenga is always worth the short boat trip, but you are much better off than the average tourist since you can visit the island in your own time and in your own boat (see below).

Another excursion certainly worth making is to the medieval walled town of Obidos, which can be reached by bus from Peniche. This town, with its beautiful renaissance and baroque buildings, is like a live museum and has in fact been declared a Portuguese national monument. An impressive castle towers over the village below, and from here you will have spectacular views of Obidos itself and the surrounding landscape.

Surprisingly, Obidos once used to be a port, although it now lies several miles inland. This was due to the gradual silting up of the lagoon over the centuries. Another curious fact is that the town was privately owned for many centuries. The Moors were chased out in 1148 by Afonso Henriques and in 1282 Dom Diniz gave the town to his wife Isabel as a wedding present. From then onwards, until 1833, Obidos always was the personal property of the Portuguese Queen.

The castle in Obidos now also houses the beautiful Pousada do Castelo, an outstanding

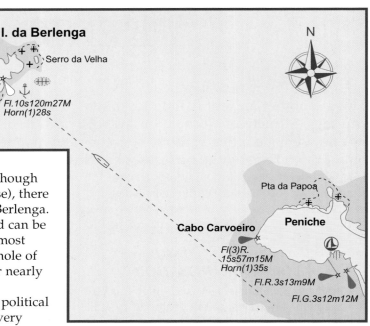

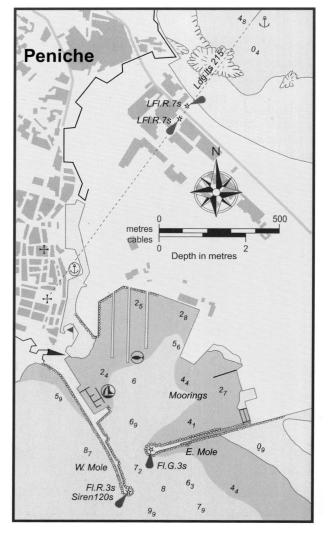

Peniche harbour seen from SW, with the yacht pontoons clearly visible just inside the entrance

luxury hotel with six rooms and three suites. In case this tempts you to spend a night ashore, the two rooms in the tower, numbers 8 and 9, are the prettiest. (Pousada do Castelo, Paco Real; telephone (262-959105).

EATING OUT

Peniche has many restaurants along the harbour-front, most of them not surprisingly specialise in fish and seafood, which is always fresh here. It is hard to recommend one above the other, so take your choice by chance and you will probably not be disappointed.

In Obidos, there are several outstanding restaurants, not least in the above mentioned Pousada. The hotel Albergaria Josefa d'Obidos (Rua Dr. Joao de Ornelas, telephone 959228, closed in January and Sundays, credit cards accepted) has a nice terrace on which to dine.

O Conquistador (Rua Josefa de Obidos, telephone 959528) is noted for its specialities, among them stuffed eel and wild boar. Moderately priced but good quality and pleasant surroundings are offered by the restaurant Alcaide (Rua Direita, telephone 959220, closed in November, credit cards accepted).

DAYTIME ANCHORAGES NEARBY

Unusual for this part of the world, Peniche actually offers several anchorages close by the harbour. Do not miss a visit to Isla da Berlenga. The anchorage is off the south-east shore of the island, but the water is quite deep and the holding only average, so make sure that your anchor is well set before exploring the island. In settled summer weather, this can also serve as an overnight anchorage, with the knowledge that if the weather plays up one can always run back to Peniche harbour for peace of mind and safety.

It is also possible to anchor just south-east of the harbour off the beach Praia de Medee or, alternatively, to the north of the peninsular in the bay between Isla de Fora and Punta da Papoa. Do not forget, however, that in the summer, the northerly wind often blows quite strongly in the afternoons, when one would probably want to move out of this bay, which is wide open to the north.

USEFUL INFORMATION

Peniche Tides (Std Port Lisboa Time Zone 0)

	MHWS	MHWN	MLWN	MLWS
Height (metres)	3·5	2·6	1·3	0·5

Radio Telephone VHF Ch 16 (H24), 11.
Local dialling code, Peniche and Obidos: 262
Tourist office, Peniche: 789571
Tourist office, Obidos: 959231

CASCAIS

Cascais - 38°41.8'N / 09°24.8'W

A very fashionable and rather elegant seaside resort on the western outskirts of Lisboa in the centre of the Costa do Sol, the so-called Portuguese Riviera. There are some remarkable beaches nearby such as the romantic Praia do Guincho, and memorable land-excursions can be made to Sintra (the Garden of Eden)

and Queluz (the Versailles of Portugal). Berthing here and visiting Lisboa by train from Cascais is a viable alternative to berthing in the Lisboa marinas.

as will, once further inshore, the lights and marks leading into the Tejo.

The marina is protected by an outer mole; the entrance opens to the north-east.

LOCATION/POSITION

Cascais is situated in the approaches to the Rio Tejo and Lisboa, south of Cabo da Roca and Cabo Raso. It is 45 miles south of Nazaré and 12 miles west of the bridge at Lisboa.

APPROACH AND ENTRANCE

The approach from the sea and the entrance do not present any difficulties. Coming from the north, the Cabo da Roca and Cabo Raso serve as landmarks. There is also a lighthouse above the marina on the Forte de Santa Maria. Coming from the west or the south, the principal lights of Cabo Raso and Cabo Espichel will be good landmarks,

BERTHING

Berthing is on pontoons with fingers. Ample visitor space has been reported by yachts visiting recently.

The new marina at Cascais seen from the west

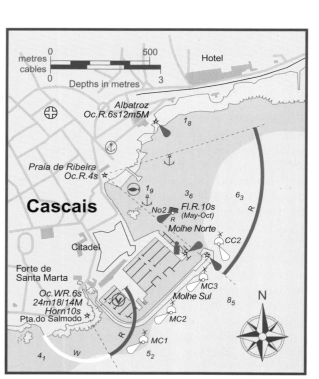

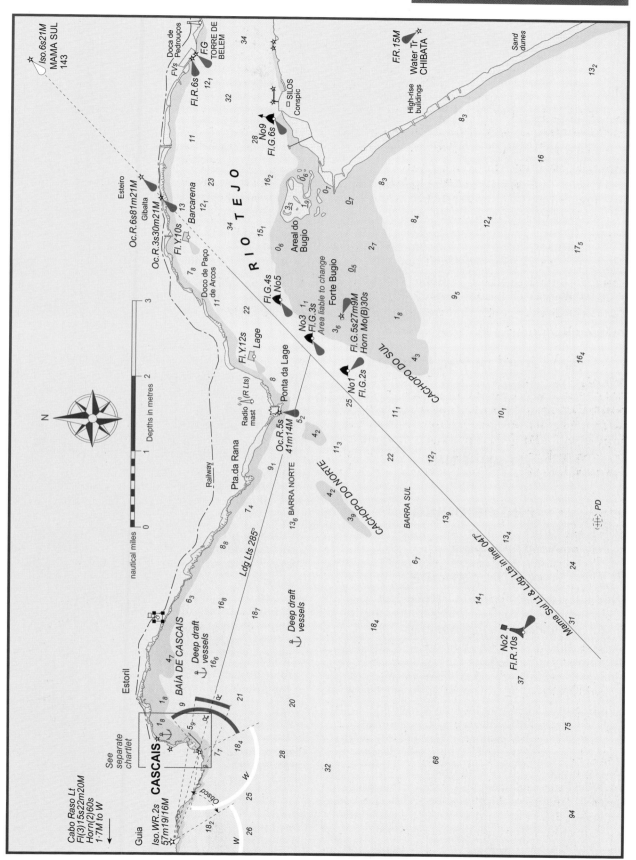

Cabo Raso Lt
Fl(3)15s22m20M
Horn(2)60s
1·7M to W

Guia
Iso.WR.2s
57m19/16M

See separate chartlet

CASCAIS

Estoril

BAÍA DE CASCAIS

Deep draft vessels

Deep draft vessels

Pta. da Rana

Railway

Ldg Lts 285°

BARRA NORTE

CACHOPO DO NORTE

BARRA SUL

Ponta da Lage

Oc.R.5s 41m14M

Radio mast

Lage

Fl.Y.12s

Fl.Y.10s

Doco de Paço de Arcos

Oc.R.3s30m21M

Oc.R.6s81m21M

Esteiro Gibalta

Barcarena

RIO TEJO

Areal do Bugio

Forte Bugio

Fl.G.5s27m9M
Horn Mo(B)30s

No5
Fl.G.4s

No3
Fl.G.3s
Area liable to change

No1
Fl.G.2s

CACHOPO DO SUL

No9
Fl.G.6s

SILOS
Conspic

Fl.R.6s

F.G
TORRE DE BELEM

Doca de Pedrouços

FVS

Iso.6s21M
MAMA SUL
143

F.R.15M

Water Tr
CHIBATA

High-rise buildings

Sand dunes

No2
Fl.R.10s

Mama Sul Lt & Ldg Lts in line 047°

PD

N

Depths in metres

nautical miles

SOUTH WEST SPAIN & PORTUGAL CRUISING COMPANION **55**

The anchorage in the bay NE of the marina

FACILITIES IN THE MARINA

There are all the usual facilities including water, electricity, and showers. Visitors have noted that security on the pontoons left a lot to be desired, but this may have been improved.

TRANSPORT

There is a fast and regular train service to Lisboa.

PROVISIONING

All shops for provisioning, and as well as elegant expensive shopping in Cascais.

A RUN ASHORE

This sophisticated resort has a wonderful waterfront promenade on which to wander up and down underneath the palm-trees. The beaches close to the town become very crowded in summer, and especially during the week-ends when at least half of Lisboa seems to congregate here. If any form of transport can be organised, it is well worth travelling the nine kilometres to the beach of Praia do Guincho which has the added benefit of a superb restaurant (see below). And once a car has been hired, why not go and see the beautiful sights a little way inland as well? These include the outstanding and wildly romantic gardens at Sintra, which have been described as a "glorious Eden" by Lord Byron. He was not the only one to become enthusiastic about this magical village - it captured the imagination of many other writers including Hans Christian Andersen ("The most beautiful place in Portugal") and William Beckford ("The best piece of land on earth").

So what is all this fuss about? The little village lies on rocky hills which give fine views to the Atlantic on the western horizon, and it is full of palaces, monasteries, quiet parks and wild gardens.

The palace of Monserrate has a remarkable story. It was originally built by William Beckford on the ruins of an ancient palace and later abandoned. Half a century later, one Sir Francis Cook came along and rebuilt the romantically decayed gardens and houses in an elaborate manner - he loved the Moorish-Gothic style - but then he left as well. Now, nature has been creeping back up the once pristine garden paths of Monserrate to give it back the morbid air of the forlorn that fascinated both owners in the first place.

Towering above Cintra Antiqua, the old quarter of the town, is the castle of Paco. It can be visited, and for the historically minded, there is a lot to be seen. Moreover, arguably the most elegant hotel in Portugal is located in Sintra - the Quinta da Capela (Estrada de Monserrate, telephone (21-9290170). It has been lavishly decorated with antiques and original pieces of art by the Portuguese film-maker Arturo da Silva Pereira, and is surrounded by wonderful gardens.

Another interesting excursion might lead to the palace of Queluz. Do not be confused by the fact

The lighthouse at Cascais

that this town lies in the heart of an industrial region. You will find here a wonderful rococo palace which was originally built between 1747 and 1755 for Pedro III. It has been likened to Versailles and Sanssouci, and both it and its gardens are indeed beautiful.

To pacify those members of the crew who might not be too interested in wonderful palaces, rococo or not, one could mention that the palace also has one of the best restaurants around. The superb Cozinha Velha in the old kitchens of the palace (telephone (21-4356158) is renowned for imaginative starters and highest quality main courses.

EATING OUT

As is to be expected in a seaside resort of this calibre, Cascais has a bewildering number of good restaurants. Most of them tend to be quite expensive, at least by Portuguese standards.

Two very nice ones are situated in the Rua des Flores: Pimentao (telephone 4840994) and O Pipas (telephone 4864501). Both specialise

in seafood and shellfish.

If you feel more like eating meat, try Dom Leitao instead (Avenida Vasco da Gama 36, telephone 4865487). If venturing out to Praia do Guincho, you might give yourself a very special treat and allow yourself the gastronomic extravaganza of a meal at Porto de Santa Maria (telephone 4870240) which is one of the very, very few restaurants in Portugal that has climbed to the heights worthy of a Michelin Star. No more needs to be said!

DAYTIME ANCHORAGES NEARBY

It is possible to anchor in the bay to the north-east of the marina.

USEFUL INFORMATION			
Cascais Tides (Std Port Lisboa Time Zone 0)			
	MHWS	MHWN	MLWN MLWS
Height (metres)	3·5	2·7	1·4 0·7
Local dialling codes for Cascais, Sintra and Queluz: 21			
Tourist office: 4868204.			

LISBOA

Lisboa - 38°39.5N / 9°19.0 W

Not only the capital of Portugal and of great maritime interest, but it is also one of Europe's cultural capitals and was the setting for EXPO 98. Moreover, Lisboa must be the most romantic and inspiring European capital and still has an exotic feel and nostalgic flair that is not found in any other major European metropolis, even in Paris or Rome.

LOCATION/POSITION

Lisboa is situated on the north bank of the Rio Tejo roughly two-thirds down the coast of Portugal. The position of the huge bridge across the Tejo is 38°41.5'N and 09°10'W.

APPROACH AND ENTRANCE

Approach and entry to the Rio Tejo are well marked and lit and should not present any problems. However, there is a (quite deep) bar across the entrance which will make for short and steep seas in westerly or south-westerly winds of substantial strength.

At low tide and in storm conditions, seas can break around the approach and entrance, but these are the only conditions that one would prefer to avoid.

BERTHING

Lisboa has a choice of five yacht basins - Doca de Bom Sucesso, Doca de Belém, Doca de Santo Amaro, Doca de Alcantara and the new Marina Expo. Of all these the Doca de Santo Amaro and Doca de Alcantara seem to be most popular with visiting yachts, offering easy access to the city. Again out of these two, the Doca de Santo Amaro has the more pleasant surroundings, with shops, bars and restaurants lining the harbour front, but it is situated more or less directly beneath the

Rio Tejo looking upstream, with the Doca de Bom Sucesso and the Doca de Belém and the monument of discoveries at Belém

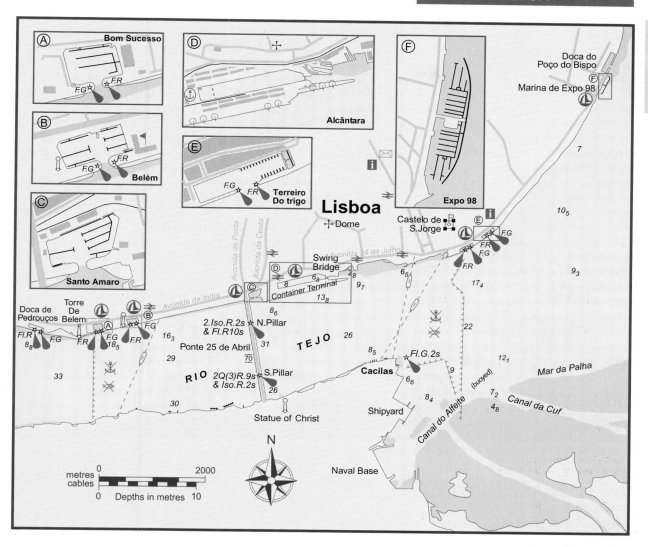

Bom Sucesso
A
F.G ☆ ✦ F.R

B
F.G ☆ ✦ F.R
Belém

C
Santo Amaro

D
⚓
Alcântara

E
F.G ☆ ✦ F.R
Terreiro
Do trigo

F
Doca do
Poço do Bispo
Marina de Expo 98
F

7

10₅

Expo 98

Lisboa
⌗ Dome

Castelo de
S.Jorge
E ⚓ F.G
F.R
F.G

F.R

9₃

Avenida da Ponta
Avenida da Ceuta
Avenida 24 de Julho

Swing
Bridge
D
Container Terminal
8
6₈
8
9₇
13₈

6₅

17₄

22

Avenida da India
C

Doca de
Pedrouços
Torre
De
Belem
A
F.G
B
F.G
Fl.R
8₈
F.G
F.R
18₅
F.R

16₃

2.Iso.R.2s ☆ N.Pillar
& Fl.R10s

8₆

8₆

Ponte 25 de Abril
29
31
70

26

T E J O

85

Fl.G.2s

12₁

Mar da Palha

33

R I O
S.Pillar
2Q(3)R.9s ☆
& Iso.R.2s
26

Cacilas

66

9

85

84

(buoyed)

7₂

4₈

Canal da Cuf

Canal do Alfeite

30

Statue of Christ

Shipyard

N

metres
cables
0   2000

0   Depths in metres   10

Naval Base

Tejo-bridge and is thus noisy from the traffic passing overhead. Besides, it only has a very limited number of visitor's berths.

Next to it, the Doca de Alcantara has many visitor's berths and is situated as close to the city as one can get in a yacht. The Doca de Belém is also attractive, situated on the outskirts of Lisboa in a place drenched in maritime history, including the well-known monument of discovery (after all, it was from this very dock that many Portuguese ships set out on their epic voyages of discovery in the 15th and 16th centuries). The excellent maritime museum is in the immediate vicinity. Using buses or the suburban train service, the city is quickly reached from here.

The Doca de Bom Sucesso was until very recently used only by the navy and lies a little bit further west, near the Tower of Belém. The new Marina Expo has the best facilities of all yacht basins but lies at the other end of Lisboa, in the

The Doca de Alcantara is probably the most popular place for visiting yachts

The small basin of Doca de Santo Amaro, underneath the massive Tejo bridge

very east, in the modern surroundings of the Expo area. Again, there are good connections to the centre of Lisboa by public transport.

My personal favourites are either the Doca de Santo Amaro for the very pleasant quayside surroundings or the marina Expo for the best facilities. Having mentioned this, others might prefer the convenience of the Doca de Alcantara or the special ambiance of the Doca de Belém - in short you are spoiled for choice.

During summer, however, berths are not readily available everywhere, so it is best to call Lisboa Port Control on VHF Ch 12, 16 or 64 in advance.

FACILITIES IN THE MARINAS

All marinas supply electricity and water on the pontoons as well as showers and toilets ashore - some in a more luxurious fashion than others. Fuel is available in Bom Sucesso, Belém and Marina Expo. For repairs, it is best to go straight to the Marina Expo which has a boatyard, with whatever mechanics and boatbuilders you might need. There are hauling out facilities as well as what appears to be well-stocked chandlery.

TRANSPORT

All forms of transport are available - buses and trains to all other parts in Portugal, hire-cars and of course an international airport. The city itself has a new metro which makes moving about in Lisboa much quicker and easier than only a few years ago.

PROVISIONING

Provisioning is certainly no problem in a major city like Lisboa, but for the visitor unfamiliar with the place, it is actually easier to organise in one of the smaller harbours where things are perhaps less confusing.

However, I am sure that the harbour staff will point you in the right direction if major provisioning is required.

A RUN ASHORE

As already mentioned above, Lisboa is definitely a most enticing European capital, with a long history and fascinating architecture to go with it. The colourful cultural life with strong bonds with

The Doca de Santo Amaro is lined with attractive bars and restaurants

north all the way to the Praca Dom Pedro, *alias* Rosso, as it is called by the Lisboans. Around the Rosso are a number of smaller squares, with many street cafés and busy stalls and kiosks - this is the vibrant centre of daytime Lisboa. An entire day could easily be spent in the Baixa, with the time divided between the delightful shops and equally inviting cafés and restaurants.

The Baixa is noteworthy for being a planned quarter, in stark contrast to other parts of Lisboa. After this part of the city was destroyed by the great earthquake of 1755, the minister Marquis de Pombal (he also planned the town of Vila Real de Santo Antonio) had it rebuilt following contemporary town planning fashion. The streets run straight and parallel to each other, and originally each was home to a specific trade or craft. They have nowadays been taken over by banks, offices and some of the more traditional shops. Modern stores can be found to the west, in the district of Chiado.

Along the waterfront, the Cais do Sodré is a bustling, lively spot with the colourful Mercado da Ribeira in its centre. This indoor market is open from Monday to Saturday, 0600 to noon, and has an impressive selection of food, spices and flowers. Most of the dockside warehouses are now being converted into upmarket cafés and restaurants.

In complete contrast, and almost a small world in itself, is Lisboa's old quarter, The Alfama is located east of the Baixa. Its narrow winding streets, too cramped for modern traffic, form a labyrinth which spills downhill from Castelo de São Jorge and the cathedral Sé to the river. Interesting bars and restaurants mingle with more traditional, cheap and cheerful eating and drinking places. Campo de Santa Clara is the setting for the local flea-market, twice every week, and the fiesta on June 12th is the annual highlight in this district. The Castelo de San Jorge can be visited (in the summer daily from 0900 to 2100) and offers some fine views on to the surrounding city. The gardens are a pleasant place to escape the hot town on a fine summer's day.

Another superb spot for a rest is the terrace Miradouro de Santa Luzia, which is located close to the museum Escola de Artes Decorativas on Largo das Portas do Sol. This museum is in fact the private collection of one of Portugal's wealthiest banking families, and the exhibits include antique furniture, carpets, chinaware and some famous paintings by Lopes, Portuense and Marques. The former cloister Mardre de Deus has one of the most remarkable museums of Lisboa,

the past contrast with the vibrant, sparkling scene of today - a curious mix of modern life with a generally slower and somehow more humane pace than will be encountered in any other major metropolis.

There is a large selection of shops, both of the wonderfully traditional type (mainly in the streets of the Baixa district) as well as the usual mainstream stores which can nowadays be found in any old capital!

A wealth of museums and churches can be visited on rainy days, and the cinemas, as everywhere in Portugal, normally show films in the original language version. The nights will be as romantic or wild as you care to make them, with Fado bars and glitzy music clubs, the more important of which are conveniently located in the old warehouses on the Alcantara dockside, close to the harbours of Doca de Santo Amaro and, of course, the Doca de Alcantara itself.

Nearly all visitors will start the day in Lisboa on the huge Praca do Comercio down by the riverside, which is surrounded by fine baroque buildings but is now sadly misused mainly as a giant car-park. From here, one can saunter up into the busy Baixa shopping district which extends the Museu Nacional do Azujelo (Tuesday to Sunday, 1000 to 1300 and 1400 to 1700). More than 15,000 hand-painted tiles are on display, not only originating from Portugal, but also many Spanish and Dutch tiled paintings. The great Azujelo painting which is the centrepiece of the exhibition dates back to the 18th century and is made up from 1300 tiles, showing the town of Lisboa before the great earthquake of 1755.

West of the city centre is the Bairro Alto, the high town. Although it is a residential area, it attracts more and more people in the evenings, who flock to the numerous Fado bars, restaurants and clubs. This quarter is reached either by bus or, better because this is quite an experience in itself, by one of the so-called elevadores, although two of the three are actually trams rather than elevators.

The Elevador da Bica leaves near the Mercado da Ribeira in Cais do Sodré (Rua de Sao Paulo). This tram climbs up steep and narrow streets and the ride is truly memorable. The Elevador da Gloria leaves from behind the tourist office on the Praca dos Restauradores, which is one of the main traffic hubs of Lisboa, and takes you to a small park off the Rua de Sao Pedro de Alcantara, from where you can enjoy a spectacular view across the city.

The third elevator actually is an elevator rather than a steeply climbing tram, and it operates inside a remarkable metal tower which was built in 1902 and has a roof-top café, again offering superb views across the Baixa. This is the famous Elevador de Santa Justa in the heart of the Baixa, off Rua Aurea just South of the Rossio.

The Alcantara district lies west of the Bairro Alto. The area near the river and yacht basins has been developed into trendy territory which now has become very popular. It has many good bars, restaurants and some of the more heavy-weight clubs in town (see below). This, of course, is especially convenient for those of us who have managed to secure a berth in one of the two adjoining Docas (de Alcantara or de Santo Amaro), but for the daytime coffee or lunch-time snack, be warned that prices in these smart cafés along the waterfront and around the yacht basins are considerably higher

Lisboa from the air, showing Belém basin with the Monumento dos Descobrimentos

The Elevator Santa Justa in Lisboa

than in the more traditional locales in town. A night-time walk up to the old quarter of Alcantara is especially worthwhile if a visit to one of Lisboa's Fado spots is featured on your evening programme.

Situated close to the Doca de Alcantara, the Museu Nacional de Arte Antiga is Portugal's main art gallery and is always worth a visit. It has a large collection of older Portuguese paintings, dating from the 15th century, and is located in a formidable Palazzo dating back to the 17th century, when it was owned by none other than the Marquis de Pombal. The gardens overlook the river, where there is a café with outdoor tables. (Rua das Janeas Verdes, open from Tuesday to Sunday, free entry on Sunday).

Anyone interested in arts should also visit the internationally renowned Museu Calouste Gulbenkian with its Centro de Arte Moderna, which is in the new town near the Parque Eduardo VII (buses 31 or 46 from

Monumento dos Descobrimentos - Monument of Discoveries in close-up

The former EXPO site is another major attraction. It is now called the Parque das Nacoes (Park of Nations), and is also home to Europe's largest oceanarium, a truly futuristic building which houses impressive tanks for 25,000 fish and sea creatures, from colourful tropical fish to the cute black-and-white penguins of Antarctica. Open daily from 1000 to 1900 hours, but be warned that it can get very crowded especially during week-ends. (Metro station Oriente).

Southwest of Lisboa along the banks of the Tejo lies the famous suburb of Belém, with some outstanding sights. Vasco da Gama set sail from here for India in 1497, and he is buried in the opulent Mosteiro dos Jeronimos nearby. Other highlights here include the Monumento dos Descobrimentos, the Torre de Belém and, in brutal contrast to these historical landmarks, the hypermodern pink marble block of the Centro Cultural de Belém (open 1100 to 2000 daily), which has an interesting design museum, contemporary art and photography exhibitions as well as various events during week-ends.

The world-famous Mosteiro dos Jeronimos dates back to 1500, when the King laid down the first stone of this ambitious building which was designed to show off Portugal's wealth and power following the successful return of Vasco da Gama from his East Indian voyage in 1499. The main entrance features a group of figures around Henry the Navigator. The monastery today also houses two museums in its buildings, the vast Museu da Marinha (maritime museum, Tuesday to Sunday 1000 to 1800) showing Portugal's great maritime past (of interest to all seafarers) and the Museu de Arqueologia (the archaeological museum).

One of Lisboa's most photographed buildings must be the Torre de Belém, which was built

Rossio, bus 51 from Belém or Metro to Sao Sebastiao, Tuesday to Sunday 1000 to 1700). This is more a cultural centre than just a museum or gallery, and it sits bang in the middle of a large, sub-tropical park. The complex is run by the Gulbenkian Foundation, named after the Armenian oil millionaire (Calouste Gulbenkian, 1869 to 1955) whose private collection is on display here. The Museu has sections on classical and Oriental as well as European art, while the Centro de Arte Moderna, across the garden, has some interesting contemporary art by Portuguese and international artists.

Lisboa Aquarium, Nations Park

Torre de Belém

Along the river at the Doca de Santa Amaro more upmarket bars and restaurants await you. The Espalha Brasas is interesting for the (lunch-time only) Tapas menu and the outdoor, dockside tables, while the restaurant Tertulia do Tejo (tel. 213 955 552) is definitely a serious enterprise, using three storeys of one of the old warehouses. Similar in architectural concept is Zeno (tel. 213 973 948) which specialises in Brazilian dishes and also has live samba music most nights.

Along the Cais do Sodre area (near the station of the same name) is yet another converted warehouse. The restaurant Cais de Ribeira (Armazem A, tel. 213 463 611) is popular and can be recommended for high quality fish and meat dishes, although it is not exactly cheap.

Arriving at the Praca do Comercio, the Martinho da Arcada (Praca do Comercio 3, tel. 218 879 259), hidden away beneath the arcades, is a must. It has the distinct and rather elegant flair of times long gone by about it, and serves solidly traditional Portuguese food.

Up in the Baixa and Chiado, we are completely spoiled for choice. A favourite with locals and visitors alike seems to be the busy Bodega 1 de Maio (Rua de Atalaia 8, tel. 213 426 840), which offers good wines and fresh fish and meat dishes of the day, usually along with the company of a cheerful crowd. A Lisboan institution is the ancient Tavares Rico (Rua de Misericordia 37, tel. 213 421 112) decorated in old-fashioned splendour and serving high quality traditional dishes. To dine and wine here in style does not, however, come cheap. Another institution in the Chiado district is the famous coffee-house A Brasiliera (Rua Garrett 120) with its beautifully traditional interior which is a superb place for a quiet coffee during the days, but it quickly fills up with a young and noisy crowd after work or shopping.

On to the Bairro Alto, the gastronomic capital inside the capital. A typical place is the Alfaia (Travessa da Queimada), decorated in the usual style with low ceilings, wine-caskets and azujelos, but always attracting a cheerful crowd for moderately priced Portuguese dishes. Definitely more fashionable (and thus also slightly more expensive) is Fidalgo (Rua da Barroca 27, tel. 213 422 900) which serves very good seafood creations

between 1515 and 1521 to defend the entrance to the Tejo. Difficult to imagine today but, it once stood isolated on a rock near the middle of the river - until a big earthquake in 1777 shifted the river-bed causing the bank at Belém to silt up and become part of the shore.

Finally, a famous sight in Belém is the monument of discoveries, the Monumento dos Descobrimentos which was built in 1960 - the 500th anniversary of Henry the Navigator's death. He is depicted leading the figures clustered around the bow of a ship, and they are the thirty two most significant explorers of Portugal's great past. There is an interesting world chart on the floor in front of the monument which shows the routes of the most important voyages of discovery - which also could make a nice incentive to plan the rest of your own trip there and then...!

EATING OUT AND NIGHT-LIFE

Obviously, there are thousands of restaurants, cafés, bars and eating-places of all descriptions in Lisboa, so the following can only be a tiny selection in the districts already mentioned above. Many smart and upmarket restaurants and bars can be found near the river and the yacht basins in Belém and Doca de Alcantara. One such example is the Vela Latina at the Doca de Bom Sucesso (tel. 213 017 118), which serves very good, imaginative Portuguese food but is fairly expensive. In Belém try the less pricey and less well known eating place Carvoeiro (Rua Vieira Portuense 66, no credit cards). It is unpretentious, has a few outdoor tables and serves good-value grilled fish.

Santos docks by night

Maritime at Doca de Santo Amaro, with live Brazilian music and a bar-restaurant attached to it.

No stay in Lisboa would really be complete without at least one authentic Fado night. The real saudade feeling, this typically Portuguese melancholy which can be so beautiful and bitter-sweet when expressed in true Fado songs, is sometimes ruined by tacky tourist shows. But there are still many authentic Fado clubs, usually small, dark and cosy Tavernas which also serve food and, of course, drinks. They usually open around nine or ten in the evening, but the action rarely gets going before midnight and then often continues well into the small hours. Nearly all of them have minimum consumption charges, starting at 2000 Escudos but may easily reach 6000 Esc per head, and the bill obviously increases if one also eats here.

The following are only a small selection: in Alcantara, go for Timpanas (Rua Gilberto Rola 24, closed Wednesdays): in the Bairro Alto, try the attractive but moderately priced NoNo (Rua do Norte 47), the Adega do Ribatejo (Rua do Diario de Noticias 23) where allegedly even the cooks sing from time to time, or the ancient Adega do Machado (Rua do Norte 91) with fine singing and a cuisine to match.

and the fabulous leitao (suckling pig) to a colourful and interesting clientele and is open throughout the day (1000 to midnight).

More formal, upmarket and elegant is Pap'Acorda (Rua da Atalaia 57, tel. 213 464 811). Further along the street is the late-night favourite Hell's Kitchen (Rua da Atalaia 176), where the decor definitely lives up to the name but has no connection with the cooking, which is simple but delicious! For a modern and sophisticated cuisine with more than just a little French touch, try the relatively expensive Pato Baton (Travessa dos Fieis de Deus, tel. 213 422 345).

NIGHT LIFE

A lot goes on around the Alcantara Docks, where the trendy clubs can be found. Amongst these is the very flashy Docks Club (Doca de Alcantara, Monday to Saturday 2200 to 0600) which is a 'huge dancing thing', complete with a bar and restaurant attached to it in - you've guessed it - an old warehouse! Of similar format is Indochina (Rua Cintura do Porto de Lisboa), an Asian restaurant which transforms itself into a dance club from around midnight onwards.

Close by is the most famous of them all, the legendary Kings and Queens which was launched as a huge high tech palace for the gay section of Lisboa's night-owls, but is now frequented (or possibly avoided) by people of all persuasions! Another hot place is Salsa Latina in the old Gare

DAYTIME ANCHORAGES NEARBY

Off Cascais (see p55). The more adventurous can venture further up the Tejo and find anchorages there, but charts are not very accurate, and there is little to lure one past Lisboa, anyway.

USEFUL INFORMATION

Lisboa Tides (Std Port - Time Zone 0)

	MHWS	MHWN	MLWN	MLWS
Height (metres)	3·8	3·0	1·5	0·5

Radio Telephone Call Lisboa Port Control (Port authority) VHF Ch 12 16; yachts entering or leaving Lisboa are required to keep watch on Ch 12 or 16 and Ch 13; Marina EXPO Ch 62

Dialling code for Lisboa: 01

Airport: 218 413 700

Emergencies: 112

Tourist Office: 3610350

Marinas

Doca de Bom Successo: 3922011

Doca de Belém: 3631246

Doca de Santo Amaro: 3922011

Doca de Alcantara: 3922048

Marina Expo: 8380727

LISBOA TO SPAIN

This section deals with the southern part of Portugal, which comprises several interesting regions. The coast can be divided into three main parts - the first being the Atlantic coast south of Lisboa as far as Cabo de Sao Vincente, the second the rocky Algarve coast from Sargres or Baleeira to Portimão,

and lastly the sandy part of the Algarve coast, mainly made up of the lagoons behind the various low-lying islands that stretch from Faro eastwards almost to the Río Guardiana on the Spanish border. These coasts front the regions of Alentejo and the Algarve respectively.

Sailing south from Lisboa, there are just three harbours until one has rounded Cabo de São Vicente and arrived at Lagos. These are Sesimbra, Setúbal and Sines, the last being an ideal starting point for any longer passage south, or if bound for Madeira or the Canary Islands. Sines is the southernmost Portuguese harbour on the Atlantic coast and has deep, safe water immediately one clears the breakwater - no offlying dangers to worry about here. Under normal circumstances, it is an easy overnight passage from Sines to Baleeira or Lagos, so this is the place to wait for the right weather.

If you are passage making late in the season a window of at least 24 hours is required before setting off. Waiting, however, is not as bad as it might sound, as Sines is a pleasant place in which to spend a few days.

Once round Cabo de São Vicente, the coast is high and rocky until well east of Lagos, with some very impressive anchorages near the Cape. Lagos is the first port with modern marina comforts, but if the weather is right a stop at Cabo de São Vicente, or Baleeira, is certainly worth while (for details see below under Baleeira/Sagres), as the scenery is simply overwhelming and there are some fascinating walks along the cliffs to the Cape itself.

These anchorages are all wide open to the

'Enterprise' sailing into Portimao

south, and indeed nearly all harbours of the Algarve suffer to a certain extent by being uncomfortable or sometimes even dangerous to enter in strong southerly winds. If these conditions prevail, one would have to time one's entry to coincide with the last part of the ingoing flood tide, in order to have as much depth as possible and to avoid wind against tide conditions. The good news is that really strong southerlies are only encountered in winter, and even then are infrequent and rarely blow for long.

Once around Cabo de São Vicente, the climate becomes milder and more Mediterranean the further east one sails along this coast, so it comes as no surprise that many Algarve harbours are popular as wintering holes for liveaboard yacht owners, as temperatures are often higher and the weather milder and drier than in many parts of the Mediterranean itself. This area is very convenient for other reasons, like cheap flights to the UK and northern Europe from Faro airport, and a large number of ex-pat English speaking residents who have brought a fair bit of home culture to this part of the world!

So, between Lagos and Faro you can buy London newspapers on the day of their publication back home, visit 'English' pubs, and even have your traditional Sunday roast dinner - and nearly everybody speaks English! Also, there is a choice of at least three modern marinas (Lagos, Portimão and Vilamoura), as well as sheltered anchorages suitable for long-term stays in Alvor, Faro and Olhão.

The western part of the Algarve, the rocky coast, is favoured by tourists and most prone to the noisy summer tourist racket. Things do become a lot quieter in this respect a bit further east, for example in the towns of Olhão, Tavira and Vila Real. The first two of these are located in the beautiful lagoons of the Rio Formosa nature reserve (see below), where one could spend days, if not weeks, pottering about and anchoring in different places.

PLACES OF SPECIAL INTEREST

Sines is certainly worth a visit, not only as a strategic stop-over harbour on the way south, but also as an interesting town full of character. The marina is nearly always at least two-thirds empty but the marina staff members are particularly friendly and helpful (and even speak some English), and Sines is a very good base from which to tour the hinterland of the Alentejo, which can be visited by hire-car or, even better in a way, by bus from Sines.

This province, between the rich regions around Lisboa in the north, and the historically important and now prosperous region of the Algarve in the south, has always been poor, sustained by agriculture

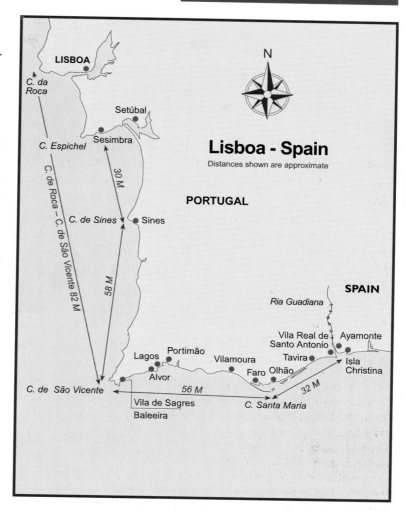

Pine Cliff Beach

Tomates beach

and little else. It has been regarded by many Portuguese as backwards and slow-developing, but this is part of its charm for today's visitor.

In the beautiful countryside, you will find scattered villages and market-towns that appear to be living in a bygone era, seeming to ignore our fast and colourful western world. Just sit in the sun with a couple of old men in front of some sleepy café, with dogs and cats dozing in the shade and nothing much else happening on the market square in front of you, and try to wind down to this slow-motion mode - and you may experience what I am trying to explain!

Another place to experience great emotions is the majestic Cabo de São Vicente. Depending on the time of year and the weather encountered at sea, you might be more than happy to round it and reach the comparatively sheltered waters of the Algarve. This cape was regarded as the end of the world by ancient settlers and as a seat of the gods by Greek and Roman philosophers, and if seen in rough weather it can be quite awe-inspiring.

If one is lucky enough to be here in settled weather, it is certainly worth trying one of the two anchorages (for details of these, see below under

Baleeira / Sagres) under the towering cliffs. It is a strange feeling indeed to anchor here, with the wide open Atlantic Ocean behind you and a wall of rocks in front, but if the conditions are right, this anchorage is as safe as any other with the added advantage that, should the weather deteriorate, it is at least easy to get out to sea!

Once in the Algarve proper, which begins with the popular holiday town of Lagos, Alvor offers a pleasant alternative to the marinas on either side, although a small marina is now under construction. This charming former fishing town has a beautiful lagoon on which one can anchor in a peaceful and safe pool not far from Alvor itself, however the

Ria Formosa

The entrance to Vilamoura marina

town is being taken over by tourists, especially at night when it then comes to life as bars and discotheques open from midnight to dawn.

The nature reserve of the Rio Formosa is a major attraction west of the Río Guadiana. This system of lagoons is separated from the sea by a long series of narrow sandbanks. There are several openings to the sea, called barras, some of which are navigable and used by local fishing boats, but only the barra at Faro and Olhão, and the one at Tavira, are usable by yachts or larger vessels without local pilotage on board.

The nature park covers an area of over 17,000 hectares and is a stop-over point for many migratory birds from Europe and Africa, as well as a nesting site for dozens of other species including storks, herons and caimans. There are numerous anchorages in the channels that run behind the sand-bars, of which only the main ones leading to the larger cities are buoyed and marked. Many more can be explored by dinghy or in the mother-ship, which is best done at low tide so that the mudbanks can actually be seen. At high water, most of the area behind the sand-bars is covered and navigation then becomes difficult, or even hazardous.

A typical fishing village beach

SESIMBRA

Sesimbra - 38°25.5' N / 09°06.5'W

Sesimbra is a pleasant little town a little way south of Lisboa but still close enough to the capital to be one of the Lisboans' week-end summer retreats. As such, it has many shops and bars and the relaxing atmosphere of a seaside town, but it is also a busy fishing harbour.

POSITION

Sesimbra lies on the rocky, south-facing coast just over 5 miles east of Cabo Espichel, about 30 miles from Lisboa.

APPROACH AND ENTRY

Sesimbra is easily approached from sea as there are no offlying dangers. Cabo Espichel is easily identified if coming from north or north-west - it is the rocky promontory at the S end of a low and sandy stretch of coast just south of the entrance to the Tejo river.

Coming from the south Sesimbra is about 5 miles east of Cabo Espichel. During daytime, the village can be seen from far off, and at night the lighthouses of Cavalo and Sesimbra are good navigation marks.

Entrance to the harbour is straightforward during the day, but can be a little confusing at night, due to the backdrop of shore lights. There are two lit buoys just outside the harbour; the red light at the end of the pier is quite weak, and the beacons east of the harbour are even more difficult to make out at night.

Once inside the harbour, the local yacht club has a few pontoons at the extreme south-west end of the harbour.

BERTHING

Yachts moor to floating pontoons with fingers. Sometimes, visiting yachts will be allocated a berth by one of the boatmen belonging to the yacht club. This club has a very annoying pricing policy where by berthing fees are not charged by the size of the boat but by the size of the berth (which is allocated by the club). Visitors also find it quite irritating that the boatman will ask them when they plan to leave again, even before the yacht is tied up! They might even ask for instant payment of the mooring charges, which should always be categorically refused.

The club's secretary told us that he was fully aware of the irritation caused to crews of visiting yachts, but was obviously not prepared to do anything about it.

FACILITIES IN THE MARINA

Water and electricity are installed on the pontoons. The club has a small office for collecting the berthing fees, but only very primitive and (most of time) refreshingly cold showers that also offer a wonderful chance to study the colourful local bug and insect life!

The harbour of Sesimbra seen from S, with the yacht club and pontoons in the W (left hand) corner

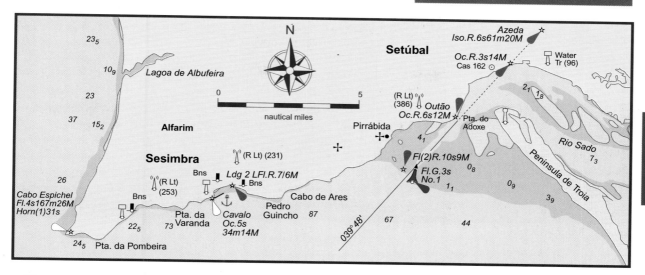

There is a yard building wooden and steel fishing vessels which might be able to haul out and repair yachts.

ANCHORAGES NEARBY

In calm weather it is possible to anchor in the bay east of the harbour entrance.

A RUN ASHORE

The marina is at the extreme end of the fishing harbour which in turn is about ten minutes walk along the seafront from the town itself. Alternatively, there is a fairly frequent minibus service from the fishing harbour into the town centre.

As already mentioned, Sesimbra has a pleasantly relaxed feel about it, and a nice beach with a waterfront promenade. There are small side streets with numerous shops, bars and restaurants, and it is easy to spend a lazy day lingering around town and on the beach.

TRANSPORT

There are buses from Sesimbra to Lisboa which take over one hour in each direction. Cars can be hired in Sesimbra.

PROVISIONING

There is a good range of small shops and supermarkets around Sesimbra.

EATING OUT

As mentioned, Sesimbra has a wide choice of restaurants and bars. Two which stand out are Ribamar (Avenida dos Naufragos 29, telephone 2234853, Amex, Mastercard and Visa accepted, fish and shellfish specialities, and medium to high

priced) and O Pirata (Rua Heliodoro Salgado 3, telephone 2230401, credit cards accepted, closed in December and slightly cheaper than Ribamar).

DAYTIME ANCHORAGES NEARBY

Portinho de Arrábida

Portinho de Arrábida is an open bay located 6M E of Sesimbra and close to the entrance to the Rio Sado. Its natural amphitheatre of high hills over looks the anchorage, which is crowded with summer moorings. Give Forte Arrábada a 0.5M offing to avoid the Baixo de Alpertiche.

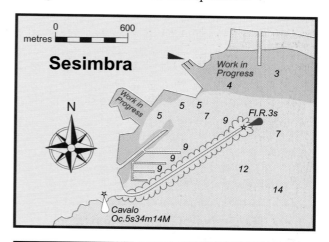

USEFUL INFORMATION

Sesimbra Tides: (Std Port Lisboa Time Zone 0)			
	MHWS	MHWN	MLWN	MLWS
Height (metres)	3·4	2·6	1·4	0·6

Radio Telephone: VHF Ch 11
Local dialling code for Sesimbra: 21
Tourist office: 2235743
Port authority: 2233048

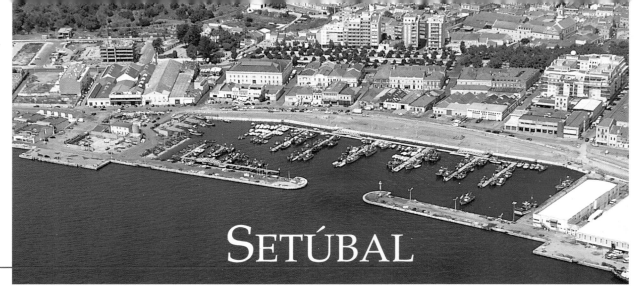

SETÚBAL

Setúbal, the town harbour

Setúbal - 38°31.2' N / 08°53.5'W.

Setúbal is a traditional fishing town, and now also something of an industrial centre, but it still has a very pretty old part noted for romantic, narrow streets and buildings in the Manueline style, such as the monastery Igreja de Jesus (see below). Close by is a natural park, and the Rio Sado can be explored a little way further inland past Setúbal by the more adventurous. Fantastic beaches can be found on the Peninsula de Troia opposite Setúbal on the south bank of the river.

POSTITION

Setúbal lies on the north bank of the Rio Sado.

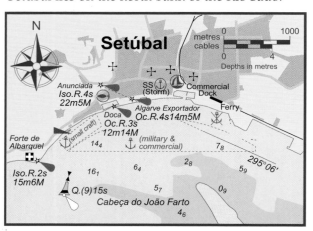

APPROACH AND ENTRY

The estuary of the Rio Sado is in the north-eastern corner of the bay of Setúbal and has a bar across it. The approach is marked by a red lightbeacon Fl(2)R.10s and a lit green buoy Fl.G.3s between which the channel leads across the bar. Beware - the water is extremely shallow outside of this marked channel and the seas will break heavily in onshore winds of any force.

From the approach marks, steer 040° (leading lights) for the harbour of Setúbal. The Fontinhas marina is in the western half of the commercial dock.

BERTHING

Yachts moor to pontoons with fingers. There are 160 berths for yachts up to 12 metres length, minimum depth is 3.8 metres. The marina office can be reached on VHF Ch 12.

FACILITIES IN THE MARINA

Water and electricity on the pontoons. Showers, launderette and toilets ashore. Fuel is available. Some (mechanical) repairs can be arranged for, but there are no other dedicated facilities for yachts.

ANCHORAGES NEARBY

There are various anchorages in the Rio Sado, which is navigable for a few miles inland, but which is not marked. Anchoring, for example, is possible west of Setúbal harbour, on the north side of the river, or in various locations behind the Troia Peninsula.

A RUN ASHORE

Setúbal is a charming and busy provincial city and is definitely worth exploring. The historical town centre is about 1.5 miles north of the marina. The town museum is inside the cloister Igreja de Jesus on the Praca Miguel Bombarda with both older and contemporary art (open Tuesday to Saturday 0930 - 1230 and 1400 - 1700 hrs as well as Sunday 0930 - 1230).

A little way out of town is the impressive

The Rio Sado (in the foreground), looking West across the Troia peninsular

Castelo da Sao Filipe with one of the nicest Pousadas (luxury hotel) of all (telephone 523844). Speaking of luxury hotels, even more charming is the Quinta des Torres (telephone 21-2180001) in the Villa Fresca de Azeitao, which must surely rank amongst the most impressive renaissance buildings in Portugal.

USEFUL INFORMATION

Setúbal Tides (Std Port Lisboa Time Zone 0)			
	MHWS	MHWN	MLWN	MLWS
Height (metres)	3·5	2·7	1·3	0·5

Radio Telephone VHF Ch 11, 16, YC Ch 12
Local dialling code for Setúbal: 265
Tourist office: 534222
Marina office: 534095

TRANSPORT

Trains and buses to Lisboa and all other parts of Portugal. Cars can be hired.

PROVISIONING

There are all types of shops and supermarkets in Setúbal, but most are a fair distance away from the marina. The best option will be to use a taxi to a Hypermarket if major provisioning has to be done.

EATING OUT

There is a wide range of restaurants around Setúbal but one fairly close to the marina which offers good quality for medium prices is the restaurant Isidro in the hotel of the same name (Rua Professor Augusto Gomes 1, telephone 535099, credit cards accepted).

Other than that, the restaurant in the Pousada de Sao Filipe is good for a special treat.

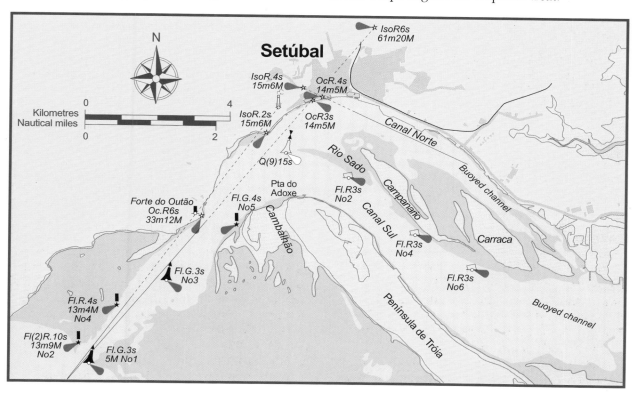

SINES

The entrance to the Rio Mira, S of Sines

Sines - 37°56.5'N / 08°53.2'W

Sines is sometimes seen as a huge commercial harbour and nothing else, but it is in fact a very picturesque, and rather sleepy, little Alentejo town. It is well worth a visit, as it has a friendly marina and a sandy beach close by. The town has special nautical interest as the birthplace of Vasco da Gama.

POSITION

Sines is just over 30 miles south of Sesimbra and the mouth of the Rio Sado, and just under 60 miles north of Cabo de São Vicente.

APPROACH / ENTRY

Cabo de Sines immediately north of the harbour and the long outer mole of the commercial harbour are easily identified from sea. There are

The inner harbour of Sines seen from the NE with the marina in the middle

SOUTHWEST SPAIN & PORTUGAL CRUISING COMPANION

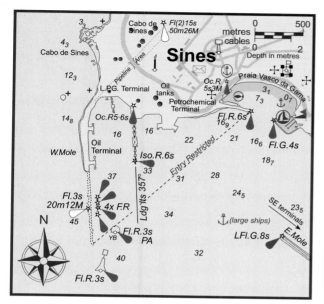

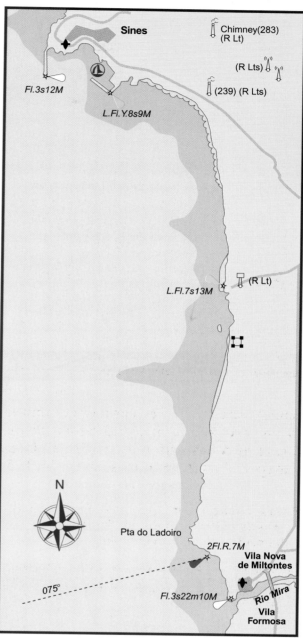

no offlying dangers and the approach is straightforward. Coming from the north, one must be careful to pass not only south of the end of the long seawall (the end is partly submerged) but also south of the red buoy marking it.

The marina is in the south-east corner of the first (more north-westerly) inner basin, and offers good shelter, although pronounced swell can enter in strong south-westerlies.

BERTHING

Yachts moor to floating pontoons with fingers in the marina. There are 88 berths for yachts of up to 20 metres in length with a least depth of 4 metres. The marina office can be called on VHF Ch 12.

FACILITIES IN THE MARINA

Water and electricity on the pontoons, showers, (free) launderette and toilets ashore. Fuel is available in the marina. Mechanical repairs could possibly be arranged, and yachts could be hauled out ashore using a mobile crane from the commercial docks. If any repairs have to be made, ask at the marina office where the staff were very friendly and helpful at the time of our visit.

SHOPPING

There are quite a few shops and a small market in town. The centre of Sines is about ten minutes walk from the marina - either along the road, or east towards the old fort and then up the steps. The shops are scattered around the town, but are still fairly close to each other. The market is across the main road at the landward end of town.

TRANSPORT

You can find buses to Lisboa and south into the Algarve, which stop in various places in Alentejo along the way. Cars can be hired, and it is easiest to inquire about this at the marina office - one will even get a small discount when booking via the marina and the car will be delivered there.

ANCHORAGES NEARBY

The Rio Mira is just under 15 miles south of Sines and scenically quite beautiful. There is a lighthouse on the small promontory at the

The statue of Vasco da Gama, gazing westwards out over the Atlantic

entrance which is rather narrow and otherwise unmarked, but yachts can enter with care on a calm day and with a rising tide.

A road bridge prevents one venturing upstream, but there is a small and normally quite sheltered anchorage just inside the river, at the tiny village of Vila Nova de Milfontes. There is also a hotel, but no other facilities.

USEFUL INFORMATION

Sines Tides (Std Port Lisboa Time Zone 0)

	MHWS	MHWN	MLWN	MLWS
Height (metres)	3·4	2·6	1·4	0·6

Radio Telephone
Call Porto de Sines (Port Authority) VHF Ch 11, 13, 16, Marina Ch 12
Local dialling code for Sines: 269
Marina office: 860600
Tourist office: 634472

Sines is a beautiful and largely unspoilt old town, despite the huge industrial harbour

A RUN ASHORE

Sines is quite a delightful little town with its own destinctive character. Tourists normally do not find their way here, and this might be part of the appeal of this friendly, sleepy little place.

This was the birthplace of Vasco da Gama (1467 to 1524) who found the sea-route to India in 1498. Before him, fellow navigator Bartolomeu Dias had already sailed around the Cape of Good Hope (in 1487-88) but had to turn back shortly afterwards. A statue of Vasco da Gama looking out to sea now stands in front of the fort, and one can even today feel his longing to venture to sea towards new lands beyond that far horizon . . .

The old fort also houses a small natural history museum, and other than that, the chapel Nossa Senhora de Salvas is noteworthy - it was rebuilt at the beginning of the 16th century at the order of Vasco da Gama.

The beach adjacent to the marina is pleasant, with a beach bar which is perfect for an early evening drink in the setting sun. More spectacular and secluded beaches for bathing or sunbathing can be found along the coast south of Sines, which are best reached by bicycle or hire-car.

A tour into the hinterland of the Alentejo with its wonderful landscapes, by bus or hire car, will certainly be worth while.

EATING OUT

Being such a quaint little town, Sines has no outstanding gourmet-type restaurants but there are many cheerful eating places where one can mix with the locals and enjoy basic but tasty food and the (usually) very drinkable Vinho da Mesa (rather cheap table-wine) for very moderate prices.

The restaurant O Migas (Rua Pero de Alenquer 17, telephone 636767, Amex accepted, closed 1 to 15 October, Saturday lunch-time and Sundays) is above average in both quality and prices.

One rather well-known speciality of this region is the Carne di Porco a Alentejana, a very tasty dish of pork and mussels with fried potatoes. The specialities of Alentejo also include acordas, a bread and garlic soup.

Finally, some very good (and strong) red wines come from the high Alentejo, far inland and close to the Spanish border.

SAGRES/BALEEIRA

Sagres/Baleeira - 37°00.6'N / 08°55.5'W

Sagres is of some historical and geographical consequence, being the most south-westerly settlement in mainland Europe. It is also thought that the first plans for Portuguese overseas expansion were made here by Henry the Navigator, although whether this is fact or fiction is much discussed by historians.

Today, Sagres presents itself as a strange, rather out-of-this world, windswept place - literally at the end of the road - which has a certain morbid charm about it.

About six kilometres away by road is the impressive Cabo de São Vicente, and tucked around the corner behind the next cape, Punta da Sagres, is the little fishing harbour of Baleeira which has a completely different atmosphere from any other Algarve harbour or anchorage.

There are anchorages near the fishing harbour of Baleeira, and in the Ensenada de Belixe in the lee of Cabo de São Vicente and E of Punta da Sagres (Ensenada de Sagres), both open to the south and subject to some swell.

All these anchorages are rather wild, set in dramatic surroundings, and are worth a try for the completely different experience compared to those further east.

LOCATION/POSITION

The south-western corner of Portugal, Cabo de São Vicente, is at 37°01.3'N / 08°59.5'W.

APPROACH AND ENTRANCE

The approach from sea presents no problems. For Baleeira, continue east past both headlands and follow the coastline about one mile offshore until the mole of the harbour can be seen. Proceed with care on a north to north-east course towards the harbour, aiming for the middle between the mole-head and the rocks Ilhotos de Martinal north-east of it.

Anchor in the bay north of the harbour mole on a rocky bottom with rather poor holding in places. A tripline, which should be brought aboard rather than buoyed (due to the amount of traffic) is also recommended, as the bottom is foul in many spots.

Sagres and the harbour of Baleeira from the south

The approaches to the two bays further west are easy and holding, in sand, is much better.

FACILITIES

There are no facilities for yachts anywhere around here. You can obtain water from a tap in the fishing harbour, and there is a rather primitive little boatyard in Baleeira which caters for rough repairs to the fishing vessels.

There are two beach-restaurants in the Ensenada de Sagres, but no facilities at all in the Ensenada de Belixe.

TRANSPORT

It is quite a steep uphill climb to the top of the cliffs and into Sagres from all three anchorages. Motorbikes and cars can be hired in some places in town, and there are buses to the other Algarve towns.

PROVISIONING

Small shops and supermarkets are scattered around Sagres and Baleeira.

A RUN ASHORE

The uphill climb to the top of the cliffs and the town is worthwhile, if only for the dramatic views. There is good walking here

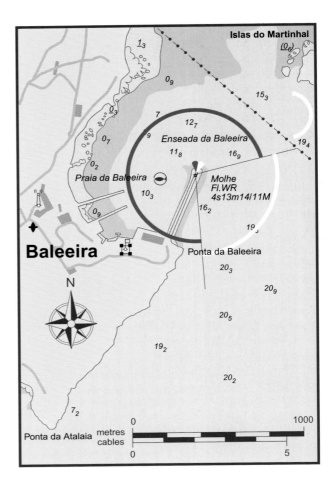

Fishing boats hauled up at the small yard at Baleeira

for those with endurance!

Cabo de São Vicente is a fantastic place from which to watch the sunset, especially if equipped with a bottle of wine and/or a small picnic! However, it may be a little too far to walk for some - six kilometres in each direction, but transport can be hired in Sagres if so desired. The cliffs here are 60 metres high and the rocky plateau itself is windswept and sparsely vegetated - impressive in a lonely way.

The Cape was the promontorium sacrum of ancient times, and the Greek philosopher Artemidoros from Ephesos allegedly said that it is here that the gods used to sleep. It is named after Saint Vincent of Saragossa, the patron of Portugal, who would have died around 304. In 1173 - goodness only knows what happened to him in between - his dead body was said to have drifted ashore here in a boat, escorted by two ravens!

There are fantastic beaches in both bays which are best reached by dinghy, although care is needed when landing - swell will almost always find its way in here and the seas break on the beach, swamping an unwary dinghy-crew.

The fortress on the Punta da Sagres is open for visitors. The Tercela Navale used to have a palace for Henriques (Henry the Navigator), an observatory, some research laboratories, a church, a chapel and a large compass rose made from small stones, which was not discovered until 1928. Scientists and historians still do not know whether this was built for astronomical or nautical reasons. Apart from this compass, the recently restored living quarters, the stables (now converted to conference rooms) and the chapel, none of the original buildings have survived.

Cabo de São Vicente, Europe's most SW-ly point

EATING OUT

There are a number of basic restaurants in both Sagres and Baleeira. On the way to the cape, about five kilometres from Sagres, is the remarkable Fortaleza de Beliche, a restaurant set in an old fortress (telephone 624124, closed in December and January, credit cards accepted). Also noteworthy is the Pousada do Infante in Sagres with a wonderful view across the Atlantic (telephone 624222, credit cards accepted).

Of the two beach restaurants in the Ensenada de Sagres, we tried the O Telheiro do Infante (telephone 624179, credit cards accepted) which served good quality meals on a pleasant terrace overlooking the beach and the yacht anchored in the bay beyond.

USEFUL INFORMATION
Local dialling codes for Sagres and Baleeira: 282   **Tourist office:** 64520   **Harbour office Sagres:** 64210

LAGOS

Lagos Marina is one of the friendliest and best sheltered in this region

Lagos - 37°05'84N / 08°39'90W

Lagos was once the capital of the region. It is a little white-washed town with attractive old buildings, and has a pleasant atmosphere, although it can become very crowded with tourists during the summer. One benefit of its popularity is the myriad of bars and restaurants to choose from, and it is always very lively, day and night!

The museum is well worth seeing, and there are some very attractive beaches in the near vicinity. The rocky coastline immediately west of the entrance is justly famous, with bizarre grottoes, clear water and sandy stretches between the cliffs. This area can be visited by foot or, even better, explored by dinghy.

There are numerous tourist activities, including para-sailing, windsurfing, jet-skiing and boat excursions. There is also a golf course near by (Palmares Golf, Tel. 282-76 29 53).

LOCATION/POSITION

Lagos lies on the Algarve coast, about 17 miles north-east of Punta de Sagres, and 20 miles from Cabo de São Vicente, the south-westernmost point of mainland Portugal.

APPROACH

Coming from the south-west, the approach to the harbour is just behind the conspicuous Punta de Piedade and its lighthouse. Coming from the east, the town can be seen between the sandy beach and the Punta de Piedade. When closing in, do not get too close to the Point or the rocky shore just north of it, as there are numerous off-lying rocks. The entrance to the harbour is between two lit moles and faces south-south-east.

ENTRANCE

The marina is reached via a fairly narrow channel between the two outer moles. It is theoretically possible to enter at any state of the tide, as the channel is supposedly dredged to 3 metres. However, the entrance is open to the south, and with strong onshore winds or a southerly swell coming in around low water, the seas will break close outside and also inside the entrance, so entering the channel under those circumstances can be quite adrenaline-quickening!

If at all possible time your arrival for any time from half flood tide onwards. Once inside the channel, pass the fishing basin (to starboard) and

The entrance and channel to Lagos seen from the S, with the fishing basin and, beyond that, the marina

continue to the waiting pontoon of the marina just before the swinging footbridge. The channel is not very wide which may present difficulties if sailing in without engine as there is very little room in which to manoeuvre.

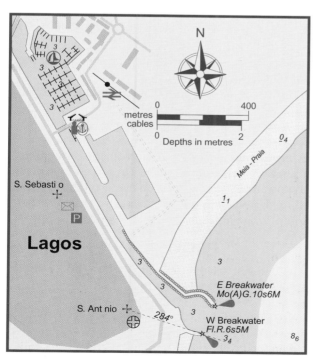

BERTHING

Lagos has one of the best and friendliest marinas on this coast. Tie up to the waiting pontoon and walk into the office, where you will be allocated a berth. Berthing inside is alongside finger-pontoons, and shelter is perfect under all conditions. The maximum length for visiting yachts is given as 30 metres.

If you want to reserve a berth in advance, call the harbour office on VHF Ch 62 or on Telephone (00351)-282-770 210. There are 462 berths and while the rates are reasonable during most of the year, they become quite high during the main summer season from 16 June to 15 October, when a boat of between 10 and 12 metres in length and up to 4 metres beam will pay 4.900 Escudos per day (2.200 per day in the off-season).

Rates include electricity and water which are on the pontoons. Fuel (diesel and petrol) is available on the reception pontoon.

FACILITIES IN THE MARINA

This marina offers the usual amenities of any modern yacht-harbour plus very good security if leaving a boat unattended over any period of time.

The marina office will receive and hold mail for visiting yachts (address as: Yacht '—' c/o Marina de Lagos, Apartado 18, 8600 Lagos, Portugal).

Lagos marina seen from the W, with Alvor lagoon just visible in the background

There is a launderette in the marina buildings, as well as various cafés and a shop selling British daily newspapers (on the day of publication), as well as cigarettes and telephone cards. Also, there is an internet service in the Marina Café where visitors can access their e-mail or the internet.

Daily weather forecasts are posted inside the marina office and broadcast on VHF Ch 62 daily at 1000 and 1600 hours.

Charts can be bought at the marina office, but other than that, there is only a very small chandlery in the fishing harbour which caters mainly to the more rugged needs of the fishing boats. Repair facilities are limited, but much better than anywhere else in Portugal. Mechanical and boat-building repairs can be made, but there is no proper hoist or Travelift for hauling out. This can only be done at a small boatyard (J. A. Pimenta, Tel. 282-762 839, fax 282-767 249) in the fishing basin, where yachts are slipped at high tide on a hydraulic wagon from a concrete ramp.

The boatyard say that they can also handle multihulls, but there is a restriction on draft, depending on the tides.

This boatyard is agent for Volvo Penta, various electronics and International paints, but do not forget that you are in Portugal - it can take a very long time to obtain any ordered spare parts.

There are also other mechanics, engineers and shipwrights about, to contact them inquire at the marina office or consult the list of mechanical, electrical and other specialists on the notice board.

TRANSPORT

Lagos is about one hour's drive away from Faro international airport, and there are also frequent train and bus connections to Faro and other major towns around Portugal. The train station is immediately behind the marina, and cars can be hired in town or via the marina office.

PROVISIONING

There is a well stocked hypermarket (Pingo Doce) very close to the marina - open seven days a week. There are also two smaller, local supermarkets in the town, across the foot-bridge, which are slightly cheaper. There is a large market (open every morning) near the quayside for fresh fish, meat and vegetables, plus a local grocery and livestock market every Saturday morning near the bus station.

A RUN ASHORE

As already mentioned above, Lagos is a very popular spot with tourists and is as lively and crowded in summer as is to be expected. Either accept this fact and enjoy yourself, or stay away until the winter, when life takes on a more relaxed pace. In fact, Lagos is one of the more popular spots for yachts to winter, which is usually very pleasant and mild, although many prefer to slip away elsewhere during the summer.

Lagos is famous for sandy beaches, but also for various interesting buildings, such as the fort dating back to the 16th century, the governor's palace (open for art exhibitions) and the two churches, the Igreja de São Sebastiao with a renaissance portal from 1530, and the Igreja de Santo Antonio which also houses the local museum. This church was built in 1769 and has many baroque features inside. The Museu Regional has an exhibition of clerical items, contemporary art and various curiosities from the town's history. This is open Tuesdays to Sundays, 0930 - 1230 and 1400 - 1600 hours.

A walk along the rocky coastline to the Punta de Piedade is well worthwhile, with many sandy coves and beach restaurants. Back in the narrow cobbled streets of the town centre there are numerous bars and cafés as well as a bewildering number of souvenir shops, handicrafts and boutiques - a treat for anyone seriously addicted to shopping.

EATING OUT AND NIGHT-LIFE

Lagos has such a wide variety of restaurants that it can be quite difficult to decide on one, and also to find a good quality place just by trial and error. Apart from the Portuguese establishments, there are two Chinese restaurants in town as well as one in the marina, a few Italian and even a very good Indian restaurant (Maharaja de Lagos, Rua Dr. José Formozinho, telephone 761507, off the road towards Punta de Piedade just on the outskirts of town opposite the fire-station (Bombeiros), and still within walking distance).

The following are a few of the better Portuguese restaurants:

Dom Sebastiao (Rua 25 de Abril, 20; telephone 762795). This is one of the best-known restaurants in town, elegant, and with a high standard of cooking - but not cheap. Major credit cards accepted, advance booking strongly recommended. The Rua 25 de Abril runs one

Lagos as seen from the fishing harbour just outside the marina

In the old part of Lagos, looking towards the restaurant Mediterraneo

Lagos Tides (Std Port Lisboa Time Zone 0)

	MHWS	MHWN	MLWN	MLWS
Height (metres)	3·4	2·6	1·4	0·6

Radio Telephone Call Marina de Lagos
VHF Ch 62 for bridge opening.
Lagos Marina Reception: 282-770216
Emergency 112
Regional Tourist Office 282-763 031
Hospita:l 282-763 034; Medilagos: 282-760181
Police: 282-762 930
Yacht Club: 282-762 256
Taxi: 282-763 587
Faro Airport: 289 800 800

hotel close to the marina (near the Pigo Doce hypermarket) which serves good quality, straightforward Portuguese food, and is thus also popular with the locals.

Escondidinho (Behind the Hotel de Lagos) is very popular with locals for fish, including sardines.

Bas Luis - a friendly bar near the entrance to the Hotel de Lagos - it is good for snacks and they will change sterling and travellers cheques without commission.

As far as the night-life after supper is concerned, the bars and night-clubs and discotheques are so numerous (and subject to change in location and popularity) that they are best left to be explored at the actual time of the visit. One place to start your research is the bar Mullens, located in a small back street (Rua Candido dos Reis, 86), which is always lively, loud and popular. They also serve bar snacks until 2200 hours, after which it's music and drinking into the early hours . . .

street upwards and parallel to the promenade alongside the entrance channel and cannot be missed. This is the main street as far as restaurants and bars are concerned.

Dom Henrique (Rua 25 de Abril, 75; telephone 76 35 63). Of a similarly high standard and prices to match. A speciality are the shellfish from the aquarium. Credit cards accepted, advance booking recommended.

A Lagosteira (Rua 1 de Maio, 20; telephone 76 24 86), supposedly has the best fish-soup and seafood in town, but also serves the more rustic Portuguese meat dishes. Credit cards accepted. Closed 10 January to 10 February.

São Roque (Estrada de Meia Praia, telephone 77 02 28) is a cosy and unpretentious restaurant in the basement of a

Mullens is situated in the old part of Lagos

DAYTIME ANCHORAGES NEAR LAGOS

In settled weather, yachts can anchor off the beach just east of the entrance. Alternative overnight anchorages can be found in Baleeira and near Punta de Sagres (see p77) or in the lagoon of Alvor (see p85).

ALVOR

Alvor - 37°07'N / 08°37'W

The landing place at Alvor with the anchorage in the background

Alvor used to be a charming old fishing village on a hill above the lagoon but, like all places in the Algarve, it has undergone a remarkable transition to a bustling, lively holiday spot. It is now bursting with restaurants, (English) bars, night-clubs and discotheques.

During the daytime, however, some of the traditional atmosphere can still be sensed when life slows down to a sleepy, more Mediterranean pace.

The lagoon offers a peaceful and sheltered anchorage - a world apart from the busy marinas at Lagos, Portimao or Vilamoura.

LOCATION/POSITION

The lagoon of Alvor is only 2.5 miles east of Lagos at the end of the long, sandy beach in the Baia de Lagos.

APPROACH AND ENTRANCE

Having identified Punta da Piedade south of Lagos, the approach is easy. The lighthouse of Alvor stands some way inland but can also be distinguished from sea. The entrance to the lagoon is protected by two lit moles, but first-time entry at night is not recommended as the lagoon is rather shallow and the channel leading to Alvor is neither buoyed nor lit.

The entrance is reported to have about 3 to 4 metres depth at low water, and the channel is supposedly dredged to 2 metres, which is also roughly the depth in the pool in front of Alvor.

Enter as soon as possible after low water with the young flood tide, so that the channel can still be seen before everything is covered, and proceed with care!

ANCHORAGE

It is possible to anchor just inside the entrance, where one will find the deepest water, or in a small pool just off Alvor itself. Multihulls and those boats with minimum draft are obviously at an advantage here, but it should be possible to

The entrance to the lagoon of Alvor, seen from S

find an anchorage for a boat drawing not more than 2 metres, at least during neap tides. There are two small pontoons at Alvor foreshore, which are reserved for local fishing boats only, but they make a good dinghy landing place. Other than this, there are no facilities whatsoever for visiting yachts.

The town of Alvor at the E end of the lagoon

TRANSPORT

The nearest train station is at Portimao, a few kilometres east, and there are also buses. Cars or motor-bikes can be hired.

PROVISIONING

There are many tiny but charming groceries in the centre of Alvor, as well as a small market, so anything that is needed in the way of day to day shopping can be found. There is also a supermarket (Alisuper) at the other end of town, but it is a longish walk from the landing pontoons.

A RUN ASHORE

The best thing to do in Alvor is to sit in the sun with an aperitif - at any time during the day - and watch the world crawl by. Or, gaze out over the peaceful lagoon and the yachts anchored there. Despite being a holiday town, this is a perfect place to relax and wind down.

There are also some superb beaches nearby, on the outsides of the sandy spits that shelter the lagoon - best reached by dinghy - which can also be used to just drift around the beautiful lagoon.

EATING OUT

There are so many restaurants here that you are spoilt for choice. But having said that, here is the good news: when coming from the boat, you need not venture far or drag your hungry body uphill into the town centre. Directly opposite the landing pontoons is the enchanting and cosy restaurant Ababuja (telephone 458979) with a small terrace overlooking the water. Specialities here not only include the usual assortment of fresh fish (priced by the kilo), but also traditional Portuguese dishes such as bean-stews like Feijado de Choco (with octopus) or Feijado de Buzina (with mussels).

Alvor's oldest restaurant, and still a favourite with many, is A Cubita, situated a little way uphill

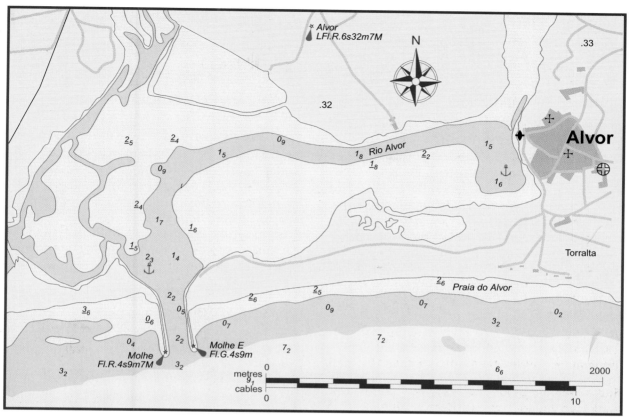

The first stop in the sun after landing at Alvor

Siesta time in Alvor is the only time in 24 hours when things are really quiet here

towards the town in the Rua Fredrico Mendes (telephone 459129). It has a nice roof-top terrace and has been run by the same owners for 25 years. Specialities here include shellfish rice, chicken piri-piri, and eels in tomato sauce.

The Vasco da Gama (Rua Pedro Alvares Cabral, telephone 457308, closed Tuesdays) is run by an English couple which is reflected in the food - next to vegetarian dishes, Indian classics feature high on the menu. And for anyone seriously

home-sick, we can recommend a very British pub - the Crow's Nest (Rua 25 de Abril, telephone 459332, closed Thursdays) with all-day English breakfast, authentic Sunday roasts and bar snacks.

USEFUL INFORMATION

Local dialling code for Alvor: 282

PORTIMÃO

Portimão - 37°06.4'N / 08°31.6'W

Portimão lies a little way upstream on the Rio Arade, and is a typical Portuguese provincial town with a busy fishing harbour. Until recently, the only option for yachts was to either moor to a small floating pontoon just outside the town centre, or anchor in the river, which has been reported as being extremely smelly!

Now, a large new yacht marina has been constructed in Praia da Rocha at the mouth of the river. Praia da Rocha used to be an exclusive summer resort frequented by the rich English during the 1930s and 1950s, but is now degraded to a tourist-ghetto with skyscraper hotels and apartments, and literally no local flavour left. The town of Portimão is about two miles away from here, which means either a short bus ride or a long walk.

POSITION

The entrance to the Rio Arade is 8 miles east of the headland of Punta da Piedade and about 32 miles west of Cabo de Santa Maria.

APPROACH / ENTRY

The approach to the Rio is straightforward: there are no offlying dangers. The entrance is immediately west of the lighthouse Punta do Altar and is easily identified from sea. It is protected by two marked and lit moles. Once inside, the river is buoyed, and the buoys are lit, so entry at night should be straightforward. The entrance to the marina is on the port hand past the first red buoy (No 2).

Approach and entrance to both the river and the marina are possible at any state of the tide and under all conditions.

BERTHING

In the marina, yachts moor to floating pontoons with fingers. There are to be 600 berths for yachts of up to 30 metres in length.

FACILITIES IN THE MARINA

The pontoons have water and electricity. Shore facilities are limited to showers and toilets, because, at the time of publication, the marina was still being built. Once finished, all facilities are intended to be there, including swimming pool, launderette, shops, and, one mile upstream on the opposite side of the river, a new boatyard with a 70-tonne Travelift and all repair facilities

Portimão marina and Praia da Rocha beyond

plus a large hard-standing area.

The marina was due to open officially in April 2000 but this does not mean that all of the above mentioned facilities would be installed by then - realistically, it may take at least another two years before everything is finished.

Until then, only mechanical repairs can be carried out in Portimão. There is a small yard catering for basic repairs to fishing boats but no place, at the time of writing, to haul out a yacht.

SHOPPING

In the village of Praia da Rocha you will find hundreds of souvenir shops selling T-shirts and sun-shades, plus many bars and rather average restaurants, but only one or two tiny grocery shops. For provisioning the boat, it is best to take a taxi to one of the hypermarkets which are situated at the far end of Portimão itself.

One can also walk into Portimão (about 25 minutes walk from the marina) and visit one of the various supermarkets there, or take the dinghy - or even the whole boat - upstream into Portimão, as there are a few pontoons at the town where yachts can moor.

TRANSPORT

There is a train station at Portimão, connecting the town with Faro and Lagos. Cars can be hired from various companies in Praia da Rocha. Portimão is just under one hours drive from Faro international airport.

ANCHORAGES NEARBY

It is possible to anchor off the beach of Praia da Rocha during the summer in the then predominantly offshore winds, and also just inside the river mouth north of the east mole. Holding is good in sand in both places. At the time of writing, it was still also possible to use the floating pontoons off Portimão itself. These offer no special facilities but have the advantage of being very close to the centre of Portimão.

As this book goes to print, we hear on the grapevine that there is a move to bar anchoring in the river, thus forcing yachts into the marina. Let us hope that this does not succeed and that those who prefer to anchor and go ashore by dinghy are still allowed so to do.

A RUN ASHORE

Towering over the marina at Praia da Rocha is the 16th century fortress of Santa Catarina, which can

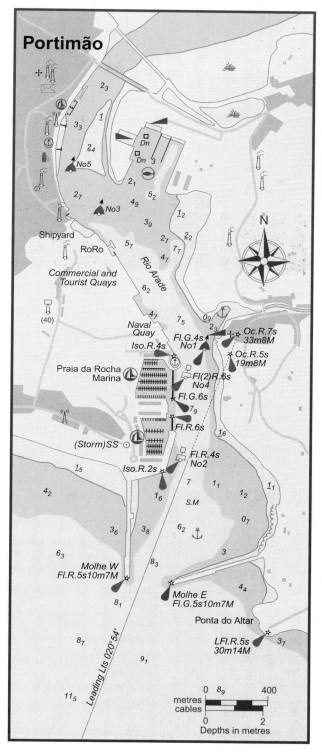

be reached by a flight of stairs. From here, one has good views over the Rio and the coastline reaching to the west. There are one or two cafés in the fortress where one can enjoy an afternoon coffee or a sundowner, but once having done so, I personally would not venture too far out of the

Portimão seen from Praia da Rocha marina

fortress into the tourist settlement of Praia da Rocha itself unless I absolutely had to. Having said that, some like Praia da Rocha so this is obviously a matter of personal taste and depends what one is looking for in the first place!

The beach just west of the harbour is long, sandy and inviting for long walks and whatever else you do on the beach. Underneath the fortress are also a handful of beach bars and restaurants. There are also some spectacular little beaches between the rocks to the east of Punta do Altar.

Portimão itself might be worth a visit especially if one is interested in a normal Portuguese town or if any shopping has to be done. As mentioned above, it is about 20 to 30 minutes walk, but buses run from Praia da Rocha to Portimão. One could also consider taking the dinghy upstream to the floating pontoon.

EATING OUT

Praia da Rocha is full of restaurants, none of which one could honestly recommend as being outstanding in any way. There is, however, an attractive restaurant in the inner yard of the fortress itself, a much more pleasant location than anything you will find in 'downtown little Manhattan' further down the road into Praia da Rocha. This is the restaurant Fortaleza de Santa Catarina (telephone 422066) which has seating either outside in the yard or inside with a nice view west towards the sunset.

Among the hotels and apartment-blocks of the village itself are at least two Indian restaurants, many English and Irish pubs, several fish & chips shops and also a few Chinese and Italian eating

The old floating pontoons opposite Portimão

USEFUL INFORMATION

Portimão Tides (Std Port Lisboa Time Zone 0)

	MHWS	MHWN	MLWN	MLWS
Height (metres)	3·3	2·6	1·5	0·7

Radio Telephone
Port VHF Ch 11 16. Marina VHF Ch 68
**Local dialling code for Portimão
and Praia da Rocha:** 282
Marina da Portimão
(Preliminary sales office number only): 425805
Tourist Office Praia da Rocha: 419132
Tourist Office Portimão: 419131
Hospital (Clinica da Rocha): 414400

places, all of which will be found when wandering about.

The Titanic might also be worth a try (Rua Eng. Francisco Bivar, telephone 422371, located in a side-street in the second row behind the main seafront road, sign-posted), where the ambience is strangely reminiscent of a 1950s theatre but the food is above average, as are the prices.

VILAMOURA

Vilamoura - 37°04'N / 08°07'W

Vilamoura is Portugal's first purpose built (during the 1980s) commercial marina and the surrounding tourist development area then enjoyed quite an upmarket reputation for some years. Today, both the concept and the architecture of Vilamoura look a bit dated, and one can easily see why it is no longer a favoured place on the Algarve coast.

Both Vilamoura (an artificial marina and golfing village) and the neighbouring town of Quarteira (dominated by modern high-rise apartment blocks) are lacking in charm and local flavour. Having said this, the marina offers all facilities for yachts.

POSITION

Vilamoura is just under 15 miles west-north-west of Cabo de Santa Maria.

APPROACH / ENTRY

Vilamoura can be identified by the high buildings of Quarteira to the east of the marina area. The entrance is protected by two lit moles; there is also a lighthouse at the entrance. There are no offlying dangers and both the approach and entrance are straightforward, although difficult to dangerous in very strong southerly winds.

There is a large outer harbour full of fishing boats and the inner basin is the marina.

BERTHING

Yachts moor to floating pontoons with fingers. When entering, first moor alongside the reception pontoon on the port side of the entrance to the inner harbour, the marina office there will allocate a berth.

There are 1000 berths for yachts up to 50 metres in length and up to four metres draft (very large yachts should contact the marina office well before arrival).

The marina office can be contacted on VHF Ch 62.

FACILITIES IN THE MARINA

All facilities for yachts are available here. Water and electricity on the pontoons, showers, launderette and toilets by the marina office - which is an extremely long walk from some of the berths and often very much quicker by dinghy.

All repairs can be carried out here, and there is a 60 ton Travelift and a mobile crane for hauling out. There are also chandlers and many independent contractors for all types of yacht repairs and services.

Weather forecasts are obtainable at the marina office, and they are also broadcast daily at 1000 on VHF Ch 20.

SHOPPING

Souvenir shops, boutiques and small stores in the marina area (including banks and pharmacies). For serious provisioning, it will pay to take a taxi to the Princessa Tesco Export supermarket at

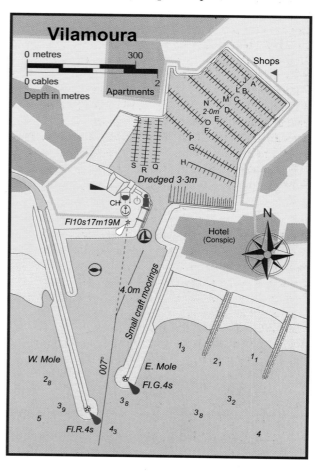

Almancil, which mainly serves the local bars and restaurants but which is also open to the public. It has a very good butchery, and stocks many British products (open Monday to Friday 0900 - 1830, Saturday 0900 - 1400).

Opposite is Griffin Bookshop, an international book-shop with books in English.

TRANSPORT

Buses and taxis run to Faro and the airport. Hire-cars are readily available in the marina area.

ANCHORAGES NEARBY

The next good anchorages are in the lagoon of Faro (see p94).

A RUN ASHORE

Apart from the service facilities for yachts, the main attraction, for some people, of Vilamoura is in the surrounding tourist developments, for there are three golf courses nearby, and numerous bars and restaurants around the marina basin.

For those culturally interested, a few Roman ruins are close by, and, a bit further away in Almancil, the Igreja de Sao Lourenco is quite impressive and reputed to be the finest baroque church in the southern part of Portugal. Inside, beautifully painted tiles tell the story of Lourenco the Martyr.

Many of Vilamoura's restaurants overlook the marina

Marina Vilamoura seen from N

A regatta off Vilamoura

USEFUL INFORMATION

Vilamoura Tides (Std Port Lisboa Time Zone 0)

	MHWS	MHWN	MLWN	MLWS
Height (metres)	3·7	2·5	1·5	0·3

Radio Telephone Call marina Vilamoura Radio
VHF Ch 62 (0900-2100/1800 off season) 16.
**Local dialling code for Vilamoura
and Almancil: 269
Marina office: 302924**

Loulé is a lively town with a slightly oriental flair. It is a little way inland (visit by bus) and has a Moorish style market-hall and the ruins of a Saracen castle dating back to the 12th century.

EATING OUT

The marina has a wide variety of restaurants including Indian, Chinese and Italian. There is also the usual mélange of fast-food places - burgers and pizzas and the like. All of these will be easily found when wandering about and none of them need be further mentioned.

Not so far away in Almancil, however, serious hedonists will find a wonderful oasis. The restaurant Ermitage (telephone 394329, closed Tuesdays, 11 - 26 January, 7 - 21 June, 1 - 21 December, major credit cards accepted except Diners Club) is decorated lavishly with antiques and

has a fantastic cuisine that is crowned with a Michelin star. Needles to say the prices are as high as the standard of cooking.

Also a few kilometres away, on the road from Vale do Lobo to Quinta da Lago, is the restaurant Sao Gabriel (telephone 394521, closed Tuesdays and 9 January - 12 February, credit cards, ex Diners Club, accepted) which also has a Michelin star and is known for exquisite and creative dishes.

The busy marina is lined with shops, bars and restaurants all round

FARO & OLHÃO

Faro and Olhão - 36°57.6'N / 07°52.2'W

The wide lagoon at Faro and Olhão is enclosed by the Ilha da Culatra

Faro is today's capital of the Algarve and a lively and attractive town of 30,000 inhabitants which has kept its own profile and way of life despite a massive tourist onslaught. It has no facilities to offer in the way of modern marinas, but has a rather beautiful lagoon with sheltered anchorages

and a national park - the Reserva Natural da Ria Formosa.

The entire area seems to be a haven for birds, but a reported difficulty for yachts is the fine floating grass which can block cooling water intakes.

While the marshy lagoon is an important habitat and migratory stop-over for many different species, the storks seem to have taken over the air-space above Faro itself (in fact, storks are quite common throughout the Algarve but are mainly seen further inland).

At the eastern end of the lagoon is the smaller fishing town of Olhão with an old quarter (Bairro de Barreto) which is reminiscent of a North African Medina. There are wonderful beaches on

the sandy islets separating the lagoon from the sea, namely on Ilha da Culatra and Ilha da Armona.

LOCATION/POSITION

The entrance to the lagoon of Faro and Olhão is by the lighthouse Cabo de Santa Maria.

APPROACH AND ENTRANCE

The sandy islets south of the lagoon are low-lying and sometimes difficult to see, but the airport and town of Faro itself are conspicuous if coming from the west, as is the lighthouse on Cabo de Santa Maria itself.

The entrance to the lagoon is sheltered by two lit sea-walls which can be seen once the lighthouse is

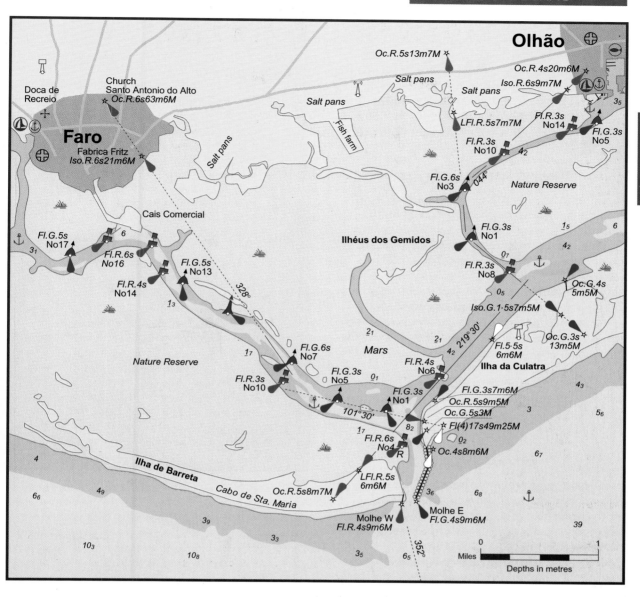

Olhão

Oc.R.5s13m7M

Salt pans

Oc.R.4s20m6M

Iso.R.6s9m7M

Doca de Recreio

Church Santo Antonio do Alto
Oc.R.6s63m6M

Salt pans

Salt pans

Fl.R.3s No14

Faro

Fish farm

LFl.R.5s7m7M

Fl.R.3s No10

Fl.G.3s No5

Fabrica Fritz
Iso.R.6s21m6M

Salt pans

Fl.G.6s No3

044°

Nature Reserve

Cais Comercial

Fl.G.3s No1

Fl.G.5s No17

Ilhéus dos Gemidos

Fl.R.6s No16

Fl.R.3s No8

Oc.G.4s 5m5M

Fl.G.5s No13

Fl.R.4s No14

Iso.G.1·5s7m5M

328°

Oc.G.3s 13m5M

Nature Reserve

Fl.G.6s No7

Mars

Fl.R.4s No6

Fl.5·5s 6m6M

Ilha da Culatra

Fl.R.3s No10

Fl.G.3s No5

Fl.G.3s No1

Fl.G.3s7m6M

Oc.R.5s9m5M

Oc.G.5s3M

101°30'

Fl(4)17s49m25M

Fl.R.6s No4

Oc.4s8m6M

LFl.R.5s 6m6M

Ilha de Barreta

Cabo de Sta. Maria

Oc.R.5s8m7M

Molhe E
Fl.G.4s9m6M

Molhe W
Fl.R.4s9m6M

355°

Miles

Depths in metres

identified. Approach from sea is straightforward; there are no offlying dangers as long as one does not get too close to the beach before having identified the entrance, so stay about a mile or so offshore until one can steer for the entrance on a northerly course. Shifting sandbanks have been reported outside and mainly west of the entrance, but there is no bar as such.

If one is planning to continue to Faro or Olhão, it is best to enter at low tide or with the first of the flood so that the sandbanks inside the lagoon and the channels can still be seen - this is also of course the easiest and safest time to pick your anchorage. The channels are buoyed, lit, and have transits, so the approaches to both places should present no real problems.

ANCHORAGES

There are various possibilities and it seems best to make your own choice from the chart. If you want to visit Faro, continue in the marked channel towards Faro until well past the commercial pier. At the junction where the channel branches off to the north towards Faro, there is a pool with moorings, one of which can be used if vacant. Depth is around three metres at low tide. From here, it is just over half a mile by dinghy to Faro, where there is a floating pontoon in the town-centre to use as a dinghy-landing. It stays afloat at low tide.

When entering the lagoon at low tide, one can easily see where to anchor just outside the buoyed fairway. There is also a good anchorage just inside the entrance north of the lighthouse and outside the channel leading to Olhão (depths between 3 and 1.2 metres depending where you pick your spot). There are various other anchorages north of the Ilha da Culatra and also just off Olhão.

There is a tiny, so-called yacht-basin behind the landing pier at Olhão but there is no room for visiting yachts so it is better to anchor off (see photograph).

FACILITIES ASHORE

Some basic repairs (mainly mechanical) could possibly be arranged in Olhão at the fishing harbour. Fuel is also available at Olhão fishing harbour, water (by dinghy and cans) from the small Doca de Recreio at Faro. There is also a chandlery at the Doca de Recreio in Faro, with only very limited stocks, as well as a mechanic who mainly repairs outboard-engines.

A very helpful mechanical shop, who also do repairs, is Sulnautica in Olhão, situated near the Pingo Doce supermarket.

TRANSPORT

Railway station, international airport, hire-cars and taxis at Faro. Hire-cars, taxis and buses (to Vila Real and Faro) at Olhão.

PROVISIONING

Faro has a good range of shops in the town centre of Faro, but for provisioning Olhão might be a more convenient place, as there is a large Pingo Doce supermarket within easy walking distance of the landing pier.

The hypermarkets at Faro are situated on the road to the airport outside town, just a short taxi ride from the centre.

A RUN ASHORE

Despite having a rather unsightly skyline when see from the sea, Faro has a pretty town centre,

Faro lagoon has some beautiful and remote parts

The anchorage in the pool off Faro

particularly in the historical Vila Adentro.

This ancient town within the city (immediately south-east of the small boat basin of the Doca de Recreio) is reached through the impressive Italian renaissance style archway called Arco da Vila, which was funded by the fishing community and built in 1814 by a Genoese architect. Inside are the town hall, and the cathedral, which shows a worrying mixture of styles as it has been changed and re-built many times over the centuries, the last time after the big earthquake of 1755. A testing subject for students of church architecture!

Immediately north of the Doca de Recreio begins the more modern town centre with its attractive pedestrian streets full of shops and boutiques of all description, plus many cafés thrown in for frequent rests! Having called this the more modern town, it is actually quite misleading, since this is the Bairro Ribeirinho which is still within the moorish and medieval town walls.

Near the Praca da Liberdade (off the Rua do Pé

larger neighbour, as it has quite a Moorish, North African feel about its narrow, shady streets, running between small, square white houses with flat roofs and minarets. Olhão is much quieter and has more character than Faro, although both towns are worth visiting and each has its merits.

The main church (built 1681 - 1698) with its impressive baroque facade was, for some unfathomable reason, paid for by the fishermen of Aveiro. Its main attraction is the church tower, which can be climbed to enjoy the unique view across the sea of white houses and roof-terraces that form the old part of Olhão.

Further east, the lagoon of Ria Formosa is quite unique. It is visited by many migratory birds and is a permanent nesting site for dozens of other species, including herons, storks, grebes, caimans and flamingos - truly a great place for bird-watching. There is also a remarkable diversity of fish in the lagoon, with allegedly over 100 species. More prosaic attractions include some superb beaches others quite deserted, as well as swimming, dinghy sailing and, alas, jet ski-ing, which seems to become ever more popular.

It is a good idea to spend some time on the lagoon, anchored in various places and exploring flora and fauna as well as enjoying the beaches, where you will find beach-bars and very basic, simple restaurants in some places, in others complete solitude.

Olhão – the small-boat harbour and the anchorage

da Cruz) is the regional museum (Museu Etnografico Regional) which is worth a visit if interested in the history of the region. Among the many exhibits are also rebuilds of typical houses of the region and many paintings showing the bygone Algarve way of life (open Monday to Friday 0930 - 1230 and 1400 - 1700).

In the port office, which is on the north side of the Doca de Recreio (you walk past it when coming from the dinghy pontoon into town), is a small maritime museum with an exhibition of fishing and shipping of the Algarve and Portugal (open Tuesday to Sunday 10 - 1230 and 1400 - 1700).

Olhão is quite different from its

Shopping street in the centre of Faro

Relaxing in the sun outside one of the many beautiful cafes in Faro

The pleasant restaurant Ciedade Velha is in the old town

EATING OUT

Not surprisingly, both these large towns have a large number and wide variety of restaurants. In Faro, the following are noteworthy: The Café Chelsea (Rua da Francisco Comer 28, telephone 28459) is a popular and lively meeting place and café during the daytime, with all day snacks and attractive lunch menus. During the evenings, diners go up to the first-floor restaurant for a colourful menu of local dishes and international cuisine.

A tradition in Faro is the restaurant Dois Irmaos (Largo do Torreiro do Bispe 18, telephone 23337) which has been there since 1925 and is still justly famous for the variety of fish dishes.

In the historical Vila Adentro, the restaurant Cidade Velha (Rua Domingos Guieiro 19, telephone 27145, closed Sunday, no food Saturday) is a pleasant, no-fuss eating place with a certain charm, serving house-made dishes of the day. This is mainly frequented by the council workers during weekday lunch-time, but is also open for informal dinners during week-day evenings.

Close by is the Mesa dos Mouros (Largo da Sé, telephone 878873) also with a friendly atmosphere, a nice terrace overlooking the square and a mixture of Portuguese and international dishes.

In Olhão, the main theme in the restaurants is seafood with grilled fish, mussels, shellfish and of course Cataplana, a delicious stew of tomatoes, onions, fish, clams and sausage. One restaurant to try is O Tamboril (Avenida 5 de Outubro 160, telephone 714625), renowned for the good quality regional food it serves - it is at the end of the Avenida which is in fact the main waterfront promenade.

Opposite the new market halls are a few small but rather good restaurants serving freshly grilled fish and shellfish which they obviously get from the market just across the road.

USEFUL INFORMATION			
Faro & Olhão Tides (Std Port Lisboa Time Zone 0)			
	MHWS	MHWN MLWN	MLWS
Height (metres)	3·4	2·6 1·4	0·6
Local dialing codes for Faro and Olhão: 289			
Tourist office Faro: 803604			
Tourist office Olhão: 713936			
Faro airport information: 800800			

The entrance to the Rio Formosa with Quatro Aguas in the centre and the anchorage to the right

TAVIRA

Tavira - 37°06.7'N / 07°36.7'W

Tavira is a pleasant, easy-going southern fishing town surrounded by salines. It may have been an old moorish settlement, but today it has more than 30 churches! It is similar in style to Olhao, but tourism is not as blatantly obvious as in many other Algarve towns.

The entrance to the fishing harbour is limited due to a low road bridge, but there is a pleasant anchorage in good holding in the Rio Formosa off the peninsular called Quatro Aguas. Separating the Rio from the sea is the Ilha de Tavira with a little palm tree park and sandy beaches close to the entrance of the Rio.

LOCATION/POSITION

Tavira is situated off the Rio Formosa which is a continuation of the Faro/Olhao lagoon. In fact, with very shoal draft craft or a multihull, it should be possible to navigate from Olhao to Tavira inside the sandy islands.

APPROACH AND ENTRANCE

The entrance is not easily seen from sea unless one is already fairly close, so keep good dead-reckoning and use GPS along this low and featureless coast. The gap through the sand dunes is protected by two seawalls with small lit towers at their ends; and there are also leading lights but these are again difficult to identify.

The entrance has a depth of around 3 metres at low water and is usually straightforward, but bear in mind that there are shoal patches close outside both moles. When steering for the gap, the course should be around 320°T to 330°T.

Once inside, the Canal de Tavira follows around

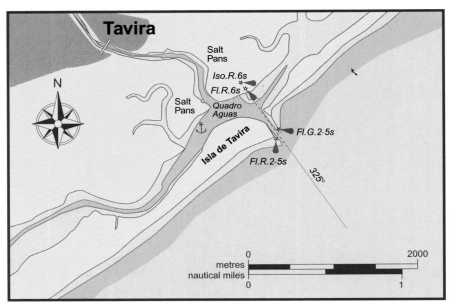

Map labels:
Tavira
Salt Pans
Iso.R.6s
Fl.R.6s
Salt Pans
Quadro Aguas
Fl.G.2·5s
Isla de Tavira
Fl.R.2·5s
325°
N
metres
nautical miles
0
0
2000
1

the end of the Isla de Tavira to port, leading to the Rio Gilao and the town (not navigable for sailing yachts), and the anchorage off Quatro Aguas.

ANCHORAGE

There are several residents moorings in front of Quatro Aguas and the local sailing club. It might be possible to use a vacant one, otherwise there is enough room to anchor clear of the moorings. Holding is good in sand, although the current runs swiftly along the Rio. Depths in the middle are 3 metres plus at low tide, but check the depth carefully and display an anchor light when anchoring to one side of the channel (which is used by fast moving fishing boats day and night).

There is also a very small basin for small craft

only just inside the Rio Gilao but it does not have room for any visiting boats, and the pontoons and fingers are not suitable for boats larger than 25 ft.

FACILITIES ASHORE

There is a sailing club and a sailing school where it is possible to shower. Water can be obtained here, by can.

TRANSPORT

From Quatro Aguas, it is about 20 minutes walk into Tavira (alternatively, take the dinghy up the Rio Gilao). In Tavira are buses and train connections to other Algarve towns, as well as taxis and hire-cars. It is about 30 kilometres by road to Faro and the international airport there.

PROVISIONING

There is a good variety of small shops and supermarkets in Tavira where all kinds of provisions can be found. There is also a large, new market just outside the town (towards Quatro Aguas - you will notice it if walking from there into town).

A RUN ASHORE

A long time ago, Tavira used to be the capital of the Algarve, but those days are gone and

The Rio Formosa is busy with fishing boats, so the anchorage is subject to wake

The landing place next to the jetty at Quadro Aguas

seemingly forgotten, for now it is a pleasant, relaxing, sleepy southern European town of provincial size and that is really all there is to it! Perhaps this is where its main attraction lies. An Italian visitor once said that Tavira was a 'peaceful and melancholic part of the world' – still true today!

The town is divided into two parts, one on each bank of the river, with a bridge joining them dating back to Roman times (it was restored in the 19th century). There are several bars and cafes along the waterfront of the fishing pier, which is where most men seem to gather for early evening drinks and gossip.

The Castro dos Maures is an old castle with Roman, Moorish and Portuguese elements, which was restored in the 18th century. Immediately adjacent to the castle is the church of Santa Maria do Castelo which was originally built in 1244 in moorish-gothic style. It has been changed, rebuilt and enlarged many times during the centuries, and now shows a typical mix of many architectural influences. Inside are the stone tombs of seven knights who were allegedly killed by the Moors during a cease-fire in 1242, thus giving Dom Paio Peres Correia the long awaited excuse to conquer the town in a particularly bloody and fierce way, liberating it from the Moors. After his death in 1275 he was also buried in this church.

The Ilha de Tavira is a particularly pleasant spot to spend a day on the sandy beach or in the palm garden on the tip of the island. And just in case you forgot to bring your picnic, there is also a restaurant and a bar here.

EATING OUT

Tavira has a good assortment of average, no-nonsense Portuguese eating places where you can get a decent meal for little money.

The restaurant Aquasul is a little bit different, as it also serves more exotic dishes from the former Portuguese colonies (Rua Silva Carvalho 13, telephone 325166). But the really good news is that the two best restaurants of Tavira are conveniently located side-by-side in Quatro Aguas, within easy reach by a short dinghy ride from your anchored boat. We tried the Quatro Aguas and found it excellent, with very good value for the money spent and well above average Portuguese and Spanish-style cooking (closed in January, telephone 325329, credit cards accepted). Apparently this restaurant has gained something of a reputation during the past years. The other one, Portas do Mar, is said to be just - well, nearly - as good (telephone 321255, credit cards accepted).

USEFUL INFORMATION

Tavira Tides (Std Port Lisboa Time Zone 0)			
	MHWS	MHWN	MLWN	MLWS
Height (metres)	3·4	2·6	1·4	0·6

Local dialling code for Tavira: 281
Tourist office: 322511
Port authority: 22438

VILA REAL DE ST ANTÓNIO

Vila Real - 37°05.5'N / 07°23.5'W

Another very sleepy town, this time on the west bank of the Rio Guadiana, which forms the border between Portugal and Spain. Vila Real has the benefit of a marina with floating pontoons and some facilities, but otherwise it has a rather dormant feel about it.

This is a good harbour to wait for a favourable tide to explore the Rio Guadiana, which is beautiful, deep, and navigable upstream for at least 15 miles as far as Alcoutim. Beyond Alcoutim there are many wilderness anchorages in great country, so if you have the time and the inclination this is a worthwile exploration.

The suspension bridge north of Vila Real has a clearance of around 20 metres at low water.

LOCATION/POSITION

Vila Real is on the west bank of the river about 2.5m from the entrance.

APPROACH AND ENTRANCE

Coming from the west, the river mouth is easily identified by the high apartment blocks of Monte Gordo about two miles west of the entrance, and the tall white lighthouse at Vila Real itself. The river mouth is sheltered by two (lit) seawalls, although the port side mole is submerged from about half tide onwards. There are dangerous shoals off the mouth to both sides of the channel. The two pairs of buoys marking the approach must be observed, especially the two inner ones (one red, one green). The entrance is rather shallow, sometimes less than 2 metres at low tide,

Vila Real and the marina seen from the W

so entry should only be attempted from half-tide onwards. Strong onshore winds against the ebb tide make this entrance very dangerous.

Once over the bar, keep closer to the west side until arriving at the marina of Vila Real.

BERTHING

Yachts moor to floating pontoons and fingers inside the marina. A strong current runs through the pontoons, and there is restricted manoeuvering space, all of which has to be taken into account when berthing. There are 350 berths for yachts of up to 20 metres overall length.

FACILITIES IN THE MARINA

Water and electricity on the pontoons, showers and toilets ashore, fuel (diesel and petrol) is available from a fuel pontoon outside and just upstream of the marina. There is a concrete ramp which could be used as a slipway.

There is also a shipyard for fishing boats near the mouth of the river.

TRANSPORT

Ferry across the Rio Guadiana to Ayamonte. Taxis, and buses go to all major towns in Portugal as well as Huelva and Sevilla.

The remarkable central square named after the town planner, Marquis de Pombal

PROVISIONING

There are small grocery shops and general stores in town for day to day shopping, but no big supermarkets within walking distance. However, a new and good mini-market has recently opened next to the square. About ten minutes walk from the marina are two cheap supermarkets, Mini Preco and Lidl. These are easily found when following the pedestrian zone past the central square.

A RUN ASHORE

Vila Real de Santo António is an artificial town, built by the then interior and defence minister, the Marquis de Pombal as a defence post against Spain in 1774, after the former border-posts of Castro Marim and Cacela were completely destroyed in the great earthquake of 1755.

This town was planned on the drawing board - as can be deduced by the grid pattern street plan - none of those narrow, twisting lanes of other Portuguese towns to be found here! Pombal encouraged shipbuilding in this area, founded a

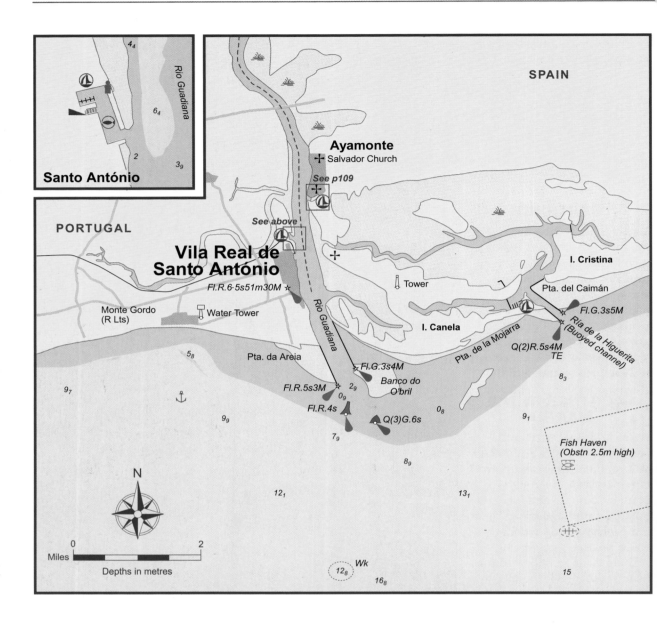

Santo António

SPAIN

PORTUGAL

Ayamonte
+ Salvador Church

See p109

See above

Vila Real de
Santo António

Fl.R.6·5s51m30M ✦

Monte Gordo
(R Lts)

⊤ Water Tower

Tower

I. Cristina

Pta. del Caimán

Fl.G.3s5M

Ría de la Higuerita
(Buoyed channel)

Río Guadiana

I. Canela

Pta. da Areia

Pta. de la Mojarra

Q(2)R.5s4M
TE

5₈

9₇

⚓

9₉

Fl.G.3s4M

Fl.R.5s3M ✦ 2₉

Banco do
O'bril

0₉

Fl.R.4s

Q(3)G.6s

7₉

8₉

8₃

9₁

Fish Haven
(Obstn 2.5m high)

N

0   Miles   2

Depths in metres

12₁

13₁

0₈

15

Wk
12₈

16₈

local fishing industry and finally installed a customs post. The latter was not particularly popular with the locals as this area had a strong smuggling tradition!

When the Marquis de Pombal fell out with the King a few years later, his town of Vila Real went downhill and was soon deserted and forgotten. It was actually not until 1879 that this ghost-town was 'discovered' once more. It is once again suffering a slight decline through being by-passed by the new road bridge.

The town has an attractive waterfront promenade along the river past the yacht marina, and the ferry pier which gives panoramic views of Ayamonte on the opposite side. The Praca Marques de Pombal in the town centre is also

worth seeing (whilst sitting in the sun for a coffee or aperitif, maybe). This square is surrounded by 18th century buildings and has an obelisk in its centre which is a monument to Pombal. The local museum is housed in the town hall (Museu Municipal Manuel Cabanas, open Tuesday to Saturday 1000 to 1400).

The historic town of Castro Marim is a few kilometres north of Vila Real and worth a visit mainly for its nature and bird reserve - Reserva Natural do Sapal de Castro Marim.

A trip with one's own yacht upstream is even more worthwhile. The Río Guadiana offers the rare chance to sail into a rural part of Portugal, amongst green hills and white villages to the historic settlement of Alcoutim with its ancient ramparts and castle. Take the tide and plan a night or two upriver.

EATING OUT

Vila Real has a few rather average Portuguese restaurants in which one can get a cheap and wholesome meal, but this is not a place for gastronomic treats or extravagances. There is a restaurant immediately by the yacht marina and, just across the road, another one in the Hotel Guadiana. There are also two basic but friendly small restaurants near the mouth of the river, about twenty minutes walk from the marina, good for sunny lunches or warm evenings overlooking the entrance of the Río Guadiana enjoying grilled fish or meat and cool wine (Restaurante Rebeirinha, telephone 543291, open lunches and evenings).

The neighbouring Dom Petisco (telephone 541853) is open mainly during the evenings and offers a slightly more sophisticated menu.

DAYTIME ANCHORAGES AND ALTERNATIVE HARBOURS NEARBY

Anchorage off Ayamonte upstream of the fishing basin (strong tides, good holding).

There are various anchorages and mooring places up the Río Guadiana: One floating pontoon at Alcoutim, anchorages off Pedra Amareta (Spain), Almada de Ouro (Portugal), Amoreira (Portugal), Foz do Odeleite (Portugal), Romeirao (Spain), Puerto Carbon (Spain), another floating pontoon at Sanlucar do Guadiana (Spain, opposite Alcoutim).

The river is deep but unmarked, just stay in mid-stream and keep to the outsides of bends. The tides run fast, so attempting to go against the tide would be a waste of time and energy, although if progress has to be made, they seem to run fastest in the last three hours.

'Enterprise' moored in the marina at Vila Real

USEFUL INFORMATION
Local dialling code for Vila Real: 281
Marina office in Vila Real: 541571
Marina Ayamonte: 959-321694 (VHF Ch 9)

CHAPTER 3

THE ATLANTIC COAST OF ANDALUCIA

The Atlantic coast of Andalucia, Spain's southernmost province, stretches from Ayamonte in the north to Tarifa at the western end of the Straits of Gibraltar. The coast becomes less and less developed as one proceeds south-east, with beautiful white beaches stretching for many miles, notably south of Cádiz.

There are quite a few harbours conveniently spaced along the coast for easy day sailing as well as some very interesting towns and sights to visit only a little way inland.

Andalucia is one of Spain's most exciting regions, birthplace of the Flamenco, home to the Sherry trade, famous for bull-fighting and so on, and the Atlantic coastline is far less developed and much more unspoilt than the various Costas along the Mediterranean coast. So it seems rather strange that so many cruising yachts rush past in the attempt to get into the Mediterranean as quickly as possible and miss out on some of the

best places in Andalucia. The climate here is as mild as on the Mediterranean side of the Straits, so this region makes a good choice for wintering on board, whilst the summers are less hot due to fresher Atlantic breezes.

PLACES OF SPECIAL INTEREST

Sevilla is the capital of Andalucia and has the great advantage that it can be reached by yacht and also has good moorings and marinas (see chapter for details). It is also one of the most exciting and beautiful cities of Spain, indeed of Europe. A visit here is a must, although not

'Enterprise' with Gibraltar's Europa Point in the background

recommended in the summer, when it definitely can get too hot. Along the coast temperatures are usually more moderate.

The so called Sherry Triangle is also worth exploring. This region is located between the towns of Jerez de la Frontera, Sanlucar de Barrameda and El Puerto de Santa Maria - the last two of which can again be visited by yacht.

Tarifa and the beaches in its vicinity are worth a special mention for various reasons: this is allegedly the windiest corner of Europe (so take care to choose your weather!) and, due to this and the fantastic long beaches, definitely Europe's prime surfing and windsurfing spot. Apart from that, Tarifa is a fascinating place with a strong Arabian feel and flavour about it.

The Rock of Gibraltar is also a must, of course. It is, strictly speaking, in the Mediterranean but it is included in this volume nevertheless for its importance. Gibraltar is of historic interest and has always been a strategic meeting-place for cruising yachts, whether bound in or out of the Mediterranean.

A land excursion from any one of these ports into the mountains of the hinterland is strongly recommended. In Ronda, for example, (which came to literary fame with Hemingway's Spanish Civil War novel "For Whom the Bell Tolls"), you will encounter a completely different world from the life down along the coast.

The whole mountain area north of the coast is fascinating - quite different from the coastal strip. It is a landscape of olive groves, fantastic gorges, the 'white villages', and several national parks and bird reserves with outstanding landscapes. All this is within easy reach by hire car, and the historic cities of Granada and Cordoba are also within a few hours drive of the Sevilla/Cadiz /Gibraltar area.

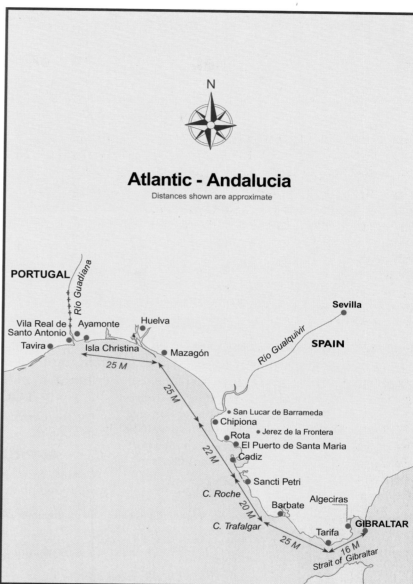

Atlantic - Andalucia
Distances shown are approximate

Another excursion well worth considering is across the Strait of Gibraltar to Africa (see final chapter). This can either be done by ferry from Tarifa or Algeciras or, much better, in one's own boat. It is only a short hop from Gibraltar across to Ceuta, a Spanish enclave in North Africa which has an easy approach and a good, friendly, secure marina. The town of Ceuta is not so different from many Andalucian cities.

From here it is possible to take a daylong coach trip into Morocco for 5,000 Pts (around £21) per head visiting Tetouan, then through the mountains to Tangier and finally back to Ceuta. The trip enables you to see a rural way of life that has not changed for centuries.

Río Guadiana looking S towards the entrance, with Ayamonte and the marina

AYAMONTE & ISLA CANELA

Ayamonte (& Isla Canela) - 37°05.5'N / 07°23.5'W

Ayamonte is the main town on the west bank of the Río Guadiana (see under Vila Real in the previous section for further information about the river). It is still a typical Andalucian town, but is quickly changing thanks to an ever increasing tourist trade. It is certainly livelier and has more shops and restaurants than Vila Real. The marina, in contrast to Vila Real, is free of the river and tidal currents.

The island of Isla Canela is the best example of the quickening pace of development on this part of the Spanish Atlantic coast, with hundreds of new apartments, four hotels, new golf courses and even a new marina being built there.

LOCATION/POSITION

The Río Guadiana is the border between Portugal and Spain.

APPROACH AND ENTRANCE

Coming from the west the river mouth is easily identified by the high apartment blocks of

Ayamonte seen from the East, with Vila Real in the background on the other side of the Río Guadiana

Monte Gordo about two miles west of the entrance, and the tall white lighthouse at Vila Real itself. The river mouth is sheltered by two lit seawalls, although the port side mole is submerged from about half tide onwards. There are dangerous shoals off the mouth on both sides of the channel. The two pairs of buoys marking the approach have to be observed, especially the inner ones (one red, one green). The entrance is rather shallow, sometimes less than 2 metres at low tide, so entrance should only be attempted from half tide onwards. Strong onshore winds against the ebb tide make this entrance very dangerous. Once over the bar, keep closer to the west side until past Vila Real.

The new marina of Isla Canela lies almost directly opposite Isla Cristina, (see p111 for approach and entry).

BERTHING

In Ayamonte, yachts moor to floating pontoons and fingers inside the marina which is located at the inner end of the former fishing basin. There are 170 berths for boats of up to 12 metres in length, larger yachts will have to anchor off the town or moor alongside the pier. The marina can be called on VHF Ch 09.

FACILITIES IN THE MARINA

Water and electricity on the pontoons, showers and toilets ashore, but no fuel was available (2000). There is a small slipway but no facilities for hauling out yachts.

TRANSPORT

There is a ferry across the Río Guadiana to Vila Real. The bus service connects with Huelva and Sevilla. Taxis and hire-cars are available in Ayamonte.

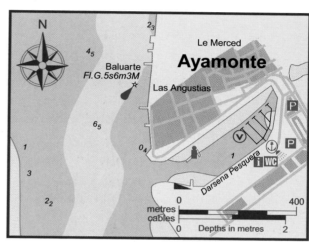

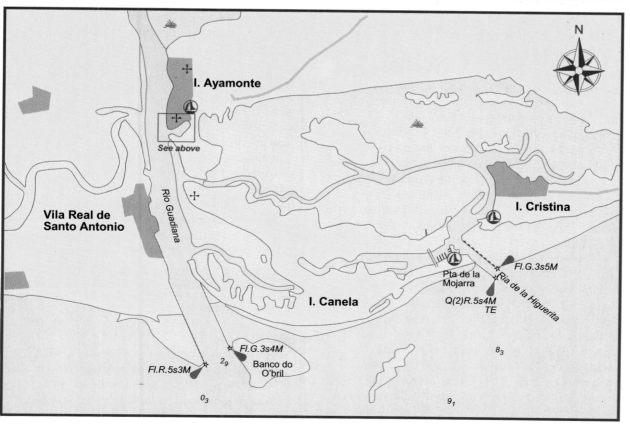

The small fishing village of El Moral near the new development at Isla Canela

The building site at Isla Canela

PROVISIONING

In Ayamonte there is a small supermarket close by the marina, as well as grocery shops, butchers, bakeries and general stores in town.

A RUN ASHORE

Ayamonte is a pretty Andalucian town, with narrow streets and white houses, shady squares and baroque churches, as well as a palm-lined promenade - Paseo de la Ribera - along the waterfront. There are castle ruins of Roman origin, an Arab tower and the 15th century church Nostra Senora de las Angustias.

Being strategically located at the border with Portugal, on the Río Guadiana and on the main road between the Algarve and Sevilla, Ayamonte has always been a busy and thriving little place. To the east of Ayamonte begin the marshlands and rivers of the region, and it is possible to go by dinghy through the marshy rivers all the way to Isla Cristina.

If you are not taking your boat up the Río Guadiana, Ayamonte is a perfect base for excursions by bus or hire-car into the inland regions of this province. Sanlucar de Guadiana is particularly worth a visit, being a picturesque and romantic rural town. From here, it is a short drive into the hills of the Andevalo or even into the much higher Picos de Aroche which are the western foot hills of the Sierra Morena. These hills and woods and mountains are wonderful for trekking and hiking and also a perfect remedy for

anybody seeking a change from the sea and longing for the smell of the Earth! There are about 700 kilometres of marked public footpaths of various distances and difficulty.

Isla Canela has some good sandy beaches and beautiful, marshy countryside - half water, half land - on the northern side, but all this is in the process of being destroyed by the development of the artificial holiday city on the tip of the island.

EATING OUT

There are quite a few bars and restaurants in Ayamonte and it is worthwhile roaming about the narrow streets to find your own place.

For a special treat, Ayamonte has a Parador. This is a short climb from the town but a very pleasant place from which to enjoy the sunset, and gaze over the Río, the town and the distant coastline before settling down to a superb dinner. Parador de Ayamonte, El Castillito, telephone 320700, credit cards accepted.

ALTERNATIVE ANCHORAGES AND MARINAS

There are various anchorages and moorings upstream on the and beautiful Río Guadiana (for details, see under Vila Real in the previous section).

The new yacht marina in the resort of Isla Canela was under construction at the time of writing (approach and entry see under Isla Cristina) and is a few miles around the corner by boat and only a few kilometres away over land. An entire resort is being built on the beach, including hotels, apartments and the like, and building will surely carry on for quite a while (the buildings were still in the early stages of construction in early 2000).

The marina was supposed to be operational from spring 2000 onwards but even if that were so, it would still be in the middle of a huge building site and there is no reason whatsoever (at the time of writing and for the foreseeable future) for a yacht to visit this port - especially as close by you have Ayamonte and Isla Cristina.

USEFUL INFORMATION			
Ayamonte Tides (Std Port Lisboa Time Zone −0100)			
	MHWS	MHWN	MLWN MLWS
Height (metres)	3·1	2·4	1·4 0·4

Radio Telephone Marina VHF Ch 09 (H24).
Local dialling code for Ayamonte: 959
Marina office in Ayamonte: 321694
Tourist information in Ayamonte: 470988

Chapter 3

Isla Cristina marina seen from S, with the 'fake lighthouse' (an apartment building) clearly visible

ISLA CRISTINA

Isla Cristina - 37°11.54'N / 07°19.36'W

Isla Cristina is a small fishing town with 14,000 inhabitants and few tourists despite some extended sandy beaches close by. It is situated in an area of low-lying, marshy river mouth and sandy islands on the left bank of the Rio Carreras. The town itself is unassuming and, at first glance, rather bland - but reveals a certain charm after a while.

LOCATION/POSITION

The entrance to the Rio Carreras is just under four miles east of the Río Guadiana. The marina itself is then another 1.5 miles upstream from the breakwater - position 37°11.54'N / 07°19.36'W.

A new, private marina is currently under construction on the right bank of the river near a new hotel complex on Isla Canela.

APPROACH AND ENTRANCE

The new hotel complex on Isla Canela and the building on the tip of Isla Cristina - which looks like a light-house from afar - are good landmarks when approaching from seaward. There is an extensive area of shoal water near the coast between Río Guadiana and Rio Carreras where the seas break even in calm weather, so it is best to stay at least 2 miles offshore here. It is also quite shallow on both sides of the breakwaters that are built in the entrance, so do not close in to

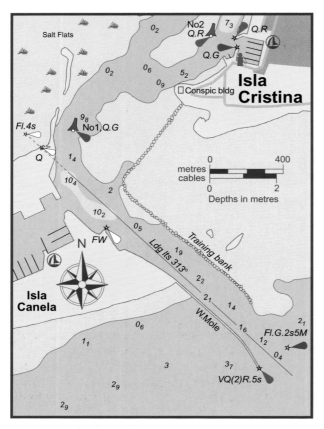

the shore before having identified the breakwater heads, which are both lit. The eastern seawall is partly submerged.

Depth in the entrance is around 3 metres but it is best to enter with the second half of the flood. Once inside the Rio, follow the green and red buoys around to starboard until you can see the marina entrance. The river is quite shallow outside this marked channel.

BERTHING

Yachts moor to floating pontoons with fingers, some of which are rather short, although the maximum length for boats in the marina is given as 15 metres. There is good shelter, but swell from passing fishing boats frequently enters the marina and makes the boats roll quite heavily at times. The marina office can be called on VHF Ch 09.

FACILITIES IN THE MARINA

Water and electricity is supplied on the pontoons, and showers and toilets ashore. Diesel is available from a fuel pontoon. There is a 32-ton Travelift and a hard-standing area, repairs of all types can be carried out (boatbuilding, mechanical, sailmaking). Nautica Levante is a yacht service

The entrance to the Rio Carreras seen from S, looking towards Isla Cristina (right) and Isla Canela (extreme left)

The wide sandy beach of Isla Cristina

company run by Rino Johansen, a Scandinavian who is also the representative of Trans Ocean (telephone 959-332730, mobile 609-508204, e-mail nlevante@teleline.es).

The other resident yacht service is Y. Lec run by Ydo Hoekstra (telephone 959-343259). There is also a diver here (Tramsub, telephone 959-343683).

TRANSPORT

There are buses to Ayamonte and Huelva, but there are no hire-cars available.

PROVISIONING

Shops and supermarkets are situated in town. Close to the marina is a small supermarket, larger ones (Lidl) are a longer walk away at the other end of town (towards the north-east from the marina, on the Ronda Norte).

A RUN ASHORE

As the younger locals would probably willingly tell you, there ain't nothing much to do here. One could wander down to the fish pier when the fleet comes in and watch the catch being unloaded, or buy some at the fish market. Or go down to the beach, which is quite close to the marina, and go for a swim or a very long walk. Alternatively, one could go into the town centre and sit in one of the cafés until enlightenment descends on one's soul!

The province of Huelva, of which Isla Cristina is a small part, also has a very interesting hinterland, but this is better explored (by hire-car) from El Rompido or Huelva (see there for details).

Cultural events at Isla Cristina include the Carnival (two weeks at the end of February) and the Carmen Festival in July.

EATING OUT

A favourite with the younger generation is the restaurant Macarena Marchena (Faneca, 44, telephone 343021), but this has the disadvantage of being a long walk from the marina.

More traditional are the two typically Spanish restaurants on the Plaza del Caudillo (follow the main street into the centre and this will lead to the plaza), Acosta (telephone 31420) and Reyes (331850). Both offer good quality Spanish food at reasonable prices in typical surroundings.

DAYTIME ANCHORAGES NEARBY

There is a pool with enough depth at low water in the river just upstream of and opposite the fishing pier at Isla Cristina - quite pleasant as a change from berthing in marinas. This is also a good base from which to explore the river further upstream in the dinghy - you can actually take a small boat as far as Ayamonte along the river.

When landing ashore in Isla Cristina, it is advisable not to use the fishing dock - better to use the marina. Dinghies have been known to disappear from the fishing dock and offered back to their owners a few days later: "We have found your boat, Señor; for a fee of 5,000 pesetas you can have it back!"

USEFUL INFORMATION

Isla Cristina RadioTelephone Marina VHF Ch 09.
Local dialling code for Isla Cristina: 959
Marina office: 343501
Tourist office: 343364

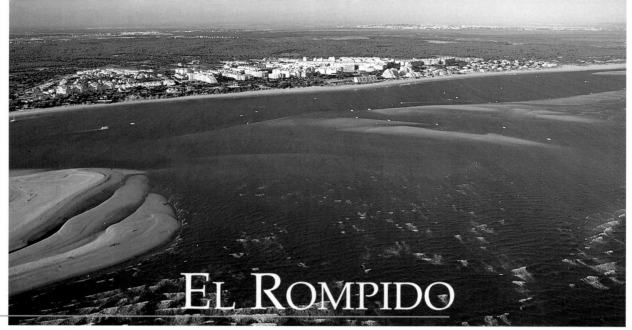

EL ROMPIDO

The entrance to the Rio Piedras, seen from S, with the buoyed channel on the right

El Rompido - 37°12'N / 07°02'W

El Rompido is an attractive fishing village offering some holiday-type activities, situated on the beautiful tree-lined banks of the Rio Piedras. The river is protected from the sea by a long and narrow sand spit with dunes and fantastic beaches.

The entrance to the Rio is quite dramatic but, given the right circumstances, entirely managable.

Once inside, you will find probably the most beautiful anchorage along the entire coast between Cabo de Sao Vincente and Gibraltar. There is a small and friendly boatyard run by Wolfgang Michalsky which mainly caters for major repairs, but otherwise there are no special facilities for yachts.

LOCATION/POSITION

El Rompido is about halfway along the coast between Isla Cristina and Mazagon and five miles upstream from the entrance. The sand-spit continually grows eastward and so the entrance moves too!

APPROACH AND ENTRANCE

Entry to the Rio Piedras can be lively so care is needed as well as local knowledge - available from Wolfgang Michalsky by mobile telephone - 959-399180, as the bar and the surrounding sands shift very frequently and the buoyage is rarely up to the latest state of affairs.

El Rompido can be identified from sea by the lighthouse, and from here the entrance is about five to six miles further east, in front of the town of El Portil. An approach buoy (red/white) and port and starboard buoys are laid to mark the entrance,

but as mentioned, this changes frequently.

Depth on the bar is as little as one metre at low water and the channel then runs very close and parallel to the beach. Entry is not advisable except in calm weather, without swell and near high water. Once inside the sand spit, the river becomes deep again and very easy to navigate.

The sheltered anchorage off El Rompido

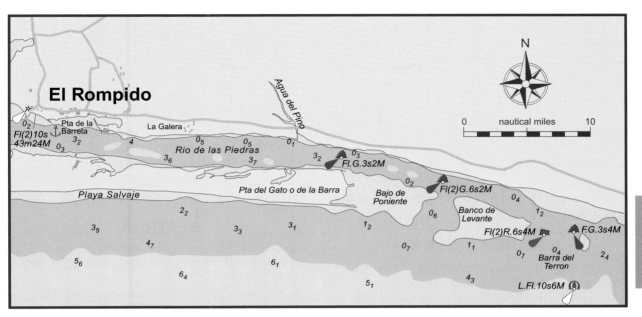

BERTHING

Anchor in the river in good holding in front of the village of El Rompido or further upstream - the river is navigable for yachts as far as the fishing village of El Terron. Dinghy landing is at the pier of El Rompido or the long floating pontoon of the boatyard.

FACILITIES

All repairs can be made by the boatyard Varadero Rio Piedras. No other facilities for yachts.

TRANSPORT

El Rompido is a rather small village and it may not be easy to organise transport.

PROVISIONING

Small local shops and supermarkets in El Rompido.

A RUN ASHORE

Walking along the shores of the river or much better, exploring by dinghy. Best of all is to cross to the sand-spit by dinghy, land there and enjoy endless stretches of dunes and sandy beaches.

EATING OUT

For a smallish village, El Rompido has a surprising number of bars and restaurants, which is, of course, a hint to the numbers of visitors coming (by land) during the summer.

The ones noted by us (although there are several others just as good) are Las Brisas, which is fairly close to the boatyard and in the second row from the beach, but with a nice terrace overlooking the river.

Directly on the water's edge, and also with a nice terrace is Carybe II (399027), as well as La Pantera which is a bit more traditional in style and ambience and only a few hundred metres along the road (or beach, depending on where you are walking).

USEFUL INFORMATION
Varadero Rio Pedras, Wolfgang Michalsky: 959-399180

HUELVA & MAZAGON

Huelva and Mazagon - 37°06.0 N / 6°49.3 W

Huelva is the capital of this region and is a busy industrial town, although not without its attractions in the centre. Mazagon is its pretty suburban offspring near the river mouth in scenically attractive surroundings; the oil refineries, commercial harbour and areas of heavy industry are all further upstream towards Huelva.

Mazagon has a convenient marina from which excursions to Huelva and other attractions in the hinterland can be organised.

LOCATION/POSITION

Both towns are on the banks of the Rio Odiel, 23 miles east of the Rio Guadiana and just under 30 miles north-west of the Rio Guadalquivir. The position of the marina in the mouth of the river is 37°07'58 N / 06°50'05 W.

APPROACH AND ENTRANCE

The entrance to the Rio Odiel can be identified from sea by the oil refineries a few miles to the east, and the lighthouse of Picacho just behind the marina itself. The entrance to the river is protected from the east by what, allegedly, is Europe's longest seawall, a mole stretching out to sea for roughly 7 miles with a small lighthouse at the end. The channel into the river is buoyed and lit, as is the marina entrance itself.

Entry is possible at all states of the tide and under nearly all circumstances.

BERTHING

In Mazagon marina, yachts moor to floating pontoons with fingers. There is a waiting pontoon just below the tower which houses the marina office which looks rather like a large gas-tank! Moor here and the staff will allocate a berth. Fuel is available here as well.

The marina basin is large and one of the few modern yacht harbours suitable for manoeuvring under sail. The marina office can be contacted on VHF Ch 09. There are 479 berths with a depth of around 4 metres, the maximum length for visiting yachts is given as 18 metres.

FACILITIES IN THE MARINA

Water and electricity is supplied to the pontoons, and there are showers and toilets ashore. There are two small chandlers in the marina as well as a hard standing area with a 32 ton Travelift. Few facilities for repairs exist, so for these one would probably be better off at Isla Cristina or the boatyard at El Rompido (see p114).

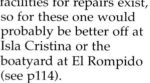

TRANSPORT

Mazagon has only a few buses per day to Huelva, but you can take a taxi for around 2,500 Pesetas for the ride. There you will find trains (to Sevilla and Madrid) and more buses and hire cars (Avis, 253329; Marina 250199; Hertz 257294-95-96).

Seville International Airport (telephone 954-510677) is about one hour by car.

The marina at Mazagon is spacious enough to manoeuvre under sail inside. This view is from the W

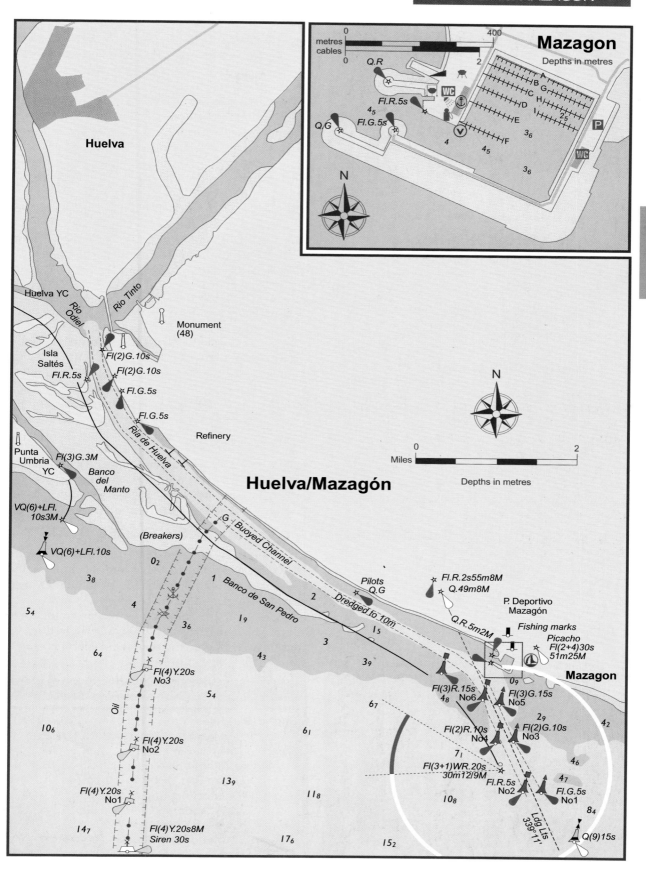

Mazagon
Depths in metres

metres
cables

0   400

Q.R

Fl.R.5s

Q.G   Fl.G.5s

WC

4_5

3_6

4_5

4

3_6

A
B
C
D
E
F

G
H
I

25

P

WC

N

Huelva

Huelva YC

Río Odiel

Río Tinto

Monument
(48)

Isla
Saltés

Fl(2)G.10s

Fl.R.5s   Fl(2)G.10s

Fl.G.5s

Fl.G.5s

Punta
Umbria
YC

Fl(3)G.3M

Banco
del
Manto

Refinery

Ría de Huelva

Huelva/Mazagón

N

0   Miles   2

Depths in metres

VQ(6)+LFl.
10s3M

VQ(6)+LFl.10s

(Breakers)

0_2

3_8

4

3_6

5_4

6_4

10_6

Oil

G

Buoyed Channel

Banco de San Pedro

1

1_9

2

3

4_3

5_4

6_1

13_9

11_8

Dredged to 10m

1_5

3_9

6_7

Pilots
Q.G

Fl.R.2s55m8M
Q.49m8M

Q.R.5m2M

P. Deportivo
Mazagón

Fishing marks

Picacho
Fl(2+4)30s
51m25M

Mazagon

0_9

Fl(3)R.15s
No6 4_8

Fl(3)G.15s
No5

2_9 4_2

Fl(2)R.10s
No4

Fl(2)G.10s
No3

7_1 4_6

Fl(3+1)WR.20s
30m12/9M

Fl.R.5s
No2

Fl.G.5s
No1

4_7

8_4

10_8

15_2

17_6

Fl(4)Y.20s
No3

Fl(4)Y.20s
No2

Fl(4)Y.20s
No1

Fl(4)Y.20s8M
Siren 30s

14_7

Ldg Lts
339°11'

Q(9)15s

Chapter 3

The town centre of Huelva is rather attractive

PROVISIONING

Mazagon has small shops and two supermarkets, but there are shops of all description in Huelva, including large supermarkets.

A RUN ASHORE

Mazagon is pretty and has fine beaches but is otherwise of little interest. The centre of this quiet little village has a few shops, restaurants, a discotheque (Galaxia), and the bus to Huelva is about a quarter of an hour's walk from the marina.

La Rabida, which is about halfway to Huelva, was where Christoper Columbus set out on his epic voyages of discovery. Here one can see a fleet of replicas of his caravels, as well as an exhibition of medieval seafaring and navigation (Caravel Wharf, telephone 959-530472). There is also a fine botanical garden with over 100 species of palm trees and many other plants. This oasis is surprisingly set in the middle of the commercial harbour and industrial area.

Huelva is 18 kilometres from Mazagon by road, and is a pleasant and lively medium sized city, where the visitor can keep his bearings and not become entirely lost. There are numerous pedestrian zones, parks, cafés and restaurants.

The surrounding province of Huelva (best

Relaxing in the 'Café de la Prensa' in Huelva

explored by hire car from Huelva town) is interesting and in places quite beautiful, its scenery ranging from the mountains of the Picos de Aroche and the Sierra de Aracena in the north, to the lowlands and marshes of the coastal regions.

The historic mines of Rio Tinto are the oldest working mines in the world, and includes a mining museum - the Corta Atalaya. This is one of the largest working mines in Europe, and a mining railway takes visitors on a 11 kilometre journey in restored mining wagons through the history of mining.

The mines were worked by British miners at one stage, and you can still see their housing at The Queen Victoria Worker's Quarter, in Huelva. These are terraced houses in the English style, built by the Rio Tinto Mining Co Ltd in 1917.

EATING OUT

There are a handful of rather average restaurants in Mazagon, which also has a Parador 6.5 kilometres to the south-east (Parador de Mazagon, telephone 536300).

A better choice of restaurants can be found in Huelva. Always a first class address is the rather formal El Estero (Gran Via, telephone 256572). Close by is the cosy and interesting restaurant and café La Prensa (Gran Via 15, telephone 240211) which serves delicious raciones all day as well as coffees and drinks. Another favourite with many is La Cazuela (Garci Fernandez 5, telephone 258096), but apart from these three there is a wide choice of tavernas and eating places scattered around town.

DAYTIME ANCHORAGES NEARBY

There are a few anchorages further upstream from Mazagon, as well as mooring buoys belonging to the local sailing club, but these are in unattractive surroundings in the industrial area. As the anchorage off Huelva is a long way from the town centre, it is still easier to choose a berth in the marina at Mazagon and take the bus or a taxi into Huelva.

USEFUL INFORMATION

Huelva (Bar) Tides (Std Port Lisboa Time Zone −0100)

	MHWS	MHWN	MLWN	MLWS
Height (metres)	3·2	2·5	1·2	0·4

Radio Telephone Marina VHF Ch 09 16.
Huelva Port Ch 06 11 12 14 16.
Local dialling codes for
Mazagon and Huelva: 959
Marina office: 376237
Tourist office, Huelva: 257403

CHIPIONA

Chipiona - 36°45.0 N / 06°25.4 W

The attractive town centre of Chipiona

Chipiona is a minor historical town near the mouth of the Rio Guadalquivir and, for sailors venturing up the Rio towards Sevilla, a good place to wait for a favourable tide. Another is anchored off the sherry producing city of Sanlucar de Barrameda on the south bank of the Guadalquivir, just inside its entrance.

Today, Chipiona is best known as a summer resort for people from Sevilla and other inland cities. Its beaches, bars and restaurants are crowded in summer. Despite this, the town has an interesting centre that is well worth exploring.

LOCATION/POSITION

Chipiona sits on a promontory about 10 miles north of the Bahia de Cadiz and just over 30 miles south-east of Mazagon.

APPROACH AND ENTRANCE

Chipiona can easily be identified from sea, and confirmed by the major lighthouse of Chipiona itself - a 68 metre high conical stone tower on a 2 story building. The entrance to the marina is just to the north-east of the town.

The approach from the north is straightforward, but take care not to get too close under the shore just north of the estuary of the Guadalquivir which is very shallow (there is also a conspicuous wreck there as a reminder to keep clear).

Coming from south or south-west, take care to round the cardinal mark off the shallow of Salmedina - a drying patch about 1.6 miles due west of Chipiona with very shallow water between it and Chipiona itself.

The approach to the marina is marked by red buoys, so keep inside these as the water shallows quickly just east of them. Apart from these dangers, approach and entry are straightforward day or night. The marina basin is fairly large and suitable for manoeuvring under sail.

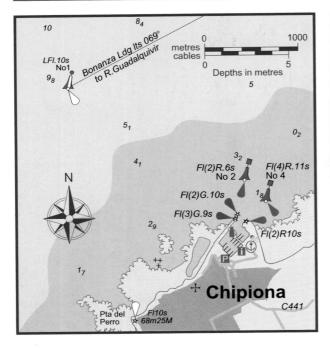

The marina at Chipiona is the perfect place to wait for a favourable tide up the Guadalquivir River

BERTHING

Visiting yachts berth in the north-eastern part of the marina on floating pontoons with fingers. The marina office can be contacted on VHF Ch 09. There are 335 berths for vessels up to 40 metres length, the minimum depth is given as 2.5 metres.

FACILITIES IN THE MARINA

The marina has the usual facilities including water and electricity on the pontoons as well as

Chipiona from S, with the town, the marina and the Donana National Park beyond the entrance to the Guadalquivir River

showers and toilets ashore. There is also a Travelift and a hard standing area, plus various mechanics and repair services. There are two chandlers in the marina area.

TRANSPORT

Hire cars are available in Chipiona, and Sevilla and Cadiz can be visited by bus from here. The nearest international airport is at Sevilla.

PROVISIONING

The town centre is about ten minutes walk from the marina and has a good range of shops and supermarkets, although they are somewhat scattered around town.

A RUN ASHORE

As mentioned above, a stroll around the town is interesting and worthwhile. Chipiona also has good beaches but these tend to be crowded in summer - especially during week-ends.

EATING OUT

There are two good restaurants by the marina (Paco and Mi Velano).

DAYTIME ANCHORAGES NEARBY

There are good and attractive anchorages just inside the estuary of the Guadalquivir, about 5 miles away from Chipiona.

USEFUL INFORMATION			
Chipiona Tides (Std Port Lisboa Time Zone −0100)			
	MHWS	MHWN	MLWN MLWS
Height (metres)	3·2	2·5	1·3 0·5
Radio Telephone Marina VHF Ch 09. Port Ch 12.			
Local dialling code for Chipiona: 956			
Marina office: 373844			
Tourist information: 370880			

SEVILLA & RÍO GUADALQUIVIR

Sevilla and Río Guadalquivir - 36°44.9 N / 07°25.6 W

Looking from the Donana National Park across the Guadalquivir River towards Sanlucar de Barrameda

To sail up the Río Guadalquivir, with the National Park of Donana and the Sherry producing town of Sanlucar de Barrameda at the entrance, and the fascinating city of Sevilla as a destination, must surely be the absolute highlight of any cruise in this region of Atlantic Andalusia.

Many cruising yachts winter in Sevilla (in Puerto Gelves, see below) whilst others who have only come for a night or two have been known to stay for weeks!

The one drawback is that while autumn, winter and especially spring are ideal times to visit Sevilla, it gets rather too hot for most northern Europeans during the summer months. It is preferable, if one is not used to excessive heat, to stay somewhere along the coast at this time - indeed most Sevillianos seem to move to the coast during July and August.

Many restaurants and other places will be closed during August, and the prices of hotels will then be at their annual lowest.

LOCATION/POSITION

Sevilla lies about 55 miles upriver from the Guadalquivir No. 1 buoy.

APPROACH AND ENTRANCE

The approach to the Río Guadalquivir is straightforward and without any offlying dangers other than the shallows north of the buoyed channel (see also Chipiona). Once inside the river,

Looking upstream towards Sevilla, with the pontoon of Marina Yachting Sevilla to the right

the buoyage becomes more and more sparse as one continues upstream, but this presents few problems. The Guadalquivir is deep (and used by quite large merchant ships), so as long as one stays in mid-channel, and towards the outsides of bends, there should be no problems. Special charts to cover the river up to Sevilla will not normally be needed.

BERTHING

There are three possible places to berth.

The Real Club Nautico, above a lock and a lifting bridge near the city centre; the pontoons of Yachting Sevilla, also above the lock; and the small marina at Gelves, a little way up the main river, past the branch that leads to the lock and into the centre of Sevilla.

The Club Nautico is most convenient, as it is within walking distance of the centre and has many luxurious facilities such as a swimming pool and tennis courts, but mooring fees are rather high. Yachts moor to floating pontoons in the river.

The pontoon of Yachting Sevilla has more basic facilities but is inconveniently placed in the middle of nowhere, about 3 miles from the town, with the nearest bus station about 20 minutes walk away, forcing reliance on taxis or cycles if

you carry them onboard. This pontoon really only serves as a waiting post if one wants to continue through the lifting bridge to the Club Nautico.

The easiest and most economic option is to go up to Gelves and either berth in the small marina or anchor in the river just outside. The marina has all the usual facilities (which may also be used by those anchoring outside for a very modest fee) and is close to the quaint little town of Gelves. Buses to Sevilla run regularly from the marina entrance and take about 20 minutes into the city.

FACILITIES IN THE MARINA

All three have the basic facilities such as water and electricity on the pontoons and showers and toilets ashore. The Club Nautico has the luxurious facilities mentioned above, while Puerto Gelves has a Travelift, hard standing, a boatyard and small chandlery, as well as a free washing machine. All three marinas can be reached on VHF Ch 09.

TRANSPORT

Sevilla has an international airport, and bus and rail connections to all other parts of Spain. Hire cars can be rented, although prices are somewhat higher than in some of the tourist areas on the Mediterranean coast.

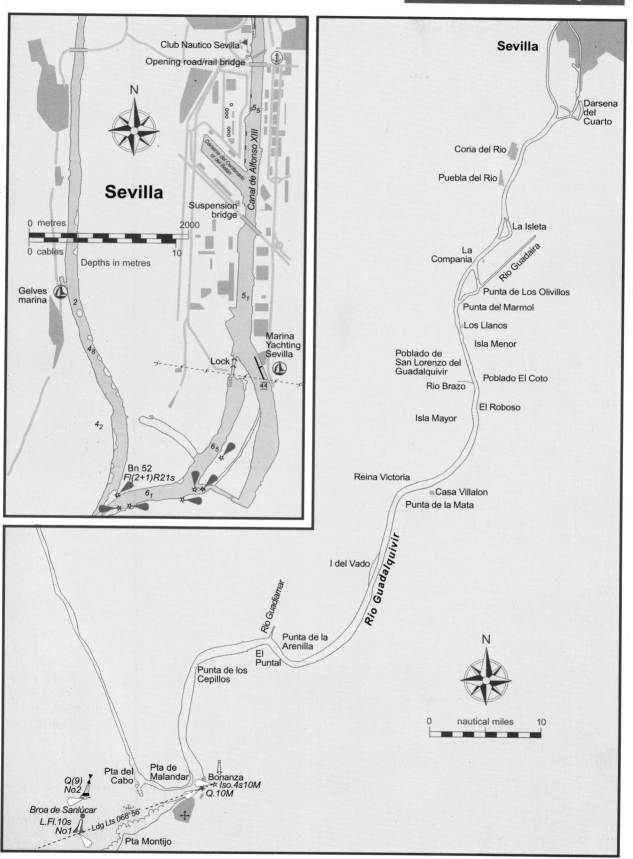

Club Nautico Sevilla

Opening road/rail bridge

Sevilla

N

Darsena del Centenario or del Batán

Canal de Alfonso XIII

Sevilla

Suspension bridge

0 metres   2000

0 cables   10

Depths in metres

5₅

5₁

Gelves marina

2

4₈

Marina Yachting Sevilla

Lock

44

4₂

6₅

Bn 52
Fl(2+1)R21s

6₁

Sevilla

Darsena del Cuarto

Coria del Rio

Puebla del Rio

La Isleta

La Compania

Rio Guadaira

Punta de Los Olivillos

Punta del Marmol

Los Llanos

Isla Menor

Poblado de San Lorenzo del Guadalquivir

Poblado El Coto

Rio Brazo

El Roboso

Isla Mayor

Reina Victoria

Casa Villalon

Punta de la Mata

Río Guadalquivir

I del Vado

Río Guadiamar

Punta de la Arenilla

El Puntal

Punta de los Cepillos

N

0   nautical miles   10

Pta del Cabo

Pta de Malandar

Bonanza
Iso.4s10M
Q.10M

Q(9) No2

Broa de Sanlúcar
L.Fl.10s
No1

Ldg Lts 068° 56'

Pta Montijo

PROVISIONING

Sevilla has all the shops and facilities of a major town, including (in 2000) a branch of Marks & Spencer, which has a small food section with British products. As far as major provisioning is concerned, the food section of the large department store El Corte Ingles is superb and they will normally deliver larger quantities of provisions to a boat moored in the Club Nautico.

In Gelves, small shops for day-to-day use are in the village - just a few minutes walk from the marina. A few kilometres up the road towards Sevilla is a huge shopping complex with various superbly stocked hypermarkets. Of these, Hypercor and Continente will normally deliver to a boat moored in Puerto Gelves (depending on the amount of provisioning), otherwise it is probably easiest to take a bus there (catch the bus to Sevilla, get out after two stops before it reaches the dual carriageway into Sevilla) and when fully burdened with shopping take a taxi back.

A RUN ASHORE

Sevilla, the capital of Andalucia, is a fascinating city with a long and varied history – reflected in its many historic buildings. It is also a lively, trendy town full of students, with a vibrant night-life and a busy cultural calendar.

The annual highlight is the Feria de Abril which usually takes place at the end of April or the beginning of May. This is the most important social event of the year for the Sevillanos, who will be parading in their finest, traditional clothes, often on horseback. As well as showing off in this way, the Feria is about eating and drinking for six consecutive days and nights on the special site of the Feria, where the wealthier family clans as well as clubs and associations will have their own tents (called casetas) in which to entertain guests and

Quite a few merchant ships use the Guadalquivir to reach Sevilla

Sevilla seen from the SW with the Club Nautico on the left bank just above the road bridge

friends. The grounds for the Feria, El Real de la Feria, are in Los Remedios on the bank of the river. The Feria is also the opening of the bull-fighting season, and Sevilla has the reputation, second only to Madrid, for the best bull-fights in Spain.

Also noteworthy is the Semana Santa, the holy week preceding Easter Sunday. During this week, incredibly opulent images and entire scenes concerning Easter are carried through the streets of Sevilla, followed by long processions. A sight not to be missed if one happens to be in the area during this time.

A guide-book or tourist map of Sevilla is an essential investment if one is interested in investigating historical sights. The main ones to see are the incredible cathedral, the Alcazar, the Museo de Bellas Artes, the Parque de Maria Luisa and Placa de Espana, the Torre del Oro, and there are many more!

Other interesting places are the shopping streets in central Sevilla, the old Jewish district of Santa Cruz between the cathedral and the University,

Another unique feature of Sevilla is the Alcazar, an ancient palace with a mix of styles which has been the headquarters and private residence of many famous rulers over the centuries. The Alcazar dates back to 912, but many palaces and buildings have been added by the various proprietors since then, which explains the intriguing mix of architectural styles. A jewel in their own right are the beautiful gardens inside the walls of the Alcazar.

Anybody interested in the arts should not miss out on a visit to the Museo de Bellas Artes which has a large collection, mainly of 16th and 17th century Spanish masters, and more modern and contemporary works from mainly Sevillian artists, in addition to periodically changing exhibitions. The museum is housed in the beautiful building of a former convent which in itself is worth the visit.

The Parque de Maria Luisa and the Plaza de Espana is an area south of the Fabrica de Tabacos (a former tobacco factory which now houses the main building of the University) which was landscaped for the 1929 Exposicion Iberoamericana, a sort of Ibero-American part-world exhibition. Quite a number of interesting buildings are scattered around, many of which are used by departments and institutes of the University.

The park is a nice area with shaded avenues and ponds to escape from the bustle of the city. The Plaza de Espana is embraced by a semicircular palace lookalike which is one of the most grandiose of the 1929 exhibition buildings.

The Torre del Oro, prominently situated on the bank of the Río Guadalquivir, is an Arab watchtower from the 13th century which, as its name implies, was once covered in golden tiles. Inside is a small but charming maritime museum - normally open in the mornings only.

A favourite with visitors is the medieval Jewish quarter of Santa Cruz, with its narrow, winding streets. A stroll along the river bank is also pleasing, especially if promenading along the Calle de Betis in Triana on the left bank. The best views of Sevilla are from here, with the added bonus of a new bar, café or restaurant literally every few metres!

An English book shop (Vertice, Calle San Fernando 33) can be found opposite the main university building (the old tobacco factory). There is also a cinema with five screens showing films in their original versions with Spanish subtitles. This is Avenida 5 Cines in Marques de Paradas 5, telephone 95-4415309 (near the

and the charming if nowadays very trendy and thus somewhat yuppifed former Gypsy quarter of Triana - full of bars and restaurants, some with superb views of Sevilla across the Guadalquivir.

Speaking of bars, the night-life in Sevilla, as everywhere in Spain, does not really get going until quite late, around midnight at week-ends. Allegedly, there are discotheques in Sevilla which only open up at nine in the morning for those who still not have had enough by then . . !

Back to the sights. The cathedral with its tower La Giralda is the central point of Sevilla and not only huge, its awesome! In terms of floor space (this church is 160 metres long and about 140 metres wide) it is outdone only by St. Peters in Rome and St. Pauls in London. It was built between 1401 and 1507 on the site of an ancient mosque which had already been used as a Christian church after Sevilla was taken from the Arabs by the Christians in 1248, and one of its interesting features is the tomb of Christopher Columbus, which is actually a little monument, containing what are thought to be his remains - brought here from Cuba in 1899.

shopping centre Plaza de Armas by the river north of the Plaza del Toros).

There are of course many more sights to be seen in Sevilla, but to list them all would be going too far - after all, many books have been written about this city. The casual visitor should just drift around town for a while, watching the lively street scenes in the different parts of the town and stopping frequently in cafés and bars to soak up the atmosphere as well as a coffee, a tapas and a manzanilla!

EATING OUT AND NIGHT-LIFE

Sevilla is one of the birthplaces of Flamenco. This emotional song, music and dance tells stories which have been handed down from the Andalucian Gypsies of the 18th century. Some songs lament the oppressed life as a Gypsy, others tell of love and hate, passion and deceit, life and death. No visit to Sevilla, or indeed Andalucia, would really be complete without seeing at least one genuine Flamenco performance.

This folk-art can be seen in several music bars and clubs around Sevilla - not to be confused with the bland tourist versions in the Tablaos Flamencos which start early evening (around seven or eight) and include dinner. Real Flamenco does not start until around 11.00pm or midnight and is so explosive and infectious that sitting at a dinner table while watching Flamenco would be truly ridiculous.

The Café Salamandra (Calle de Torneo 43) is well known for good Flamenco performances on Thursday nights, as is the small Café Sonanta in Triana (live Flamenco also Thursday nights). The Teatro Central (telephone 4460780) which, despite its name is not centrally located but in the grounds of the Expo 92, often has big Flamenco names on stage.

La Carboneria (Calle Levies, 18) is a very special music pub in a beautiful ancient building - a converted coal-yard - on the edges of Santa Cruz, which frequently has live music (often spontaneous as well). This used to be a meeting place for young politicians opposing the Franco regime. Today, it is still an intellectual meeting place with many artists as regular guests. Some of them will hang their paintings on the walls, others might recite from their latest lyrics - anything goes in this remarkable place.

El Rinconcillo (Gerona 32) is one of Sevilla's oldest bars, dating back to the 17th century, and yet another haunt of intellectuals, with frequent readings by new novelists. El Tamboril on the

Slightly more central but much more expensive are the moorings at the Club Nautico Sevilla

Puerto Gelves marina near Sevilla is the best option for visiting yachts

Plaza de Santa Cruz is also very popular and has live music nearly every night - from midnight onwards.

Instead of pub-crawling, people in Sevilla prefer the more civilised custom of Tapas-hopping. Tapas are small delicious snacks which are available in most of the bars around town. They are served either hot or cold, and can consist of anything - meat or fish or salads or shellfish (for example fried baby squid, called Puntillitas) or, a Sevilliano speciality, spinach and chick peas (Espinacas con garbanzos). Best of all is the Jamon Serrano or, better still, Jamon Iberico - delicately cured ham carved off the bone.

Drifting from bar to bar, either in Santa Cruz or Triana, having a Tapa and a glass of sherry or wine or beer in each, can be one of the more pleasurable ways in which to spend a night in town. For daytime Tapas two well known places are the Bar Giralda (Mateos Gago at the entrance to Santa Cruz district near the cathedral) and Bar Estrella

The Calle Sierpes in the centre of Seville is the main shopping street

(Calle Estrella 3 in the centre of town).

Like any major city, Sevilla is full of restaurants of all possible descriptions. Many are in the Santa Cruz district, and although most of these are geared for the tourist trade, they are still good. Some have very pleasant courtyard seating and offer reasonably priced menus, such as La Cueva (C Rodrigo Caro 18), Dona Elvira (Plaza de Dona Elvira), El Rinon de Pepe (C Gloria 6), El Giraldillo (Plaza Virgin de los Reyes) or Corral del Agua (Callejon del Agua 6).

If one is looking for a special place in which to enjoy a really top-of-the line meal, the elegant and quite beautiful Egana Oriza (Calle San Fernando 41, telephone 954 22 72 11) springs to mind, as well as maybe the Taberna del Alabardero (Calle Zaragoza 20, telephone 954 56 06 37) situated in an old palace, and serving imaginative fine food.

Many good restaurants can also be found along the river bank in Triana (Calle Betis), such as Ox's (as the name implies, a meat-eater's paradise with

The magnificient Plaza del Salvador in the centre of Sevilla, a popular place also for extended drinks in the sunshine

USEFUL INFORMATION

Sevilla Tides (Std Port Lisboa Time Zone −0100)
	MHWS	MHWN	MLWN	MLWS
Height (metres)	2·1	1·8	0·9	0·5

Río Guadalquivir, (Bar) Tides
	MHWS	MHWN	MLWN	MLWS
Height (metres)	3·2	2·5	1·3	0·4

Radio Telephone - Sevilla Marinas VHF Ch 09.
Port, lock and road/rail bridge Ch 12.
Río Guadalquivir Ch 12.
Local dialling code for Sevilla: 95
Club Nautico: 95-4454777
Marina Puerto Gelves: 95-5761212
or 95-5760728
Main Tourist Office (Avenida de la Constitucion
21 - near the cathedral, 95-4221404)
British Consulate (Plaza Nueva 8B,
95- 4228875)

top quality grills - telephone 954 27 95 85) or the Argentinian La Maria (telephone 954 33 84 61). For good fish in Triana, try Kiosco de las Flores by the bridge (Plaza el Altozano, telephone 954 33 38 98). There are a few good Italian restaurants along Calle Betis.

For a change from European food altogether, good Sushi (and other Japanese dishes) can be had at the Japanese Restaurant in Calle Salado 6 (between Triana proper and the Avenida de Argentinia). Returning to original Spanish cuisine, something of an insiders tip seems to be Casa Joaquin Marquez (Calle Felipe II, 8; telephone 95 4241229).

Apart from the few restaurants mentioned here, there is a multitude more. Obviously, it would be neither possible nor useful to list them all here, so the best recommendation is that you be guided by your own tastes and instincts.

DAYTIME ANCHORAGES NEARBY

It is possible to anchor nearly anywhere along the Río Guadalquivir as long as one keeps out of the main fairway used by merchant ships. The most attractive anchorages are downstream near the National Park, and opposite or off Sanlucar de Barrameda. There are also some small floating pontoons in this part of the river.

In Sevilla, it is quite convenient to anchor off the Marina Gelves, where the holding is good, although ample room should be left for swinging with the tide which normally runs at one to two knots, and up to three at springs. Only in the very rare event of prolonged rainfall during winter can the tide reach up to an alleged eight knots, in which case one would definitely be

The Plaza de Toros (bull ring) is the setting for some of Spain's finest bull-fights

better off inside the marina.

The tidal range at Sevilla is about 0.8 to 1.5 metres.

ROTA

Rota - 36°36 N / 06°20.8 W

A pleasant and charming old town with a useful new marina situated at the northern end of the Bahia de Cadiz. Nearby is one of the largest US naval bases in Europe which leaves its mark on Rota itself as a higher than usual proportion of night-clubs, discotheques etc. due to the large American clientele stationed close by.

LOCATION/POSITION

Rota is about 9 miles south of Chipiona at the entrance to the Bay of Cadiz.

APPROACH AND ENTRANCE

Coming from south or from the Bay of Cadiz, approach and entry are simple, and one can head direct for the harbour entrance. From the north or west, however, beware of shoal patches of under 2 metres extending west for over one mile from the coast between the harbour and Punta Candor north of the harbour.

BERTHING

Yachts moor to pontoons with fingers in the northern half of the harbour to starboard of the

fuel berth and control tower. There are 344 berths up to a maximum length of 18 metres.

FACILITIES IN THE MARINA

Water and electricity is available on the pontoons, and showers and toilets ashore. Fuel is obtainable from a fuel berth just inside the entrance. There is also a 32-ton Travelift, a large hard-standing area as well as a small trailer ramp. An engine service company also sells some chandlery items.

TRANSPORT

Rota is at the end of the road and not a convenient place for overland travel connections, arrangements for which are better made from either Cadiz or Puerto de Santa Maria, both just across the bay.

Chapter 3

Rota Harbour and Marina seen from the S

PROVISIONING

Small shops are fairly close by in the town, but for serious provisioning one would have to take a taxi to one of the large hypermarkets in the area.

A RUN ASHORE

Rota is a traditional fishing village which dates back a long time, as shown by the remains of the medieval city walls and the 14th century castle. The church - Nuestra Senora de la O - dates back to the 16th century and is quite beautiful.

The charm of Rota lies in its busy, bustling streets full of cafés and shops, and quiet Plazas in between, rather than its ancient monuments. A stroll through this town is pleasant and there are

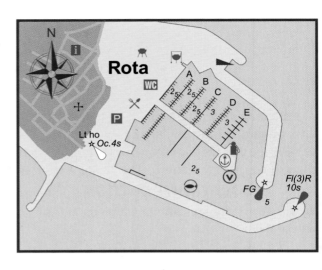

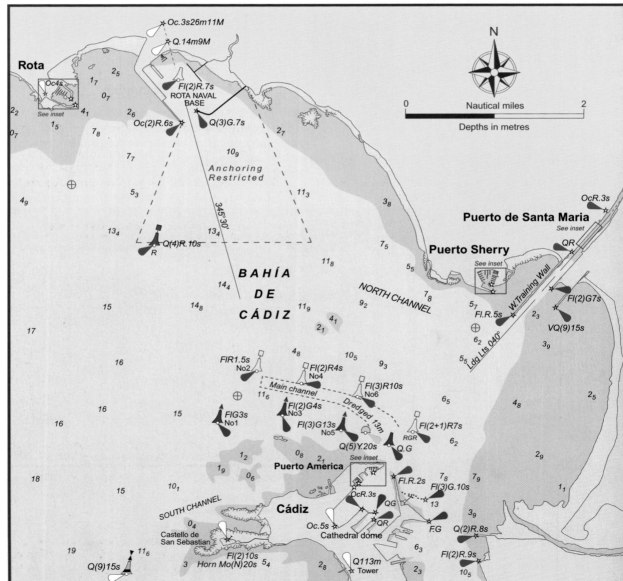

Rota lighthouse which stands just outside the old part of town

EATING OUT

As mentioned above, there are numerous bars, cafés and restaurants in town. Close to the marina in the archway by the lighthouse is an Irish pub which is open every night until the early hours. A few steps further on is the very cosy bar with traditional Spanish cooking; La Concha (Plaza de Bartomlome Perez), which also has a few tables on the plaza opposite the church - a particularly nice spot for a drink or a meal.

For a first class dinner in more posh and cosmopolitain surroundings, the restaurant El Embarcadero in the hotel Duque de Najera is a sure bet. The restaurant is decorated in the ambiance of a maritime club (including a low ceiling with fake deck beams) and serves high quality international cuisine.

many inviting places to sit and have a drink or just watch the life go by. There is also an agreeable beach promenade for relaxing afternoon strolls.

The American naval base was installed during the Cold War of the 1950s, in return for American aid to a then very poor Spain, almost starving under Franco's dictatorship.

Looking down towards the sea front and beach at Rota

DAYTIME ANCHORAGES NEARBY

If one is careful with the depths (the water shallows rapidly here) it is possible to anchor for the day off the beach between Rota harbour and the US naval base.

The luxurious Hotel Duque de Najera close to the harbour, which has a first class restaurant

USEFUL INFORMATION			
Rota Tides (Std Port Cádiz Time Zone −0100)			
	MHWS	MHWN	MLWN	MLWS

Rota Tides (Std Port Cádiz Time Zone −0100)

	MHWS	MHWN	MLWN	MLWS
Height (metres)	3·1	2·4	1·1	0·4

Radio Telephone Marina VHF Ch 09.
Local dialling code for Rota: 956
Tourist information: (Plaza de Espana) 82 91 05
Marina office: 81 38 11

CÁDIZ

Cádiz - 36°33.6 N / 6°19.0 W

Cádiz is a port of great historic importance, a unique location at the end of a long promontory, on which the superb old city is situated. However, the marina is quite a long way from the town and there is no bus service, so explorers will have to be willing to walk, or call a taxi, which might be one reason why this interesting city is missed by many yachts cruising the area.

LOCATION/POSITION

Cádiz effectively forms a breakwater of the large and well protected Bahía de Cádiz. The marina is at the very tip of the promontory, its position is 36°32 N / 06°16.0 W.

APPROACH AND ENTRANCE

Entrance into the wide Bay of Cádiz is straightforward. There is a well marked deep water channel for large commercial shipping which one would normally avoid. However, in heavy onshore weather, large seas may break in the shallower water so under those circumstances it might be wise to use the main fairway.

BERTHING

The marina has about 150 berths with a maximum length of 15 metres. Mooring is to floating pontoons with fingers, depths in the harbour are given as 7.5 metres. The visitor's marina (Puerto America) is the first basin at the very tip of the promontory. The yacht harbour next to it belongs to the local sailing club and all berths are private. Visitors who stray here are asked to move to Puerto America.

FACILITIES IN THE MARINA

Water and electricity is available on the pontoons, and showers and toilets ashore. Fuel is available from a fuel berth. There is a large hard standing area, with a 10 ton crane and a trailer ramp.

A small chandler is located on the marina

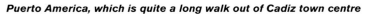

Puerto America, which is quite a long walk out of Cadiz town centre

premises, another one next door at the Club Nautico. There is also a diesel mechanic and Volvo Penta Service.

TRANSPORT

Cádiz has a train station and buses with connections to everywhere in Spain, and of course taxis and hire cars. A warning - if you are not accustomed to driving in a Spanish city, take care not to get lost in the maze of tiny one-way streets and dead ends that make up the old town - you might get stuck somewhere and never get out again!

PROVISIONING

Due to the distance from the city, this is not really convenient. There are small local shops in the old part of town, but most shopping and supermarkets are located in the modern half of Cádiz, which is still further away from the port, towards the landward end of the peninsula.

A RUN ASHORE

Cádiz is believed to be Europe's oldest city, with historical proof for this claim going back some

A typical grand, Spanish 'balcony house' in the old centre of Cádiz

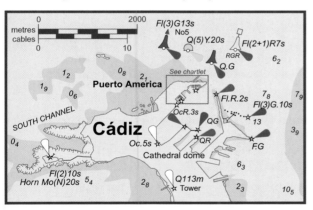

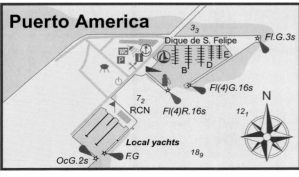

3,000 years. It was very probably founded in 1100 BC by the Phoenicians and later taken over by the Romans. As it was located on the geographical fringe of Europe Cádiz it then faded away, but staged a great comeback with the discovery of America, after which most of the lucrative trade with the New World was conducted through it.

Cádiz was burnt down several times by the English; firstly in 1587 by Sir Francis Drake who thus delayed the departure of the Armada, then again in 1596. During the Napoleonic Wars Cádiz was bombarded and the Spanish fleet destroyed off nearby Cabo de Trafalgar by the British Navy under Nelson. Despite these setbacks, Cádiz enjoyed long periods of prosperity, of which the grand buildings in the old town are evidence.

If walking from Puerto America you will eventually emerge on Cádiz's northern seafront that skirts the old town. Either dip into the attractive labyrinth of small and very narrow streets straight away, or carry on along the Alameda gardens to the first small fortification, Baluarte de la Candelaria, and from there go south-westwards to the castillo de Santa Catalina. Just south of this star-shaped fort lies one of the city's beaches, which, like all of them, get quite crowded at times.

Bang in the middle of the town is the Torre Tavira (Calle Marques del Real Tesoro, open from 10:00 to 20:00 in summer), and this former watchtower is a great spot from which to get an overview of Cádiz. They also have a little slide show which has a running commentary, unfortunately in Spanish only. South of this tower

The attractive labyrinth of streets just inside the northern seafront

is one of the liveliest districts, the Plaza de Topete, next to the Mercado Central.

One might also want to see the impressive cathedral, the city museum (Museo Historico Municipal, Calle Santa Ines 9, tel. 956-223747) which sports a large model of 18th century Cádiz, or the main museum (Plaza de Mina, tel. 956-212281) which has Roman statues and a fine arts collection with some ancient works as well.

The beaches stretch out along the western seafront, mainly south of the Castillo de San Sebastian on its little rocky island, but all of them get crowded and, cruising in a yacht, we have access to nicer ones in other places, like Sancti-Petri, for example (see p138).

The carnival of Cádiz is one of the wildest in Spain and justly famous. Every spring, this turns into a 10-day non-stop party out on the streets where everybody joins in.

EATING OUT

A small restaurant/cafeteria serving very basic meals and drinks is located in Puerto America. For those who do not want to venture into town and still feel an urge to obtain freshly cooked food, try TelePizza, who will deliver to the harbour (956-808484).

Once in town, Cádiz has the usual assortment of restaurants and bars. A very typical Spanish place, which will be crowded with Spanish families during Sunday lunchtimes, with high quality food but otherwise unassuming, is San Antonio on Plaza San Antonio in the centre of the old town. Another place worth mentioning is El Faro in the south-western part of the old town (San Felix 15, telephone 956-211068) which is very pleasant but a little more expensive.

DAYTIME ANCHORAGES NEARBY

Cádiz has a large commercial harbour, but yachts are not encouraged to moor there.

USEFUL INFORMATION			
Cádiz Tides (Standard Port)			
MHWS	MHWN	MLWN	MLWS
Height (metres) 3·3	2·5	1·2	0·5
Radio Telephone Marina VHF Ch 09.			
Cádiz port 11, 12, 14, 16.			
Local dialling code for Cádiz: 956			
Puerto America: 224220			
Tourist offices: 241001 or 211313			

PUERTOS DE SANTA MARIA AND PUERTO SHERRY

Puertos de Santa Maria/Puerto Sherry - 36°35.0 N / 06°15.0 W

An aerial view of the busy and modern marina at Puerto Sherry, just outside Puerto de Santa Maria

This is a corner of the so-called Sherry Triangle (joining El Puerto de Santa Maria, Sanlucar de Barrameda and Jerez de la Frontera) which is just one good reason for a visit! Santa Maria is an interesting little town, while Puerto Sherry has a large marina development with all facilities for yachts, but otherwise has little charm.

LOCATION/POSITION

Both harbours are very close to one another in the Bahia de Cadiz, just opposite Cadiz itself.

APPROACH AND ENTRANCE

Approach to the Bay of Cadiz, see p132 & 129 and Rota. Coming from the north, there is a channel north (inshore) of the main Cadiz fairway, which is called Canal del Norte. When using this, which is straightforward, take care to avoid the bank of La Galera, with about two metres over it, by keeping closer to the mainland shore near Punta Santa Catalina. The entrances to both harbours are easy to identify and enter; Puerto Sherry lies just north of the entrance to El Puerto de Santa Maria.

BERTHING

In Puerto Sherry, floating pontoons with fingers provide 800 berths up to a maximum length of 50 metres.

In El Puerto de Santa Maria berth on floating pontoons in the river at the Real Club Nautico. Both harbours can be called on VHF Ch 09.

FACILITIES IN THE MARINA

Water, electricity, showers and toilets are provided in both harbours. Puerto Sherry has extensive

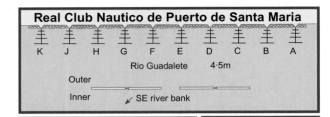

Real Club Nautico de Puerto de Santa Maria

K J H G F E D C B A

Rio Guadelete 4·5m

Outer

Inner SE river bank

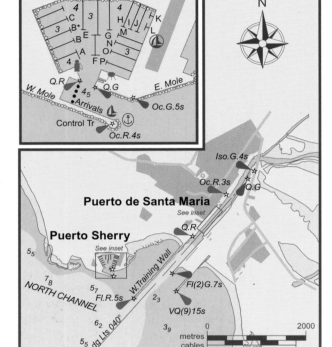

Puerto Sherry

4 4
C 3 H
B* I J K
3 E G L
B M
A N
4 O 3
F P

Q.R Q.G E. Mole
W. Mole 4 5
Arrivals Oc.G.5s
Control Tr
Oc.R.4s

N

Iso.G.4s
Oc.R.3s Q.G

Puerto de Santa Maria
See inset

Puerto Sherry
See inset Q.R

5₅
7₈ 5₇ W. Training Wall
NORTH CHANNEL Fl.R.5s Fl(2)G.7s
2₃
VQ(9)15s
6₂ 3₉
5₅ Ldg Lts 040°

metres 0 2000
cables
0 10
Depths in metres

The river at Puerto de Santa Maria seen from N

The floating pontoons of the Club Nautico at Puerto de Santa Maria, which has space for visitors

repair and laying-up facilities with hoists, 50 ton Travelift, hard standing, boatyard and several specialist services including mechanical and sailmaking.

Fuel is available from a fuel berth in the entrance to Puerto Sherry.

TRANSPORT

Puerto Sherry is a longish way from the town of Santa Maria, which can be reached by taxi or bus. There are trains and buses with connections to the rest of Spain in Santa Maria. National airport at Jerez. Car hire available in both Puerto Sherry and Santa Maria.

Most Sherry Bodegas in Santa Maria can be visited

PROVISIONING

There is only a very small supermarket in Puerto Sherry, but the shops in Santa Maria are all quite close to the Club Nautico.

A RUN ASHORE

Puerto Sherry has little touristic appeal, but El Puerto de Santa Maria is much more interesting. The town used to handle a lot of the sherry traffic, with barges coming down the Rio Guadalete and unloading into big warehouses, from which the sherry was shipped overseas. Some famous Bodegas in Santa Maria (conveniently close to the Club Nautico!) can be visited, among them Bodega Osborne.

The town is also of historical interest - this was where Columbus met Juan de la Cosa, the owner of the Santa Maria and who was his pilot on the voyage of 1492. Juan de la Cosa also drew the first world map in 1500.

The town has some remarkable 18th century private palaces, some of which can be visited

(information at the Tourist Office). The Plaza de Toros is certainly well worth seeing, even without a bull-fight going on, and is open from Tuesday to Sunday from 11.00 - 14.00 and 17.30 - 19.30 (summers only).

The sherry bodegas are usually only open during the mornings, for more information 'phone them, or ask at the Tourist Office.

A very worthwhile excursion by bus (several daily) or hire-car is to the old town of Jerez which, thanks to the sherry industry, is an elegant and rich town with shops to match. For those interested in equestrianism, this is the horse capital of Andalucia.

Apart from visits to the sherry bodegas, the old city should be explored, starting with the Alcazar. The Tourist Office in Jerez is located in Calle Larga (closed Sundays, telephone 956-331150) and can give you information about the sherry business, visits to the bodegas and the history of Jerez itself.

EATING OUT

El Puerto de Santa Maria has a reputation for its seafood. Most of the seafood restaurants are upstream of the Club Nautico near the Parque Calderon.

Worth a special mention is Los Portales (Ribera del Rio 13, telephone 541812, credit cards accepted) which serves very good food at reasonable prices. Also noteworthy is Casa Flores, just along the road (Ribera del Rio 9, telephone 453512), but apart from these two, there are plenty more to choose from.

DAYTIME ANCHORAGES NEARBY

It is possible to anchor off the beach between the two harbours in about two metres over sand, but beware of shoal patches and do not forget the tidal range (2.8m Sp)! This is quite a sheltered anchorage except in south-west winds.

USEFUL INFORMATION

Sta Maria/Pto Sherry Tides
(Std Port Cadiz Time Zone −0100)

	MHWS	MHWN	MLWN	MLWS
Height (metres)	3·2	2·6	1·1	0·4

Radio Telephone Marina VHF Ch 09.
Local dialling code for
El Puerto de Santa Maria: 956
Tourist Office: 542413
Bodega Osborne: 855211
Bodega Terry: 483000
Puerto Sherry: 870303
Real Club Nautico de Santa Maria: 852527

Chapter 3

SANCTI-PETRI

Looking into the entrance to Sancti-Petri, with the Bay of Cadiz to the N just visible in the background. The beacons marking the lagoon entrance can be clearly seen

Sancti-Petri - 36°22.0 N / 6°13.0 W

This sandy lagoon makes one wonder why one should sail another 4000 or so miles to the Caribbean if you can get similar scenery here! Set in beautiful surroundings, Sancti-Petri has a small harbour and a good anchorage, but no other facilities. It is a perfect spot to pause for a few quiet days and nights -

as long as one is not here during summer weekends when the beaches and lagoon get crowded with people from the towns surrounding the Bay of Cadiz.

The marina at Sancti-Petri offers visitors berths on floating pontoons, but there is also space to anchor off

LOCATION/POSITION

Sancti-Petri is 11 miles south of the Bay of Cadiz and 15 miles north of Cabo Trafalgar. The marina position is 36°23.5'N and 06°12'W.

APPROACH AND ENTRANCE

The approach from sea is not difficult, once the small Isola de Sancti-Petri with its Castillo and light are identified, but actually entering the lagoon is a different matter. This manoeuvre requires some care, and settled weather, preferably on the second half of a rising tide, as there can be nasty seas on the bar at low water (depths are then around 2 - 3 metres) even in otherwise calm conditions.

For the final approach pick up the outer leading marks at Coto de San Jose (difficult to see) south of the Castillo and proceed with care, as there are a few shallow spots on each side of the leading marks. Close the shore on 050° until you can turn onto roughly 350° for the second set of leading marks/lights before passing between the two beacons marking the entrance to the lagoon. The marina can be called on VHF Ch 09 and might be able to help with pilotage in cases of doubt.

BERTHING

There is a small marina with 100 pontoon berths up to a maximum length of 12 metres, least depth 1.5 metres. Otherwise anchor off, taking care not to foul any moorings, in depths that vary between 3 and 12 metres. The tide runs at 1 to 1.5 knots and there is a tidal range of about 2.5 metres (Sp).

FACILITIES IN THE MARINA

There is water and electricity on the pontoons and showers and toilets ashore as well as a public telephone, 3.2 ton crane, small trailer ramp, and mechanical repair facilities.

TRANSPORT

There is a very infrequent bus service to Chiclana de la Frontera.

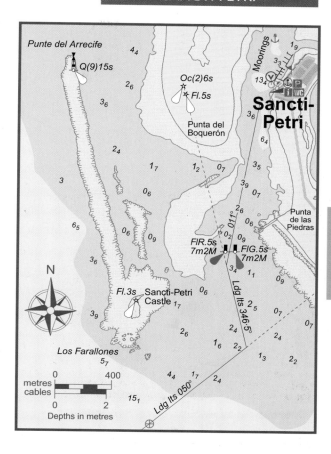

The pontoons at Sancti-Petri, looking E towards the anchorage and the sand dunes

Sailing into the beautiful lagoon at Sancti-Petri

PROVISIONING

No provisions can be obtained here.

A RUN ASHORE

Sancti-Petri is a former fishing village which has long been deserted, giving it quite a morbid atmosphere, with several ruins of buildings still standing. Although there is no permanent population it functions as a summer resort with some cafés, but no shops or facilities, other than those at the marina.

There are superb beaches in the area, the Parque Natural de la Bahia de Cadiz is close by (upriver towards the salines) with an abundance of bird-life and opportunities for exploration.

EATING OUT

There is a small Cerveceria in the harbour area which serves beers and snacks if open. The local Club Nautico runs a restaurant which is crowded during week-ends, and a few metres along the road, there is a second, smaller restaurant. Both have good food and pleasant outside seating in the shade.

The little restaurant near the pontoons gets very busy during the weekends

USEFUL INFORMATION			
Sancti-Petri Tides (Std Port Cádiz Time Zone −0100)			
	MHWS	MHWN	MLWN MLWS
Height (metres)	2·8	2·2	1·2 0·5

Radio Telephone
Marina Puerto Sancti-Petri VHF Ch 09.
Local dialling code: 956
Marina office: 496169
Tourist office (in Chiclana de la Frontera, some miles away): 956-440501

BARBATE

Barbate - 36°10.5 N / 5°55.5 W

Barbate is a fishing harbour in a scenic surroundings, with a marina in the W part of the harbour

Barbate is a pleasant small coastal town with a large fishing harbour, about half of which has been transformed into a modern and spacious marina. It lies in natural unspoilt surroundings, and land excursions into the dunes and the marshlands just to the south are definitely well worth while (see below).

More important, perhaps, Barbate is a convenient place to wait for the right weather to continue into the Mediterranean through the Straits of Gibraltar. In fact, because it has good marina facilities, Barbate is much to be preferred over Tarifa if one has to stay in harbour for any length of time due to a spell of contrary weather.

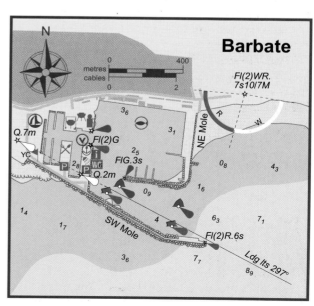

LOCATION/POSITION

Barbate is tucked around the corner from Cabo Trafalgar, about six miles west along the coast, and can easily be identified from sea.

APPROACH AND ENTRANCE

From the north: care must be taken to avoid the shallows and tidal races that are found south-west of Cabo Trafalgar. These stretch out from the Cape (which looks like an island from the north) for about four to six miles, depending on the weather. In heavy onshore winds, nasty seas can also build up on the Banco de Trafalgar, a few miles further out, in which case it would be wise to stay well offshore and not close in for Barbate until well south of the cape.

From the south: keep a good lookout for a tunny net which is laid close south of the harbour entrance, forming an east-west barrier which will have to be rounded at either end. The final approach from the south is straightforward.

The marina is located in the westernmost part of the harbour and reached through a second entrance. Depths in the entrance 4.5 metres, inside the marina 3.0 metres.

BERTHING

Yachts moor to floating pontoons with fingers. There are 170 berths for yachts of up to 25 metres length.

FACILITIES IN THE MARINA

The marina has the usual facilities - water and electricity on the pontoons, showers and toilets ashore, diesel and petrol are available. There is a 32-ton Travelift and a small yard for repairs, as well as a ramp for small trailer craft.

TRANSPORT

Taxis and hire-cars available from the marina. Buses (to Cadiz, Sevilla, Tarifa, Algeciras) leave from a bus station at the north end of the town.

PROVISIONING

Barbate has the usual assortment of smallish shops for a town of this size.

The marina part of the harbour at Barbate

A RUN ASHORE

Barbate is a rather sleepy place that only really comes to life at the height of the summer holiday season. One of its main attractions are the surrounding beaches - fine golden sand stretching for almost 25 kilometres along the coast, beginning virtually next to the harbour. Behind the dunes is the national park of La Brena and the Barbate marshes, an important bird sanctuary. Long walks are the thing to do here.

Barbate itself is a whitewashed town, typical of this corner of Spain. Drift around the narrow back streets or just relax somewhere along the Paseo Maritimo over a coffee.

An interesting land excursion could also be made to Zahara de los Atunes a few kilometres down the coast - another decaying, crumbling seaside town in the middle of a long beach - nothing much else to see. Except that Zahara is now becoming fashionable and can become very lively during summer nights. The action takes place in July and August along the beach, when tents and shacks are set up as bars and beach-discos. They get going from about midnight onwards, and some even have 'live' Flamenco!

EATING OUT

There are many seafood places along the waterfront (Paseo Maritimo) and it is impossible to recommend one above the other. One outstanding restaurant in town is Torres (Ruiz de Alda 1, telephone 956-430985, credit cards accepted) which offers exceptional quality for the price asked. Specialities are again seafood and mussels.

DAYTIME ANCHORAGES NEARBY

In calm and settled weather it is possible to anchor off the beaches for the day, but the coast is open and unsheltered and there are no real overnight anchorages until Tarifa is reached.

USEFUL INFORMATION			
Barbate Tides (Standard Port Cadiz Time Zone −0100)			
	MHWS	MHWN	MLWN	MLWS
Height (metres)	1·9	1·5	1·0	0·6

Radio Telephone Marina VHF Ch 09. Barbate is at W end of Gibraltar Strait VTS; monitor Tarifa Traffic Ch 10 16.

Local dialling code for Barbate: 956

Harbour office: 431907

Tourist office: 431006

TARIFA

The harbour of Tarifa looking NW

Tarifa - 36°00.0 N / 5°36.5 W

Tarifa is an interesting Moorish town at the western end of the Straits of Gibraltar offering a choice of anchorages either side of the isthmus linking Isla de Tarifa to the mainland at the harbour, and a rather run-down fishing harbour which is not very convenient for yachts.

It also is considered the European headquarters of windsurfing, and it has the ingredients to match: a wonderful sandy beach with a lot of breaking surf that stretches for several miles away to the north-west of Tarifa, and - cruising sailors beware - a lot of wind!

Tarifa is known as one of the windiest corners of Europe. These winds are mainly due to high pressure over the Azores, and low pressure over the Mediterranean and Morocco. It also stems from a strong high pressure area over central Europe and a deep low over the coasts of Morocco or North Africa. A third possibility is a low pressure area over the sea-area to the south of the Balearics. With these conditions very strong winds can occur, mostly in spring and autumn. The locals hate these strong winds, because they come from inland and raise the temperature a few degrees, and blows at night, disturbing sleep.

The Poniente is a light onshore wind from the west which blows only by day and in summer, if its sunny, it becomes strongest at the end of the day. It blows as a result of low pressure areas over Spain. In winter this wind can reach storm force.

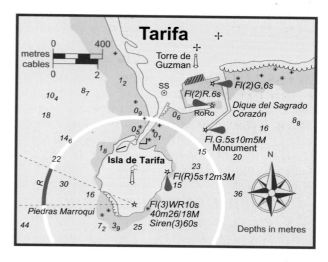

In the Strait of Gibraltar the wind becomes two forces stronger. For the locals this is the best wind; in summer it brings cooler temperatures and is less strong.

Having said all this, Tarifa itself is very attractive and lively, although at times somewhat dominated by the typically cool surfing crowd who party from 1 am onwards!

LOCATION/POSITION

Tarifa is the southernmost point of mainland Spain. The harbour entrance position is 36°04.0 N / 05°36.2 W.

APPROACH / ENTRY

The approach from sea is straightforward under normal conditions. The little island - Isla de Tarifa - with a lighthouse at its southern tip can easily be recognised from sea. In rough conditions, overfalls can form south of the island and seas will break on the shallow bank of Los Cabezos, about five miles west of Tarifa.

The harbour entrance is immediately to the north-east of the island and entry can be difficult when a strong Levanter is blowing from the east. Under those circumstance, it will be easier to use the anchorage in the lee of the island instead of trying to enter the harbour (see below) - especially as the harbour has no dedicated facilities for yachts.

BERTHING

The harbour of Tarifa is rather rough, and derelict in places. The inner side of the eastern seawall is used by ferries and passenger vessels and is unsuitable for yachts, as is the small pier in the north-eastern corner. The southern mole and nearly all other berths are used by fishing boats.

It might be possible to find a space alongside the fishing quay or at the outer end of one of the small moles that make the former naval berths at the north end of the harbour (which are now used by small local fishing boats). Beware of lines and bits and pieces of wreckage, find a clear spot and use long lines and a hefty fender-board. It might also be possible to secure to the quay and lie to a bow or stern anchor, although this obviously has the danger of fouling the hook on the debris which certainly litters the bottom.

FACILITIES IN THE MARINA

No facilities for yachts.

SHOPPING

Tarifa has a good selection of shops of all sizes and descriptions but no large supermarkets. Day-to-day stores can be obtained in town but this is not a good place for stocking up with basic provisions.

TRANSPORT

Buses (to Cadiz, Sevilla, La Linea/Gib and the

The harbour itself has no dedicated berths for yachts and is rather run-down

beaches west of Tarifa), taxis, hire-cars. Ferries to Tangier.

ANCHORAGES NEARBY

There are two possible anchorages, and due to the nature of the harbour I would almost certainly recommend that visitors anchor off rather than having the hassle of trying to find an alongside berth.

In westerly winds, one can anchor in the little bay between the island and the harbour entrance, but take care to keep clear of the entrance by moving in as close as one dares to the island and the causeway. The depths here are three to four metres unless one goes too close inshore, and holding is good in sand.

In easterly winds, use the anchorage off the beach to the north-east of the island, again 3 to 4 metres on sand, and well sheltered from the seas.

A RUN ASHORE

Tarifa is well worth seeing. With the narrow streets and small, white cubes of houses it has a distinctly Arabian feel about it - this setting is in strange contrast to the summer visitors in the lively cafés and bars, but Tarifa for some reason never feels

Chapter 3

The harbour entrance, looking out across the Strait of Gibraltar to Morocco's Rif Mountains

spoiled by tourism.

The old town stretches out beyond the castle to the north-east of the harbour. For a small fee (or *tariff* - this word is believed to originate from Tarifa where pirates used to extract fees from any ships passing through the Straits) of 100 Pesetas you can walk along the castle ramparts and enjoy spectacular views of Africa - only about eight miles away. The castle was built by Muslims in the 10th century to help defend the town against Christians, Vikings and any other hostile folk who happened to sail by.

A stroll through the old town is interesting, and there are many cafés and bars for potential pit-stops. The market is located in Calle Colon at the northern end of the old town, close to the tourist office at the northern end of the palm-lined Paseo de la Alameda that runs along the western edge of the old district.

One of the main attractions of Tarifa is the long stretch of wonderful, sandy beach which culminates in a huge dune about 10 kilometres north-west of the town. Buses going there leave just opposite the castle, at the beginning of the Calle Sancho IV El Bravo. Apart from walking, swimming and (if so inclined and equipped) surfing, one can also visit one of the few beach-

bars, or go horse-riding along the beach.

The Hotel Dos Mares (956 68 40 35) and the Hurricane Hotel (956 68 49 19) rent out horses, and both are a few kilometres out of town.

SURF SPOTS

Las Dunas is a about 10 kilometres west of Tarifa, in the Valdevaqueros bay. The road, however, is very poor. It is a good surfspot with tuition and equipment for hire. It is best with westerly winds with higher waves. When there's a weak poniente, this is the place with the strongest wind.

Bolonia is 22 kilometres to the west in Bolonia bay. Here the wind is stronger than in Tarifa due to a thermic effect caused by the hills. The beach is beautiful like surfspot Las Dunas, fine white sand and flat water.

USEFUL INFORMATION			
Tarifa Tides (Std Port Gibraltar Time Zone −0100)			
	MHWS	MHWN	MLWN MLWS
Height (metres)	1·4	1·0	0·6 0·3
Radio Telephone monitor Tarifa Traffic Ch 10 16.			
Local dialling code for Tarifa: 956			
Tourist office: 68 09 93			

Speedbeach is THE surfspot for speedfreaks and lies close to Tarifa. You can only surf here when there is a weak levante or poniente.The sea is flat and the wind can be very strong and many records have been set here.

EATING OUT

During the day, the Café Central (Calle Sancho IV El Bravo) seems to be the meeting-point. They offer breakfast and some good lunch dishes. Out of town, the Terrace Restaurant at the Hurricane Hotel is very nice for a good, long lunch in the shade overlooking the beach and the Atlantic beyond, listening to the rollers thundering on to the nearby beach.

For the evenings, Tarifa has a good choice of restaurants. The Mandragora (Calle Independencia 3) is always a sure tip for some more imaginative than usual Spanish food.

A 'well known' secret is Juan Luis (Calle San Francisco 15) which has no sign outside. It has fixed price menus and you can eat as much as you like until you fall over! Not only is the quantity convincing, the quality of the dishes tempts one to eat on and on and on . . !

There is often live music at the Café Continental (Paseo de la Alameda), and the Bodega Casa Amarilla (Calle Sancho IV El Bravo) sometimes has live Flamenco. There are quite a few discos around town which can easily be found!

Tarifa has an attractive and exotic old town which already has a flavour of Morocco

The busy and pleasant Cafe Central in Tarifa

The not even half finished marina at Algeciras, looking over the bay towards Gibraltar

ALGECIRAS

Algeciras - 36°09.0 N / 5°25.5 W

Algeciras is a busy town with a large commercial harbour, and it handles the bulk of the ferry traffic between Spain and Morocco. Unfortunately, there are (as yet) no facilities for yachts, and the town itself is not as attractive as many other places along the Andalucian coast.

Unless one had a very special reason to go here, it would be more convenient for a yacht to anchor off La Linea (immediately north of Gibraltar, see there) or to visit Gibraltar itself.

LOCATION/POSITION

Algeciras is at the western end of the Bay of Algeciras (Bay of Gibraltar), opposite Gibraltar. The position of the northern harbour entrance is given above, the southern one is at 36°07.2 N / 5°25.7 W

APPROACH AND ENTRANCE

As long as one stays about a mile or two offshore when rounding the headland south of Algeciras (coming from the Atlantic), the approach to Algeciras is easy and straightforward - noting, however, that there is a lot of ferry traffic which also includes fast catamaran ferries. The only place for visiting yachts is the Darsena del Saladillo, south of the main commercial harbour.

BERTHING

There are some small floating pontoons in the Darsena del Saladillo, suitable only for smaller yachts. Opposite, on the other side of the bay are some concrete piers (the first signs of the planned marina) and mooring to these or anchoring off would be possible. There is a small Club Nautico tucked away at the inner end of the main commercial harbour further north, but they only have few berths which are all permanently occupied.

FACILITIES IN THE MARINA

Water on the floating pontoons in Darsena del Saladillo, but no other facilities for yachts there. Water and electricity at the Club Nautico, if one has a berth there.

TRANSPORT

Buses to other major towns in Spain and to La Linea (Gibraltar), ferries to Morocco, hire-cars, taxis.

Algeciras town centre, which has a strong Moroccan feel about it

PROVISIONING

Being a major town, Algeciras has the usual range of shops and supermarkets. A few miles outside Algeciras, on the road towards Malaga, is a huge commercial centre with many megastores including a vast Continente hypermarket. There is also a market not very far from the fishing harbour.

Coming from the Darsena del Saladillo on foot, the city centre is a longish walk of maybe 20 minutes.

A RUN ASHORE

As already mentioned above, Algeciras holds no special attractions for visitors. There is a bustling city centre with pedestrian shopping areas, but many parts of the town are crumbling and rather derelict.

USEFUL INFORMATION

Algeciras Tides (Std Port Gibraltar Time Zone −0100)			
MHWS	MHWN	MLWN	MLWS
Height (metres) 1·1	0·9	0·4	0·2

Radio Telephone Marina VHF Ch 09 16.
Port Ch 09, 12, 13, 16.
Local dialling code for Algeciras: 956
Tourist information: 572636

*The market at Algeciras,
close to the commercial harbour*

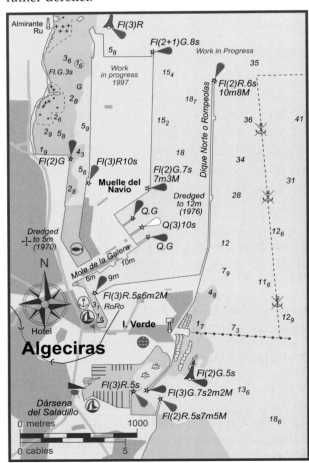

GIBRALTAR

Looking S over the Bay of Gibraltar with La Linea in the foreground

Gibraltar - 36°09.0 N / 5°23.0 W

The Rock sits like a capsized birthday cake at the eastern end of the Straits of Gibraltar and holds great fascination for passing yachts, most of which call here for at least a few days – some for a much longer time. Most Gibraltarians speak English and almost anything for yachts is either obtainable or can be ordered from the UK (VAT free if marked 'for yacht in transit').

Despite this, the times where anything here was cheaper than in mainland Europe are long gone - with the exception of cigarettes and, to some extent, liquor. The cost of day-to-day-life is alarmingly high when compared to other southern European countries and provisioning for example is certainly more expensive than in neighbouring Spain. Gibraltar, with its interesting history, is certainly well worth seeing - at least once - as it is a unique and, some say, anachronistic place.

LOCATION/POSITION

Located at the eastern end of the Straits of Gibraltar, Europa Point (the southern tip of Gibraltar) is at 36°06.5 N / 05°20.6 W. The approach position to Marina Bay given above.

APPROACH AND ENTRANCE

Gibraltar would be hard to miss! The approach from sea is straightforward once through the Straits, although there is a lot of shipping movement, which increases dramatically inside the Bay of Algeciras (called the Bay of Gibraltar by the Gibraltarians) when closing in towards the port. A good lookout is essential.

A night approach presents no undue difficulties, although things can become confusing as many harbour lights are impossible to identify due to the backdrop of shore lights, and others are not actually working - according to the latest pilot books!

When approaching Marina Bay at night, be especially careful not to hit the end of the airport runway which should be lit by yellow lights but was completely dark on at least one occasion when we came into Gibraltar around midnight.

Sheppard's Marina, with 'Enterprise' moored here and 'The Rock' towering above

Aerial view of Marina Bay (left) and Sheppard's Marina

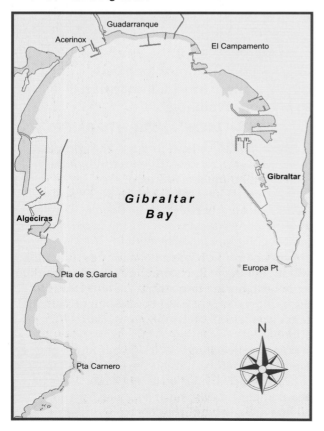

BERTHING

There are three marinas to choose from. The oldest (and scruffiest) is Sheppard's Marina, originally constructed in 1961. Little seems to have been done to the piers and floating pontoons since, but they do offer cheap mooring if you berth stern-to using your own anchor. They have alongside berths which are charged for at about the same rates as the ones in the other two marinas. Swell often finds its way into the corner of the bay where both Sheppard's Marina and Marina Bay are located and staying here can be decidedly uncomfortable, especially in strong westerly winds.

Marina Bay is located just next door to Sheppard's, but has concrete piers and either alongside or stern to berths, using mooring ropes.

The latest development is Queensway Quay Marina around the corner in the commercial harbour which is normally more sheltered than the other two, but nevertheless can become dangerously exposed in the very strong westerly gales that may be encountered during the winter

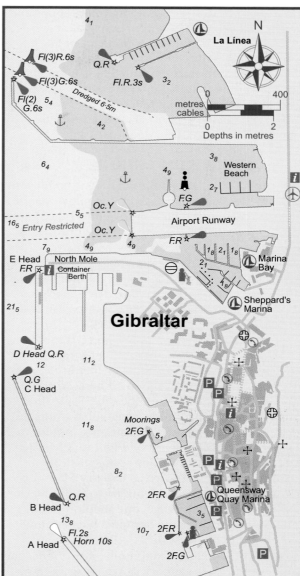

and the equinox periods. Again, mooring is stern-to using mooring lines.

FACILITIES IN THE MARINAS

All three marinas have the basic facilities one requires - water and electricity at the berths and showers and toilets ashore. Sheppard's also offer extensive repair and refit services, with a boat-yard catering for all kinds of repairs, a 40-ton Travelift, a 10-ton crane, and a hard-standing area where crews and owners are allowed to work on their boats themselves. There is also a large chandlery and a brokerage on the premises.

There is a chandlery and a laundrette in the buildings at Marina Bay.

ENTRY FORMALITIES

Customs and Immigration have to be cleared upon first arrival. This can be at the customs and immigration hut in Marina Bay, to starboard as you come in, and opposite the two marinas. It has a floating pontoon at which to secure.

Alternatively, these formalities will be dealt with by the marina staff in Queensway Quay Marina when you check in.

TRANSPORT

Direct flights to UK are available of course. Taxis offer tours of the Rock, and hire-cars and scooters are available. La Linea, which is just across the border in Spain, is easiest reached on foot, and from here buses run to Algeciras, Cadiz, Malaga and many other destinations. The next nearest international airport is at Malaga.

PROVISIONING

Expensive but convenient. There is a Tesco supermarket at Marina Bay, very close to both

Sheppard's and Marina Bay, and more shops and supermarkets in town within easy walking distance. You will find an abundance of tax-free shops for cigarettes and liquor.

If you want to store up with Spanish food (or rather, international food at Spanish prices), consider taking a bus or taxi from La Linea to the Continente hypermarket which is a few miles along the road towards Algeciras.

A RUN ASHORE

Although Gibraltar is quite small (one could walk around the base of the rock in a couple of hours), there is a lot to see - including quite a bit of family entertainment. The town itself is not only full of tourists, but also 'english pubs' and many of the usual UK High Street Shops.

The museum gives a good insight into the long and varied history of Gibraltar, dating back to early man. There is also a full size Moorish bath house dating from the 14th century.

At the southern end of Main Street, through Southport Gate, is a small Trafalgar cemetery for sailors who were wounded in the battle of Trafalgar and subsequently died here. Nearby is the Botanical Gardens and the cable car station, from which a trip uphill is well worth while, the price for which includes the entrance fees for the Upper Rock Nature Reserve with the Ape's Den and St. Michael's Cave. The apes, cute little creatures correctly known as Barbary Macaques, roam around freely and jump on to taxis and cars expecting to be fed (which one shouldn't do). They are probably quite harmless but certainly very entertaining to watch.

After visiting these two (family) attractions, one can take the cable car back down, or walk the pleasant, mainly downhill, route back into town. There are taxi and coach tours which also visit this upper part of the Rock, but the value of these

Queensway Quay Marina

is debatable - they do not go to any places that cannot be reached by cable car and on foot.

Other sights to be seen up here are the Great Siege Tunnels, the Military Heritage Centre and the Moorish Castle. Back at sea level, Europa Point has a famous lighthouse (white with red stripe) situated next to a mosque which was built in 1997, funded by King Fahd of Saudi Arabia.

If cruising close by in calm weather, these two can be viewed from on board as you pass the Point.

HISTORY

Gibraltar's history dates back to the Neanderthals of about 50,000 years ago. Much later, Greeks and Phoenicians came here, as well as the Muslims, for the Islamic invasion of Iberia started here (in 711 AD), when Tariq Ibn Zyad landed with a huge army. The name Gibraltar is derived from this occasion - Jebel Tariq means Tariq's mountain.

The Spanish conquered Gibraltar back in 1462 but lost it again to the next invaders, a mixed Anglo-Dutch fleet in 1704 who took the Rock during the war of the Spanish Succession. Spain

One of Gibraltar's guardians, the famous apes ...

tried hard to get it back, culminating in the Great Siege of 1779 to 1783 which, however, failed to change the status quo. After this, the British really made themselves at home here. Gibraltar was an important military base during both World Wars and has only recently been de-militarised to some extent.

For decades, ownership of Gibraltar has been an extremely sore point between Spain and Britain and the debate about the Rock is far from closed. Some years ago, this controversy was fiercely fuelled by the fact that Gibraltar was considered as a haven for money laundering and drug smuggling from nearby Morocco - both of which activities have now been stopped.

Gibraltar has about 30,000 inhabitants, most of which are Gibraltarians (with a rather mixed ancestry of Genoese, Jewish, Spanish and British) who speak both English and Spanish and more often than not a curious melange of the two, switching from one to the other in mid-sentence.

EATING OUT

Gibraltar is not famous for its gastronomic and culinary delights. There is, however, a choice of restaurants and pubs, and the latter will serve the usual UK style pub food.

Amongst the restaurants, Bunters (College Lane, telephone 70482, closed August, credit cards

The waterfront bar at Marina Bay

Europa Point lighthouse and the mosque beside it

accepted) with strong French influence in la cuisine, is considered to be the best, but it will invariably tear quite a big hole into the ship's kitty.

Both Marina Bay and Queensway have some shoreside restaurants. At Marina Bay Da Paolo (Tel 76799, closed Sunday) has a more international than genuinely Italian cuisine, and Charlie's Taverna on the Port (Tel 79993) has a large menu including Tandoori and seafood

dishes. Raffles Restaurant (Tel 40362, credit cards) at Queensway Quay also has a huge menu, and is one of Gibraltar's most popular places for eating out.

In a small yard off Main Street is the pleasant Indian restaurant Viceroy of India (Horse Barrack Lane, telephone 70381, Visa accepted, closed Sunday) which serves good quality tandooris and other Indian specialities.

For a light snack or an easy going meal, the House of Sacarello (57 Irish Town, telephone 70625) seems very popular. This is located in a former coffee warehouse and serves meals - and also fresh scones!

ALTERNATIVE ANCHORAGES NEARBY

You can anchor either north of the airport runway and south of the mole (which is the border between Spain and Gib), or north of the mole in Spanish waters. Both anchorages offer good holding and are well sheltered, but if shelter from westerly winds is sought, tuck in behind the mole on the Spanish side.

There is dinghy landing on small floating pontoons in either case.

USEFUL INFORMATION

Gibraltar Tides (Standard Port Time Zone –0100)

	MHWS	MHWN	MLWN	MLWS
Height (metres)	1·0	0·7	0·3	0·1

Radio Telephone Marina Bay VHF Ch 73; Queensway Quay and Sheppards Ch 71. Civil port Ch 06; Gibraltar Bay Ch 12; QHM Ch 08.
Dialling code for Gibraltar (international): ++350.
Dialling code from Spain: 9567.
Sheppard's Marina: 75148/77183
Marina Bay Marina (Pier Office): 73300
Queensway Quay Marina: 44700
Tourist Information: 45000
Taxi tours: 70027

SPANISH NORTH AFRICA

Sailing off Morocco

No one has sailed into the Strait of Gibraltar at night with a newly risen moon hanging over the mountains of North Africa and not felt the urge to land and explore this mysterious shore which at times seems almost close enough to reach out and touch.

All you need is a good excuse and with Ceuta, a Spanish enclave, sitting patiently at the eastern gate to the Straits you need wait no longer, for when the Levanter blows from the west the Ceuta option as a place to wait for a break can seem much more attractive than Gibraltar.

CROSSING THE STRAITS

Sailing between Gibraltar and Ceuta is generally straightforward, as one will sail across both tides and predominant winds. The complex tidal and current situation here is described in the chapter dealing with Gibraltar, but as we are now crossing it, we can do so at any state of the tide or with any flow of the current – as long as one keeps a careful check on leeway and current in the process, either by GPS or frequent land-bearings.

There are also some quite impressive overfalls around Europa Point (shifting with the tide and currents) and, to a slightly lesser degree to the NE of Ceuta, quite close to the harbour entrance.

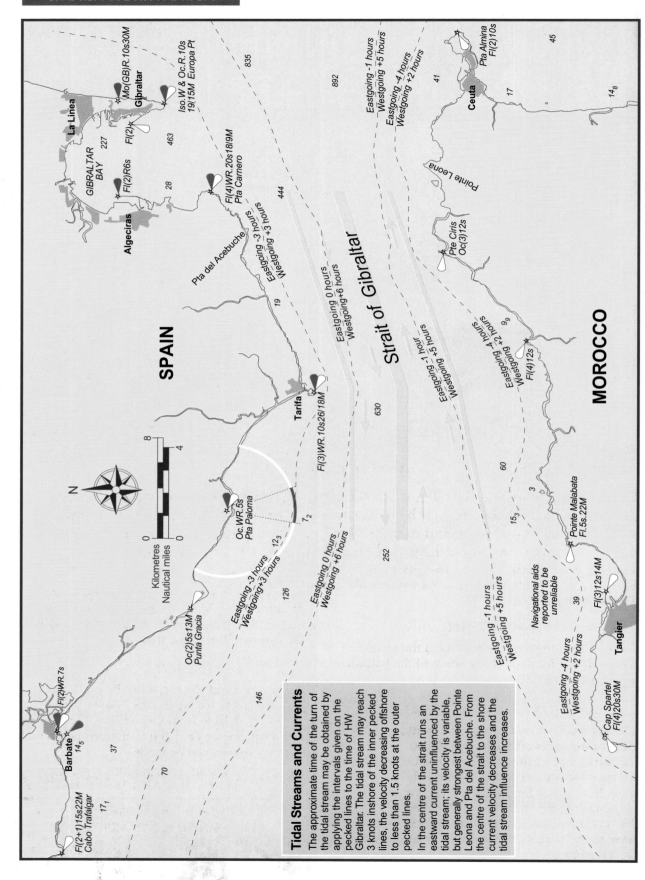

SPAIN

La Linea

Mo(GB)R.10s30M *Gibraltar*

Iso.W & Oc.R.10s
19/15M *Europa Pt*

Fl(2)

GIBRALTAR
BAY

227

Fl(2)R6s

463

Algeciras

28

Fl(4)WR.20s18/9M
Pta Carnero

444

Pta del Acebuche

Eastgoing -3 hours
Westgoing +3 hours

19

630

Tarifa

Fl(3)WR.10s26/18M

252

Eastgoing 0 hours
Westgoing +6 hours

Oc.WR.5s
Pta Paloma

7₂

12₃

Eastgoing -3 hours
Westgoing +3 hours

126

N

Kilometres
Nautical miles
0   4   8

Oc(2)5s13M
Punta Gracia

146

Fl(2)WR.7s

Barbate
14₅

37

70

Fl(2+1)15s22M
Cabo Trafalgar

17₁

Strait of Gibraltar

835

892

Eastgoing -1 hours
Westgoing +5 hours

Eastgoing -4 hours
Westgoing +2 hours

41

Pta Almina
Fl(2)10s

45

Ceuta

17

14₈

Pointe Leona

Pte Ciris
Oc(3)12s

Eastgoing -4 hours
Westgoing +2 hours

Fl(4)12s

9₉

60

Eastgoing -1 hour
Westgoing +5 hours

3

15₃

MOROCCO

Pointe Malabata
Fl.5s.22M

Navigational aids
reported to be
unreliable

39

Fl(3)12s14M

Eastgoing -1 hours
Westgoing +5 hours

Tangier

Eastgoing -4 hours
Westgoing +2 hours

Cap Spartel
Fl(4)20s30M

Tidal Streams and Currents

The approximate time of the turn of
the tidal stream may be obtained by
applying the intervals given on the
pecked lines to the time of HW
Gibraltar. The tidal stream may reach
3 knots inshore of the inner pecked
lines, the velocity decreasing offshore
to less than 1.5 knots at the outer
pecked lines.

In the centre of the strait runs an
eastward current uninfluenced by the
tidal stream; its velocity is variable,
but generally strongest between Pointe
Leona and Pta del Acebuche. From
the centre of the strait to the shore
current velocity decreases and the
tidal stream influence increases.

Chapter 4

CEUTA (SEBTA)

Ceuta marina

Ceuta - 36°45.0 N / 06°25.4 W

Ceuta, along with Melilla 130 miles to the East, has been a Spanish enclave since the 16th century. Nowadays, it has lost some of its military importance, although still a Spanish naval base, and mainly thrives as a duty-free port. Fuel and other provisions are much cheaper than across the straits in Gibraltar and also cheaper than in most other places in Europe. There is an excellent marina which offers all the usual amenities.

POSITION

Ceuta is located on a promontory at the SE end of the Strait of Gibraltar. The position of the harbour is 53°53N and 5°19W.

APPROACH AND ENTRANCE

The approach should be from the north, keeping clear of the rocks off the Monte Hacho immediately E of the harbour. If heading due S for the entrance, all is clear, but one should keep a good lookout for ferries and other commercial shipping coming in and out of the main harbour. The marina is due S of the harbour entrance, so if ferry traffic permits, just continue straight on for the yacht basin.

BERTHING

Yachts moor to pontoons, either alongside finger pontoons or with Mediterranean-style mooring lines. Depths in the harbour are around 4 metres in the forward part of the marina.

FACILITIES

There is water and electricity on the pontoons, and showers and toilets ashore. A key to these facilities is available from the marina office. There is also a small boat-yard and a small crane, so that temporary repairs can be made.

Useful Information

Ceuta Tides (Std Port Gibraltar Time Zone –0100)			
	MHWS	MHWN	MLWN	MLWS
Height (metres)	1·0	0·8	0·4	0·2

ENTRY FORMALITIES

These are the same as on the Spanish mainland. Checking in at the marina office is all that is required, although customs and immigration may sometimes make a random check of the papers of yachts moored here.

PROVISIONING

This is quite a strong point in favour of Ceuta due to the low prices of food and many other items. There are supermarkets close by the harbour, as well as the very colourful and interesting local market, situated in a multi-storey market hall more or less opposite the marina, reached through a pedestrian-tunnel beneath the main road.

A RUN ASHORE

The main attraction for visitors here might be the day coach trip into neighbouring Morocco described in the introduction to chapter 3. This is a good sight seeing Moroccan expedition while one can still leave the boat in a secure place.

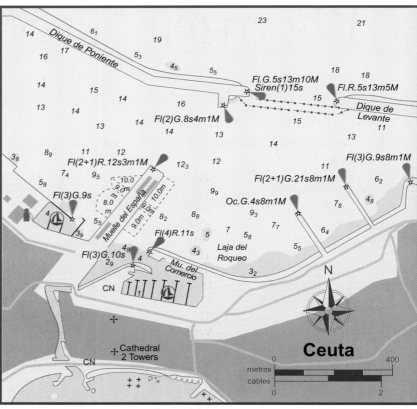

Ceuta marina

WEATHER FREQUENCIES

NORTH AND NORTH WEST SPAIN

Coast Radio Stations

The following Coast Radio Stations broadcast in Spanish gale warnings, synopsis and forecasts for Areas 1-9 at the times and on the VHF or MF frequencies shown below:

Pasajes	VHF Ch 27	at 0940 1140 2140 UTC
Machichaco	1707 kHz	at 0903 1233 1733 UTC
Bilbao	VHF Ch 26	at 0940 1140 2140 UTC
Santander	VHF Ch 24	at 0940 1140 2140 UTC
Cabo Peñas	VHF Ch 26	at 0940 1140 2140 UTC
	1677 kHz	at 0803 1203 1703 UTC
Navia	VHF Ch 27	at 0940 1140 2140 UTC
Cabo Ortegal	VHF Ch 02	at 0950 1150 2150 UTC
La Coruña	VHF Ch 26	at 0950 1150 2150 UTC
	1698 kHz	at 0833 1233 1733 UTC
Finisterre	VHF Ch 26	at 0950 1150 2150 UTC
	1764 kHz	at 0803 1203 1703 UTC
Vigo	VHF Ch 20	at 0950 1150 2150 UTC
La Guardia	VHF Ch 82	at 0950 1150 2150 UTC
Tarifa	VHF Ch 81	at 0940 1140 2140 UTC
	1704 kHz	at 0803 1233 1703 UTC

Coastguard MRCC/MRSC

Broadcast in Spanish and English gale warnings on receipt, plus synopsis and forecasts for the Areas, times (UTC) and VHF channels listed below:

Bilbao MRCC	VHF Ch 10	every 4h from 0033 for Areas 2-4.
Santander MRSC	VHF Ch 11	every 4h from 0245 for Areas 2-4.
Gijón MRCC	VHF Ch 10 16	every even H+15 from 0015 to 2215 for Areas 3 & 4.
Coruña MRSC	VHF Ch 12 13 14	every 4h from 0005 for Areas 1-5.
Finisterre MRCC	VHF Ch 11	every 4h from 0233 for Areas 1-5.
Vigo MRSC	VHF Ch 10	every 4h from 0015 for Areas 3-6.

Radio broadcasts - Radio Nacional de España (National Radio)

Broadcasts in Spanish storm warnings, synopsis and 12h or 18h forecasts for Spanish Areas 3 & 4 at 1100, 1400, 1800 and 2200 LT. Stations and frequencies are:

San Sebastián	774 kHz
Bilbao	639 kHz
Santander	855 kHz
Oviedo	729 kHz
La Coruña	639 kHz

Recorded telephone forecasts

A recorded telephone marine weather information service in Spanish is available for the Spanish forecast areas 1 to 4, i.e. Gran Sol, Vizcaya (North Biscay), Cantábrico and Finisterre. The service also provides forecasts for Coastal waters from the French to Portuguese borders i.e. Guipuzcoa, Vizcaya, Cantabria, Austurias, Lugo, Coruña and Pontevedra. This service is only available within Spain or for Autolink equipped vessels. Tel 906 365 372.

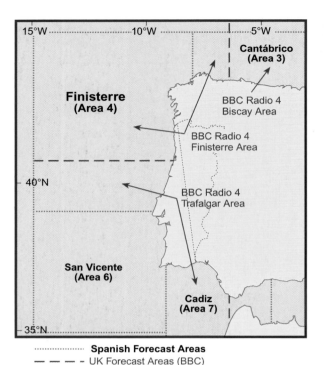

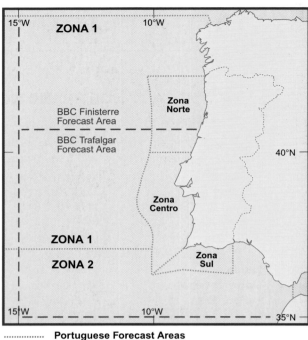

⋯⋯⋯⋯ **Spanish Forecast Areas**	⋯⋯⋯⋯ **Portuguese Forecast Areas**
— — — - UK Forecast Areas (BBC)	— — — UK Forecast Areas (BBC)

PORTUGAL

Coast Radio Stations

The following Coast Radio Stations broadcast in Portuguese gale warnings, synopsis and coastal waters forecasts
for Portugal, up to 50M offshore for Zona Norte, Zona Centro and Zona Sul.

Leixões	Ch 11	0705 1905 UTC	For Norte and Centro
Lisboa	Ch 11	1030 1730 UTC	For Porto de Lisboa
Setúbal	Ch 11	1030 1630 UTC	For Porto Setúbal

Naval Radio weather broadcasts

Gale warnings are Broadcast in English, on receipt, for the coastal waters of Portugal, including the Azoresand Madeira. The weather bulletins at 0905 and 2105 UTC give gale warnings, a synopsis, a 24h fcst, in Portuguese, for coastal waters of Portugal, up to 50M offshore.

The times and Channels/frequencies are listed below.

Monsanto	MF 2657 kHz	0905 2105 UTC	Gale warnings & fcst for Norte, Centro, Sul, Zona 1 & 2
	VHF Ch 11	1000 1630 UTC	Gale warnings & fcst for Alges

Radio broadcasts - Radiofusão Portuguesa (National Radio) - Programa 1

Broadcasts 24h forecasts for North, Central and South Zones in Portuguese at 1100 UTC. Transmitters and frequencies are:

Porto	720 kHz	**Coimbra**	630 kHz	**Lisboa 1**	666 kHz, 95·7 MHz
Miranda do Douro	630 kHz	**Elvas**	720 kHz	**Faro**	720 kHz, 97·6 MHz

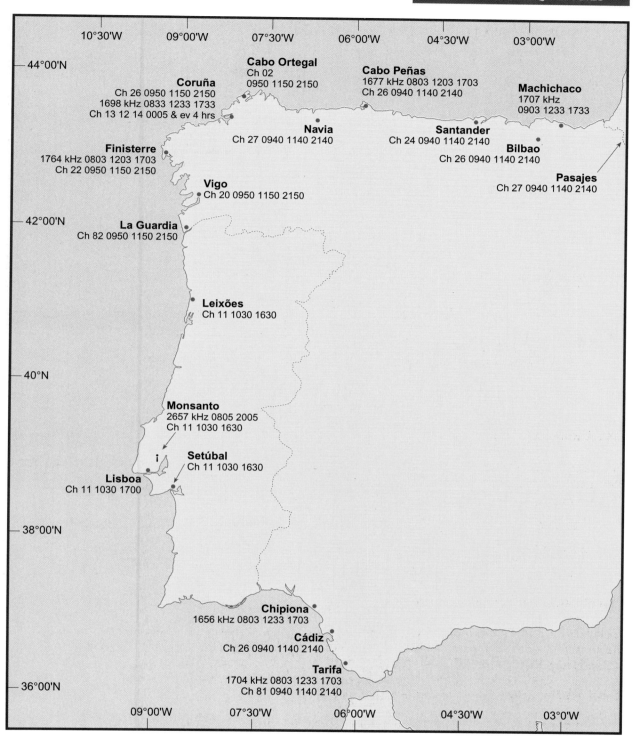

Cabo Ortegal
Ch 02
0950 1150 2150

Coruña
Ch 26 0950 1150 2150
1698 kHz 0833 1233 1733
Ch 13 12 14 0005 & ev 4 hrs

Cabo Peñas
1677 kHz 0803 1203 1703
Ch 26 0940 1140 2140

Machichaco
1707 kHz
0903 1233 1733

Navia
Ch 27 0940 1140 2140

Santander
Ch 24 0940 1140 2140

Bilbao
Ch 26 0940 1140 2140

Finisterre
1764 kHz 0803 1203 1703
Ch 22 0950 1150 2150

Pasajes
Ch 27 0940 1140 2140

Vigo
Ch 20 0950 1150 2150

La Guardia
Ch 82 0950 1150 2150

Leixões
Ch 11 1030 1630

Monsanto
2657 kHz 0805 2005
Ch 11 1030 1630

Setúbal
Ch 11 1030 1630

Lisboa
Ch 11 1030 1700

Chipiona
1656 kHz 0803 1233 1703

Cádiz
Ch 26 0940 1140 2140

Tarifa
1704 kHz 0803 1233 1703
Ch 81 0940 1140 2140

Recorded telephone forecasts

Within **Portugal** Tel 0601 123, plus 3 digits below:

	Offshore	Inshore
N border-Lisboa	140	123
Lisboa-C St Vincent	141	124
C St Vincent-E border	142	125

For a 9 day general forecast Tel 0601 123 131. All forecasts are in Portuguese.

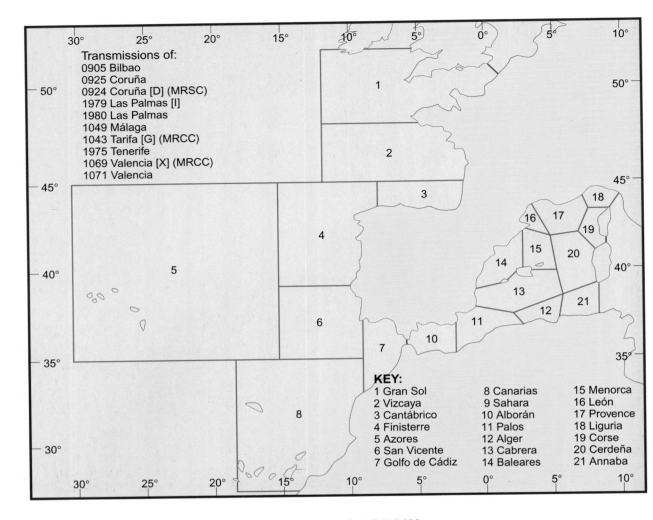

Transmissions of:
0905 Bilbao
0925 Coruña
0924 Coruña [D] (MRSC)
1979 Las Palmas [I]
1980 Las Palmas
1049 Málaga
1043 Tarifa [G] (MRCC)
1975 Tenerife
1069 Valencia [X] (MRCC)
1071 Valencia

KEY:

1 Gran Sol	8 Canarias	15 Menorca
2 Vizcaya	9 Sahara	16 León
3 Cantábrico	10 Alborán	17 Provence
4 Finisterre	11 Palos	18 Liguria
5 Azores	12 Alger	19 Corse
6 San Vicente	13 Cabrera	20 Cerdeña
7 Golfo de Cádiz	14 Baleares	21 Annaba

SOUTH WEST SPAIN

The following CRS broadcast in Spanish gale warnings, synopsis and forecasts for Areas 1-21, in Spanish, at the times and on the VHF or MF frequencies shown below:

Chipiona	1656 kHz	at 0803 1233 1703 UTC
Tarifa	VHF Ch 81	at 0940 1140 2140 UTC
	1704kHz	at 0803 1233 1703 UTC
Cadiz	VHF Ch 26	at 0940 1140 2140 UTC

Coastguard MRCC/MRSC

Broadcast in Spanish and **English** gale warnings on receipt, plus synopsis and forecasts for the Areas, times (UTC) and VHF channels listed below:

Tarifa MRCC VHF Ch 10 74 every even H+15 for actual wind and visibility at Tarifa, followed by a forecast for Strait of Gibraltar, Cádiz Bay and Alborán, **in English** and Spanish. Fog (visibility) warnings are broadcast every even H+15, and more frequently when the visibility falls below 2M.

Algeciras MRSC VHF Ch 15, 74 At 0315 0515 0715 1115 1515 1915 2315 UTC

Recorded telephone forecasts

In SW Spain Tel 906 365 372 for offshore bulletins for forecast areas San Vicente, Cádiz, Alborán, Azores and Canaries; also coastal bulletins from Portugal to Gibraltar, and Canaries. All forecasts are in Spanish. The service is only available within Spain and to Autolink-equipped vessels.

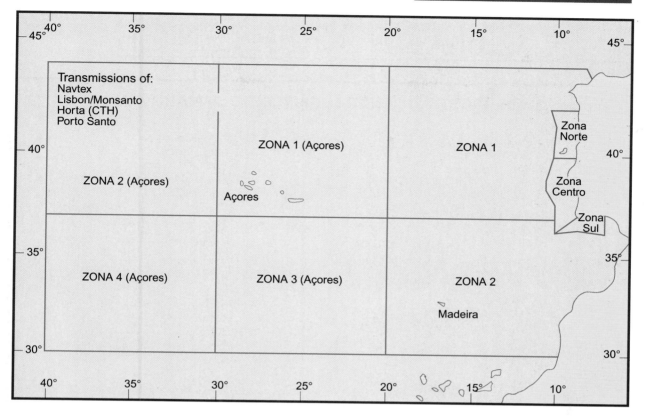

Transmissions of:
Navtex
Lisbon/Monsanto
Horta (CTH)
Porto Santo

ZONA 2 (Açores)

ZONA 1 (Açores)

Açores

ZONA 1

Zona
Norte

Zona
Centro

Zona
Sul

ZONA 4 (Açores)

ZONA 3 (Açores)

ZONA 2

Madeira

GIBRALTAR

a. Radio Gibraltar (Gibraltar Broadcasting Corporation)

Broadcasts in **English:** General synopsis, situation, wind direction and strength, visibility and sea state for area up to 50M from Gibraltar. Frequencies are 1458 kHz, 91·3 MHz, 92·6 MHz and 100·5 MHz. Times are:

Mon-Fri: 0610 0930 1030 1230 1300 1530 1715 UTC
Sat: 0930, 1030 1230 1300 UTC
Sun: 1030 1230 UTC

General synopsis, situation, wind direction and strength, sea state, visibility and Sailing forecast, for area up to 50M from Gibraltar.

Mon-Fri: 0630 0730 0830 1130 1740-1755 LT
Sat: 0630 0730 0830 1130 LT
Sun: 0730 0830 1130 LT

b. British Forces Broadcasting Service (BFBS) Gibraltar

Broadcasts in **English:**   Shipping forecast, wind, weather, visbility, sea state, swell, HW & LW times for local waters within 5M of Gibraltar.

Frequencies are: **BFBS 1** - 93·5 and 97·8 MHz FM and **BFBS 2** 89·4 and 99·5 MHGz FM.

BFBS 1 times are:
Mon-Fri: 0745 0845 1130 1715 2345 LT
Sat/Sun: 0845 0945 1230 LT

Mon-Fri: Every H+06 (0700-2400) LT
Sat-Sun: Every H+06 (0700-1000, 1200-1400) LT

Fcst for Gibraltar area; general synopsis, situation, wind direction and strength, sea state, visibility together with HW/LW times.

BFBS 2 times are:
Monday-Fri: 1200 UTC

CHART REFERENCE

Spanish Charts – INSTITUTO HIDROGRÁFICO DE LA MARINA

441	De Río Guadiana a la Ría de Huelva	50,000		**445**	Estrecho de Gibraltar De punta Camarinal a punta Europa y de cabo Espartel a punta Almina	60,000
441A	Desembocadura del Río Guadiana y Ría de Isla Cristina	20,000		**445B**	Bajo de los Cabezos e isla de Tarifa	25,000
441B	Río de las Piedras	25,000		**451**	De punta Leona a cabo Mazarí	50,000
442	De punta del Picacho a Rota	60,000		**453**	De punta Europa a la torre de las Bóvedas	50,000
443	De Chipiona a cabo Roche	50,000		**4438**	Barra de Sancti-Petri	5,000
443A	Aproches del puerto de Cádiz	25,000				
444	De cabo Roche a punta Camarinal	50,000				

Vila Real de Santo Antonio - Gibraltar

Spanish Chart Agents

Instituto Hidrográfico de la Marina
Plaza de San Severiano, 3
11007 CADIZ

Yacht Scene Publications
GIBRALTAR

Producciones Gráficas Para Instituciones Públicas, S.L
Avda. Fernández Latorre, 28-30
LA CORUÑA

Papelería D Manuel Pereira González
C/ Pelota, 14 bajo
CADIZ

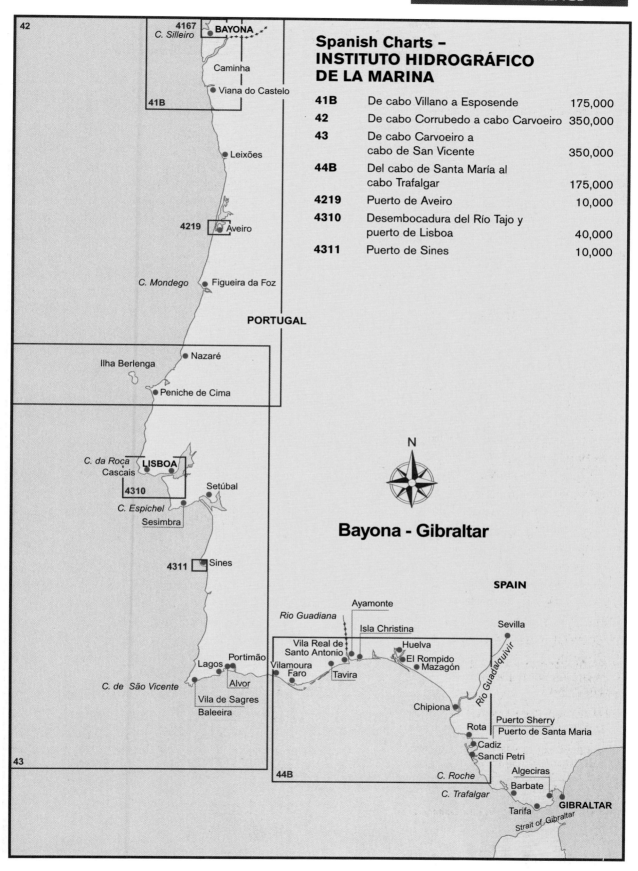

Spanish Charts – INSTITUTO HIDROGRÁFICO DE LA MARINA

41B	De cabo Villano a Esposende	175,000
42	De cabo Corrubedo a cabo Carvoeiro	350,000
43	De cabo Carvoeiro a cabo de San Vicente	350,000
44B	Del cabo de Santa María al cabo Trafalgar	175,000
4219	Puerto de Aveiro	10,000
4310	Desembocadura del Río Tajo y puerto de Lisboa	40,000
4311	Puerto de Sines	10,000

Bayona - Gibraltar

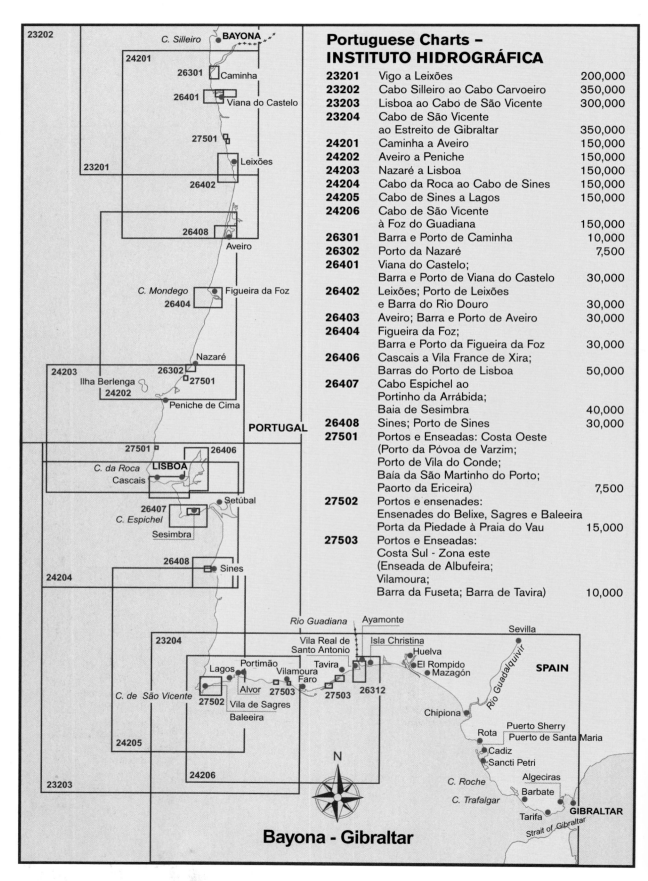

Portuguese Charts – INSTITUTO HIDROGRÁFICA

23201	Vigo a Leixões	200,000
23202	Cabo Silleiro ao Cabo Carvoeiro	350,000
23203	Lisboa ao Cabo de São Vicente	300,000
23204	Cabo de São Vicente ao Estreito de Gibraltar	350,000
24201	Caminha a Aveiro	150,000
24202	Aveiro a Peniche	150,000
24203	Nazaré a Lisboa	150,000
24204	Cabo da Roca ao Cabo de Sines	150,000
24205	Cabo de Sines a Lagos	150,000
24206	Cabo de São Vicente à Foz do Guadiana	150,000
26301	Barra e Porto de Caminha	10,000
26302	Porto da Nazaré	7,500
26401	Viana do Castelo; Barra e Porto de Viana do Castelo	30,000
26402	Leixões; Porto de Leixões e Barra do Rio Douro	30,000
26403	Aveiro; Barra e Porto de Aveiro	30,000
26404	Figueira da Foz; Barra e Porto da Figueira da Foz	30,000
26406	Cascais a Vila France de Xira; Barras do Porto de Lisboa	50,000
26407	Cabo Espichel ao Portinho da Arrábida; Baia de Sesimbra	40,000
26408	Sines; Porto de Sines	30,000
27501	Portos e Enseadas: Costa Oeste (Porto da Póvoa de Varzim; Porto de Vila do Conde; Baía da São Martinho do Porto; Paorto da Ericeira)	7,500
27502	Portos e ensenades: Ensenades do Belixe, Sagres e Baleeira Porta da Piedade à Praia do Vau	15,000
27503	Portos e Enseadas: Costa Sul - Zona este (Enseada de Albufeira; Vilamoura; Barra da Fuseta; Barra de Tavira)	10,000

Bayona - Gibraltar

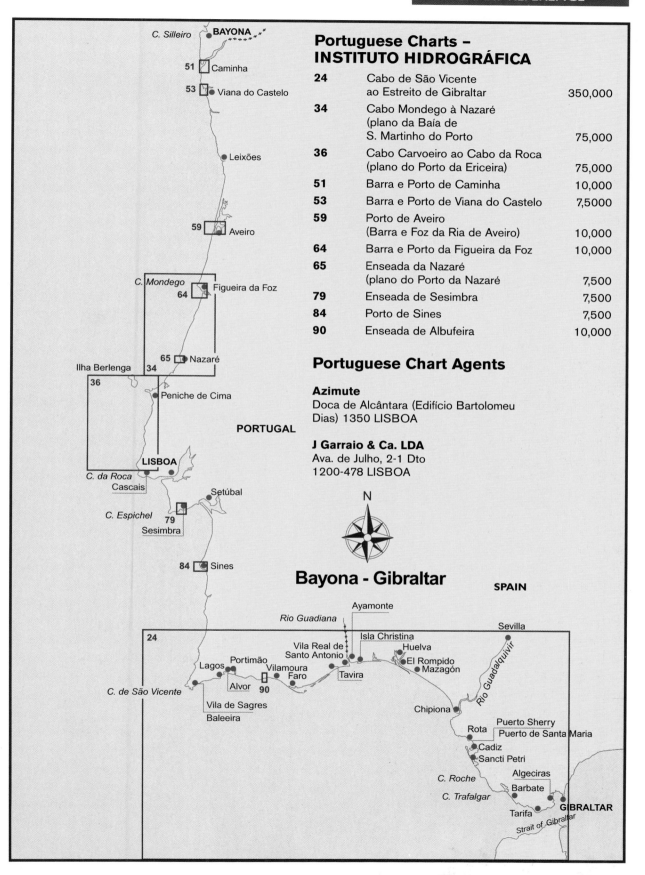

Portuguese Charts –
INSTITUTO HIDROGRÁFICA

24	Cabo de São Vicente ao Estreito de Gibraltar	350,000
34	Cabo Mondego à Nazaré (plano da Baía de S. Martinho do Porto	75,000
36	Cabo Carvoeiro ao Cabo da Roca (plano do Porto da Ericeira)	75,000
51	Barra e Porto de Caminha	10,000
53	Barra e Porto de Viana do Castelo	7,5000
59	Porto de Aveiro (Barra e Foz da Ria de Aveiro)	10,000
64	Barra e Porto da Figueira da Foz	10,000
65	Enseada da Nazaré (plano do Porto da Nazaré	7,500
79	Enseada de Sesimbra	7,500
84	Porto de Sines	7,500
90	Enseada de Albufeira	10,000

Portuguese Chart Agents

Azimute
Doca de Alcântara (Edifício Bartolomeu Dias) 1350 LISBOA

J Garraio & Ca. LDA
Ava. de Julho, 2-1 Dto
1200-478 LISBOA

Bayona - Gibraltar

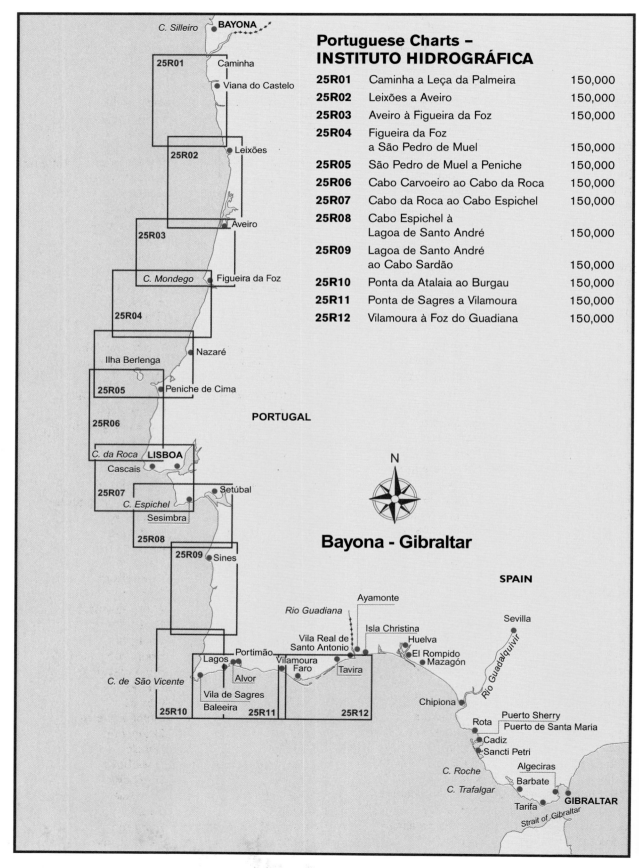

Portuguese Charts – INSTITUTO HIDROGRÁFICA

25R01	Caminha a Leça da Palmeira	150,000
25R02	Leixões a Aveiro	150,000
25R03	Aveiro à Figueira da Foz	150,000
25R04	Figueira da Foz a São Pedro de Muel	150,000
25R05	São Pedro de Muel a Peniche	150,000
25R06	Cabo Carvoeiro ao Cabo da Roca	150,000
25R07	Cabo da Roca ao Cabo Espichel	150,000
25R08	Cabo Espichel à Lagoa de Santo André	150,000
25R09	Lagoa de Santo André ao Cabo Sardão	150,000
25R10	Ponta da Atalaia ao Burgau	150,000
25R11	Ponta de Sagres a Vilamoura	150,000
25R12	Vilamoura à Foz do Guadiana	150,000

Bayona - Gibraltar

GLOSSARY

English	Spanish	English	Spanish
Abeam	Por el través	Carburettor	Carburador
Aft	Atrás	Catwalk	Pasarela
Ahead	Avante	Centre	Centro
Air filter	Filtro a aire	Centreboard	Orza
Air mass	Massa de aire	Certificate of registry	Documentos de matrìcuia
Airport	Aeropuerto	Chandlery	Efectos navales
Anchor	Ancia	Channel	Canal
Anchor chain	Cadena	Charging	Cargador
Anchor warp	Cabo	Chart	Carta náutica
Anchor winch	Molinete	Check in	Registrar
Anchoring	Fondear	Chemist	Farmacia
Anticyclone	Anticiclón	Clouds	Nube
Area	Zona	Coastguard	Guarda costas
Ashore	A tierra	Cockpit	Bañera
Assistance	Asistencia	Cold	Frio
Astern	Atrás	Cold front	Frente frio
Babystay	Babystay	Commercial port	Puerto comercial
Backing wind	Rolar el viento	Companionway	Entrada cámera
Backstay	Estay de popa	Compass	Compás
Bandage	Vendas	Compass course	Rumbo de aguja
Bank	Banco	Compression	Compresión
Barometer	Barómetro	Cooling water	Agua refrigerado
Battery	Baterìas	Cruising chute	MPS
Bearing	Maración	Current	Coriente
Beating	Ciñendo a rabier	Customs	Aduana
Bilge	Sentina	Customs office	Aduanas
Bilge keel	Quillas de balance	Cutter stay	Estay de tringqueta
Bilge pump	Bomba de achique	Cyclonic	Ciclonica
Binoculars	Prismáticos	Dead reckoning	Estimación
Block	Motón	Deck	Cubierta
Boat	Barco	Declare	Declarar
Boathoist	Travelift	Decrease	Disminución
Boatyard	Astilleros	Deep	Profundo
Boom	Botavara	Deepening	Ahondamiento
Bow	Proa	Degree	Grado
Breakwater	Escolera	Dentist	Dentista
Breeze	Brisa	Depression	Depresión
Bridgedeck	Bridgedeck	Depth	Profundidad
Buoy	Boya	Deviation	Desvio
Bureau de change	Cambio	Diesel	Gas-oil
Burns	Quemadura	Diesel engine	Motor a gas-oil
Bus	Autobús	Dinghy	Chinchorro
Cabin	Cabina	Direction	Direción
Cable	Cadena	Dismasted	Desarbolar
Calm	Calma	Dispersing	Disipación
Can I moor here please	Puedo atracar aqui por favor?	Distance	Distancia
		Distress	Pena
Cap shrouds	Obenques altos	Distress flares	Bengalas
Capsize	Volcó	Disturbance	Perturbación

English	Spanish	English	Spanish
Doctor	Médico	Garage	Garage
Downstream	Rìo abajo	Gearbox	Transmisión
Dries	Descubierto	Generator	Generador
Drizzle	Lioviena	Genoa	Génova
Drying port	Puerto secarse	Good	Bueno
Dynamo	Alternador	Gradient	Gradiente
EPIRB	Baliza	Grease	Grasa
East	Este	Grounded	Encallado
Ebb	Marea menguante	Guest berths	Amarradero visitantes
Echosounder	Sonda	Gust, squall	Ráfaga
Eight	Ocho	Hail	Granizo
Electrical wiring	Circuito eléctrico	Halyard	Driza
Emergency	Emergencias	Handbearing compass	Compás de
Engine mount	Bancada del motor	marcaciones	
Engine oil	Aceite motor	Harbour	Puerto
Engineer	Mecánico	Harbour entrance	Entradas
Estimated position	Posición estimado	Harbour guide	Guia del Puerto
Exhaust pipe	Tubos de escape	Harbour master	Capitán del puerto
Exhaustion	Agotamiento	Harbourmaster's office	Capitania
Extending	Extension	Harness	Arnés de seguridad
Extensive	General	Hazard	Peligro
Falling	Bajando	Haze	Calina
Fathom	Braza	Head gasket	Junta de culata
Feet	Pie	Headache	Dolor de cabeza
Fender	Defensa	Heart attack	Ataque corazón
Ferry	Ferry	Heavy	Abunante
Ferry terminal	Terminal marìtmo	Height	Alturas
Fever	Fiebre	Helicopter	Helicóptero
Filling	Relleno	High	Alta presión
Fin keel	Quilla de aleta	High water	Altamer
Fire extinguisher	Extintor	Holding tank	Tanque aguas negras
Firing range	Zona de tiro	Hospital	Hospital
First aid	Primeros auxillos	How far is it to....?	A que distancia esta ...?
Fishing harbour	Puerto de pesca	How much does that cost?	Cudnto cuesta ...?
Five	Cinco	Hull	Carena
Flood	Flujo de marea	Illness	Enfermo
Fog	Niebla	Inboard engine	Motor intraborda
Fog bank	Banco de niebla	Increasing	Aumentar
Forecast	Previsión	Inflatable	Bote Hinchable
Foresail	Foque	Injectors	Inyectores
Forestay	Estay	Injury	Lesión
Foul ground	Fondo sucio	Insurance	Seguro
Four	Cuatro	Insurance certificate	Certificado deseguro
Fracture	Fractura	Is there enough water?	Hay bastante agua?
Frequent	Frecuenta	Isobar	Isobara
Fresh	Fresco	Isolated	Aislado
Front	Frente	Jackstay	Violìn
Fuel filter	Filtro de combustible	Jetty	Malecón
Fuel tank	Tanque de Combustible	Jumper	Violìn
Fuse	Fusible	Keel	Quilla
GPS	GPS	Landing place	Embarcadero
Gale	Temporal	Latitude	Latitud
Gale warning	Aviso de temporal	Leading lights	Luz de enfilación

English	Spanish	English	Spanish
Leeway	Hacia sotavento	Pilotage book	Derrotero
Let go aft	Suelta los cabos del amarre de popa	Please direct me to ...?	Por favor, digame a ...?
Let go foreward	Suelta los cabos del amarre de proa	Please take my line	Por favor cojan mi cabo
		Police	Policìa
Lifeboat	Lancha de salvamento	Poor	Mal
Lifejacket	Chaleco salvavidas	Port	Babor
Liferaft	Balsa salvavidas	Post office	Correos
Lighthouse	Faro	Pratique	Prático
Lightning	Relampago	Precipitation	Precipitación
List of lights	Listude de Luces	Pressure	Presión
Local	Local	Prohibited	Prohibido
Lock	Esclusa	Prohibited area	Zona de phrohibida
Log	Corredera	Propeller	Hélice
Long keel	Quilla corrida	Propeller bracket	Arbotante
Longitude	Longitud	Pulpit	Púlpito
Low	Baja presión	Pulse	Pulso
Low water	Bajamar	Pushpit	Balcón de popa
Lower shrouds	Obenques bajos	RDF	Radio-gonió
Main engine	Motor	Radar	Radar
Mainsail	Mayor	Radio receiver	Receptor de radio
Make fast aft	Asegurar los amarres de popa	Radio transmitter	Radio-transmisor
Make fast foreward	Asegurar los amarres de proa	Railing	Guardamencebos
		Railway station	Estación de ferrocanil
Man overboard	Hombre al agua	Rain	lluvia
Marina	Marina	Reaching	Viento a través
Mast	Mast	Register	Lista de tripulantes/rol
Mast crane	Grúa	Regulator	Regulador
Metre	Metro	Rest	Reposo
Minute	Minuto	Ridge	Cresta
Mist	Nablina	Rigging	Jarcia
Mizzen	Mesana	Rising	Subiendo
Moderate	Moderado	River outlet	Embocadura
Moderating	Medianente	Rope	Cabo
Mooring	Fondeadero	Rough	Bravo o alborotado
Motoring	Navegar a motor	Rudder	Pala de Timón
Moving	Movimiento	Running	Viento a favor
Nautical almanac	Almanaque náutico	Running backstay	Burde volanto
Nautical mile	Milla marina	Sail batten	Sables
Navigate	Navegar	Sailing	Navegar a velas
Neap tide	Marea muerta	Sailmaker	Velero
Nine	Nueve	Scattered	Difuso
North	Norte	Sea	Mar
Occluded	Okklusie	Seacock	Grifos de fondo
One	Uno	Seasickness	Mareo
Outboard engine	Motor fuera borda	Seaway	Alta mar
Passport	Pasaporte	Seaworthy	Marinero
Permitted	Permitido	Seven	Siete
Petrol	Gasolina	Shackle	Grillete
Petrol engine	Motor a gasolina	Shaft	Eje
Pier	Muelle	Sheet	Escota
Pilot	Práctico	Ship	Buque
		Ship's log	Cuaderno de bitácora
		Ship's papers	Documentos del barco

English	Spanish	English	Spanish
Shock	Choque	VHF	VHF
Shops	Tiendas	Variable	Variable
Shower	Aguacero	Variation	Variación
Shrouds	Obenques	Veering	Dextrogiro
Sinking	Hundiendo	Village	Pueblo
Six	Seis	Warm front	Frente calido
Sleep	Sueño	Water pump	Bomba de agua
Slight	Leicht	Water tank	Tanque de agua
Slip	Varadero	Waypoint	Waypoint
Slow	Lent	Weather	Tiempo
Snow	Nieve	Weather report	Previsión meteorologica
South	Sud, Sur	West	Oeste
Spark plug	Bujia	Wheel	Rueda
Spinnaker	Spi	Where can I get...?	Donde puedo
Spinnaker boom	Tangon		conseguir ...?
Spring tide	Marea viva	Where can I moor?	Dondo puedo atracar?
Stanchion	Candelero	Winch	Winche
Starboard	Estribor	Wind	Viento
Starter	Arranque	Working jib	Foque
Staysail	Trinquete	Wound	Herida
Steamer	Buque de vapor	Wreck	Naufrago
Stern	Popa	Yacht	Yate
Stern gland	Bocina	Yacht club	Club náutico
Storm	Temporal	Yacht harbour	Puerto deportive
Storm jib	Tormentin		
Storm trysail	Vela de capa		
Sun	Sol		
Supermarket	Supermercado		
Superstructure	Superestructura	**English**	**Portuguese**
Surveyor	Inspector	Alternating	luz alternada
Swell	Mar de fondo	Anchorage	fundeadouro
Swing bridge	Puente giratorio	Antibiotic	antibiótico
Taxi	Taxis	Ashore	A Terra
Ten	Diez	Bakery	padaria, pastelaria
Tender	Anexo (bote)	Bandage	ligadura
Three	Tres	Basin	doca, bacia
Throttle	Acelerador	Bar	barra
Thunder	Tormenta	Bay	baía
Thunderstorm	Tronada	Beach	praia
Tide	Marea	Beacon (Bn)	baliza
Tide tables	Anuario de mareas	Beam	boca
Tiller	Caña	Bell	sino
Toe rail	Regala	Black (B)	preto
Topsides	Obra muerta	Bleeding	sangrar
Tow line	Cabo	Boat hoist (BH)	portico elevador
Trough	Seno	Boatyard (BY)	estaleiro
True course	Rumbo	Breakers	arrebentação
Two	Duo	Breakwater, mole	quebra-mar, molhe
Unconscious	Inconsciente	breeze (F2)	vento fraco
Underwater	Debajo del agua	Bridge	ponte
Underwater hull	Obra viva	Buoy	bóia
Upstream	Rìo arriba	Burn	queimadura
Upwind	Vienta en contra	Bus station	estação de camionetas
		Butcher shop	açougue
		Calm (F0)	calma

English	Portuguese
Can (PHM)	cilíndrica
Chandlery (CH)	aprestos
Chart Datum (CD)	zero hidrográfico
Chemist	farmácia
Choppy	mareta
Cloudy	nublado
Coastguard (CG)	policia marítima
Cone, conical (SHM)	cónica
Conspicuous (conspic)	conspicuo
Crane (C)	guindaste
Customs (n)	alfândega
Dehydration	desidratação
Dentist	dentista
Diesel (D)	gasóleo
Draught	calado
Dredged	dragado
Drizzle	chuvisco
Drown, to	afogar-se
East (E)	este
Engineer (ME)	engenheiro
Facilities	Facillidados
Fever	febre
First aid	Primeiros socorros
Fixed (F)	luz fixa
Flashing	luz relâmpagos
Flood/ebb stream	corrente enchente/vasante
Fog	nevoeiro
Fresh breeze (F5)	vento frêsco
Fresh water (FW)	aguada
Front, warm/cold	frente, quente/fria
Gale (F8)	vento muito forte
Gentle breeze (F3)	vento bonançoso
Green (G)	verde
Gust	rajada
Hail	saraiva
Harbour Master	capitanía
Haze	cerração
Heart attack	ataque de coração
Height, headroom, clearance	altura
High (anticyclone)	anticiclone
High Water (HW)	preia mar (PM)
Insurance certificate	certificado de seguro
Ironmonger	ferreiroa
Island	ilha
Isolated danger (IDM)	perigo isolado
Jetty	molhe
Knot (kn)	nó
Landfall (SWM)	aterragem
Launderette	lavanderia
Leading light	farol de enfiamento
Leading line, transit	enfiamento

English	Portuguese
Length overall (LOA)	comprimento
Lifeboat (LB)	barco salva-vidas
Light airs (F1)	aragem
Light Low (depression)	depressão
Lighthouse	farol
Lightship	barco-farol
Lock	eclusa
Low Water (LW)	baixa mar (BM)
Market	mercad
Meteorology	Meteorologia
Methylated spirits	alcool metílico
Mist	neblina
Moderate breeze (F4)	vento moderado
Mooring buoy	bólia de atracação
Mussel beds/rafts	viveiros
Navigation	Navegación
Neaps (np)	águas mortas
Near gale (F7)	vento forte
North (N)	norte
Obscured	obscurecido
Occulting (Oc)	ocultações
Overfalls (tide race)	bailadeiras
Pain	dôr
Painkiller	analgésico
Paraffin	petróleo
Petrol (P)	gasolina
Point, headland	ponta
Poisoning	envenenamento
Port (side)	bombordo
Post Office	correio (CTT)
Pressure, rise/fall	pressão, subida/descida
Quick flashing (Q)	relâmpagos rápidos
Railway station	estação de comboios
Rain	chuva
Range	amplitude de maré
Rate/set (tide)	força/direcção
Red, (R)	vermelho
Reef	recife
Registration number	número do registo
Ridge (high)	crista
River	rio
Rock	rocha
Rough sea	mar bravo
Sailmaker (SM)	veleir
Sandhill, dunes	dunas de areia
Severe gale (F9)	vento tempestuoso
Shoal	baixo
Shock	choque
Short/steep (sea state)	mar cavado
Shower	aguaceiro
Slack water, stand	águas paradas
Slight sea	mar chão
Slipway (slip)	rampa

English	Portuguese	English	Portuguese
South (S)	sul	Swelling	inchação
Special mark (SPM)	marca especiá	Thunderstorm	trovoada
Splint	colocar em talas	Tide tables	Tabela de marés
Springs (sp)	águas vivas	Tidal stream atlas	Atlas de marés
Squall	borrasca	Toothache	dôr dos dentes
Stamps	sellos	Topmark	alvo
Starboard	estibordo	Trough	linha de baixa pressão
Sticking plaster	adesivo	Unconscious	sem sentidos
Stomach upset	cólicas	Visibility, poor; good	fraca, má; bôa
Storm (F10)	temporal	West (W)	oeste
Strait(s)	estreito	Whistle	apito
Stretcher	maca	White (W)	branco
Stripe/band	faixas verticais/horizontais	Wreck	naufrágio
		Yacht harbour, marina	doca de recreio
Sunburn	queimadura des	Yellow (Y)	amarelo
Swell	ondulação		

DISTANCE TABLE: COASTS OF NW SPAIN, PORTUGAL AND SW SPAIN

Approximate distances in nautical miles are by the most direct route, whilst avoiding dangers and allowing for Traffic Separation Schemes. Places in italics are off UK and North West coast of France.

		1	2	3	4	5	6	7	8	9	10	11	12	13	14	15	16	17	18	19	20
1	*Lands End*	1																			
2	*Ushant (Créac'h)*	100	2																		
3	La Coruña	418	338	3																	
4	Cabo Villano	439	365	43	4																
5	Bayona	510	436	114	71	5															
6	Viana do Castelo	537	468	141	98	32	6														
7	Leixões (Pôrto)	565	491	169	126	63	33	7													
8	Nazaré	659	585	263	220	156	127	97	8												
9	Cabo Carvoeiro	670	596	274	231	171	143	114	22	9											
10	Cabo Raso	710	636	314	271	211	183	154	62	40	10										
11	Lisboa (bridge)	686	652	330	287	227	199	170	78	56	16	11									
12	Cabo Espichel	692	658	336	293	233	205	176	84	62	22	23	12								
13	Sines	726	692	370	327	267	239	210	118	96	54	57	34	13							
14	Cabo São Vicente	777	743	421	378	318	290	261	169	147	104	108	85	57	14						
15	Lagos	797	763	441	398	338	310	281	189	167	124	128	105	77	20	15					
16	Vilamoura	820	786	464	421	361	333	304	212	190	147	151	128	100	43	27	16				
17	Cádiz	911	877	555	512	452	424	395	303	281	238	242	219	191	134	120	95	17			
18	Cabo Trafalgar	928	894	572	529	469	441	412	320	298	255	259	236	208	151	139	115	28	18		
19	Tarifa	952	918	596	553	493	465	436	344	322	279	283	260	232	175	163	139	52	24	19	
20	Gibraltar	968	934	612	569	509	481	450	360	338	295	299	276	248	191	179	155	68	40	16	20

INDEX